BEHIND THE FRONT PAGE

Organizational Self-Renewal
in a Metropolitan Newspaper

Chris Argyris

BEHIND THE
FRONT PAGE

Jossey-Bass Publishers

San Francisco · Washington · London · 1974

BEHIND THE FRONT PAGE
Organizational Self-Renewal in a Metropolitan Newspaper
        by Chris Argyris

Library of Congress Catalogue Card Number LC 73–22558

International Standard Book Number ISBN 0–87589–223–X

Manufactured in the United States of America

JACKET DESIGN BY WILLI BAUM

FIRST EDITION

Code 7416

*The
Jossey-Bass
Behavioral Science Series*

To Alfred J. Marrow,
whose dedication to enhancing
the quality of our lives
has made him a rare combination:
humane and effective activist and researcher

Preface

The research reported in *Behind the Front Page* was guided by two interdependent objectives. The first, a policy-oriented objective, was to discover what must be done to create newspapers that are self-examining and self-regulating. The second, a scholarly objective, was to add to our knowledge of the processes needed to enhance organizational health and to create effective, on-going renewal activities within organizations. A few words about each seem necessary.

Creating self-examining newspapers. The press in this country has been under attack from many elements of society: the angry and the quiet, the thoughtful and the thoughtless, the old and the young, the minorities and the establishment, the left and the right. The call for change has also come from some of the more thoughtful people in journalism (Brucker 1972, Raskin 1967, Reston 1966). The credibility of the press has been shaken to the point where a national blue-ribbon task force, privately financed by the Twentieth Century Fund, has recommended that a national press council be established (Balk 1972). All this is happening at time when the press in the United States can be

ix

shown to be among the finest and most responsible in the world.

The underlying reasons, the Twentieth Century Fund panel suggests, are that the press has grown remote and unresponsive to its constituencies; the public feels a sense of alienation and helplessness in its relationship with the press. The causes of remoteness, frustration, lack of credibility, and unresponsiveness include too much emphasis on the dramatic (emphasizing the shocking, negative, and deviant), a lack of nationwide standards for the profession, non-competitive salaries, decreased competition between newspapers (Balk 1972), and control of newspapers by individuals who are forced to be profit-conscious (Brucker 1972).

Although these causes are certainly important, when I first chose to study a large metropolitan newspaper I had no idea that my research would be relevant to them. I elected to study the newspaper which I shall call *The Daily Planet* for three reasons. First, my long-range interest has been in learning how healthy organizations can be designed and managed effectively. Organizational health requires continual self-examination and self-renewal. Yet, as far as I could see, the communications media had shown little interest in such activities. The *Planet,* I had been told by my informants, would be especially resistant to a behavioral science inquiry. "To put it mildly," said one informant, "they would consider your views to be nonsense."

That comment led to my second reason. I had never studied an organization that was skeptical about the value of behavioral science. All the organizations I had studied had asked to be studied, which meant that my sample was highly self-selective. If I could be admitted to an organization that was skeptical and not particularly cooperative, then I might learn more about the processes of gaining credibility where, given a behavioral scientist's bias, we are needed most. How do you get cooperation from a skeptical organization? One strategy is to speak to the top, ask for their cooperation, and be honest about your motives as well as about the possible pay-off for the clients. I did this and was invited in. That was a start. The problem of getting cooperation from that point on is the subject of most of this book.

My third reason for selecting this newspaper was my interest in the basic problem of the relationship between thought and action. I wanted to learn what impact, if any, the internal system and the quality of life within the organization had upon the perceptions, thoughts, and writing of the participants. I did not realize then how relevant this issue was for understanding the credibility gap that exists between newspapers and the public and for developing insights into the creation of self-examining systems.

The realization of the connection between my research and the possibility of self-examining newspapers came as I was reading the Twentieth Century Fund report. *The Daily Planet* was acknowledged in this report to be a newspaper with high professional standards and one not plagued with the causes of low credibility identified above. Nevertheless, this newspaper, even though an excellent one, was having credibility problems with many of its constituencies. I knew, from first-hand observations, that the causes for this credibility gap were as much internal as external. Moreover, many members of the newspaper expressed a genuine sense of helplessness about changing these internal conditions, which included the win-lose dynamics among reporters and between reporters and copywriters, management by crisis and with hypocrisy, and the conception of advocacy journalism held by many of the top young reporters. If the public feels helpless in relation to newspapers, newspapermen themselves feel the same way. "Not you or anyone else will ever change this place" was a prediction I heard often at *The Daily Planet*—and it was backed up by serious offers to bet large sums of money on it.

It is doubtful that a newspaper or any organization can develop effective self-examination processes if its personnel hold these pessimistic attitudes about change. However, unlike most organizations, newspapers are protected by law. This protection can be healthy to the extent that newspapers are able to manage themselves effectively to produce news and editorial products of the highest quality. But, as the reader will see, most of the top news and editorial officials on *The Daily Planet* eventually admitted that they were not ready to become the open system that they have said newspapers should be, and that they have argued that our societal institutions should become. One question that I

hope this book raises is whether newspapers should be protected if, by their own admission and behavior, they are not
capable of creating an open learning system within their own
boundaries.

The genuine autonomy of newspapers therefore may depend ultimately upon their being able to manage themselves. But,
in order to accomplish this objective, newspapers will have to
find ways to reduce the repetitive, compulsive processes of their
internal systems. A system that behaves compulsively in ways
that its members acknowledge are ineffective creates the conditions for organizational neurosis and invites outside intervention
and control.

The self-sealing, non-learning processes that lead to
organizational dry-rot and inhibit self-examination are not unique
to this newspaper or to all newspapers. These processes of decay
are so prevalent in all our organizations that a law of organizational entropy has been proposed (Argyris 1964, 1970, 1971).
And an outside regulatory agency, such as a national press council, would probably develop the same processes of deterioration
just as many other regulatory commissions and courts have
become rigid and ineffective.

Acquiring knowledge about organizational health. My
second primary objective is to add to our knowledge about the
factors that determine organizational health and about the kind
of interventions that can effectively enhance organizational
health. Specifically, the objectives are (1) to understand the inner
workings of the upper managerial and editorial activities of a
newspaper so as (2) to be able to explain why events occur as
they do, (3) to be able to predict, under specified conditions,
what will happen, and (4) to help the participants redesign their
system to become more effective. The objectives are listed in
order of increasing difficulty. The easiest task for the action researcher is to describe and understand; the most difficult one is
to describe and understand in such a way as to make new things
happen.

The same is true for the participants. Publishers, top
editors, and for that matter managers and administrators in any

organization must understand the inner workings of their systems in order to be able to predict behavior and alter it wherever and whenever necessary. As the analysis here shows, the participants find that understanding human behavior in their organization is difficult; that making valid predictions about it is even more difficult; and that altering it seems nearly impossible. There is, therefore, a high degree of compatibility between the interests of a researcher committed to understanding complex systems and the interests of administrators responsible for managing these complex systems.

Several differences between the researcher and the administrator, however, are important if for no other reason than that they affect what is included in this book. The researcher conducts research and develops models or theoretical frameworks to explain his findings in such a way that they may apply to other organizations which may have similar problems. Thus the intention, in this research, is to produce some knowledge that may help to understand other newspapers. If this were a study of *The New York Times,* it would not satisfy us to learn about the everyday trials and tribulations described by Gay Talese. We would need to go beyond learning the intimate details of the "Washington fiasco" to predict, for example, whether the top people at the *Times,* if faced with a a similar problem, would behave again in a similar fashion. Or, more importantly, how one can help the people at the top avoid repeating such an episode.

In addition, my objective is to be of help to other communications-producing organizations. Indeed, I hope that some of the findings, such as the existence of a star system of reporters and columnists, may be of help to executives in many fields, ranging from radio and television to university administration. A university president, for example, is faced with a faculty which contains a few stars. The stars provide the attraction for graduate students and other faculty members, but the rest of the faculty members do the bulk of the teaching and are largely responsible for the everyday effectiveness of the university. How can an organization be designed that rewards both groups justly and simultaneously minimizes the jealousies and fears that usually go along with differentiations that place people in first- and second-class status? The hope is to bridge the two worlds with a minimum of falling out between them.

The phases of research. The Daily Planet was studied in depth and over a long period of time. The study began with interviews and observations of the top forty news, editorial, and business personnel. This phase lasted approximately one year. I was free to observe and tape-record any naturally occurring meeting between two or more people. During the diagnostic phase, I was never excluded from any meeting that I chose to attend. Interviewing and observing for a year made it possible for me to sample meetings, problems, and issues over a long period of time and under many different conditions. (I varied my visits to the newspaper so that I systematically covered all the days of the week.)

On the basis of these data (and others described in the first two chapters) I prepared a diagnosis of the internal workings of the *Planet*. The diagnosis showed that the credibility problems of the paper were related to its internal system, which in turn caused top people to have credibility problems with each other.

The next phase was a series of interventions, which lasted for two years. They provided additional longitudinal information about the internal system of the newspaper. More important, they were designed to become a test of the potential for self-examination on the newspaper. In other words, the objective of the second phase was to try to solve problems which the participants agreed (after studying the diagnosis) were critical for self-regulation and self-renewal *and* which up to that point had seemed to them unsolvable.

For the intervention to become a legitimate test of the potential for self-examination and self-renewal, the intervention processes had to be so designed and executed that their success or failure could be traced explicitly to the participants. Under these conditions, a "failure" of progress could become a valid indicator of the lack of capacity for self-renewal within the system.

It was also important to show that I did not intervene in ways that unilaterally, made success or failure more or less probable. This does not mean that I was a passive observer. I was very active, continually suggesting strategies and courses of action which, if carried out, could become genuine tests for the members of their own capacities to learn and change. However, I believe the data also show that I worked patiently and actively to encourage the participants to reject my suggestions whenever they could not accept them fully as their own. The participants could reject their own ideas, or mine, even after they had translated them into objectives to be accomplished.

This is a case study, therefore, with some qualities not frequently found in case studies. The organization (1) was studied with multi-research methods, (2) over a three-year period, where not only (3) was a diagnosis developed but (4) it was fed back to begin a process of intervention within the system, which led to (5) the creation of statistically rare events which in turn (6) provided learning for the participants (about their system and themselves) and which (7) became tests for the capacity for self-examination and self-renewal within the system.

The organization of the book. A tension exists between the several themes of this book which may frustrate some readers, especially those whose main interest is to learn about newspapers and how they can examine themselves. First, this is a study that focuses on the internal processes by which one newspaper maintains itself as a system. Second, it is also a study of an attempt to change parts of that system. Finally, these two studies are intended to shed light on the problem of self-examination within a newspaper.

One way to make sense of these three themes is to view the diagnosis of the internal workings of the system as helping us to discover what forces inhibit or facilitate self-examination. The intervention activity may be viewed as an attempt to change the system. Therefore, if the intervention strategy is designed to enhance self-examination, it becomes a living test of the capacity of the organization to change itself. In order to be such a test, the intervention strategy cannot be based on the typical management-consulting philosophy, which usually dictates that the experts diagnose and manage the change. The intervention program must be designed and executed so that every step becomes a test of the ability of the client organization to learn how to become self-examining. Such a theory of intervention has already been developed (Argyris 1970, 1971), and it was in this study. Therefore the focus on newspaper self-examination cannot be developed without first presenting the diagnosis and making explicit the steps and processes of intervention.

Part One presents the diagnosis. Because reality is so complex, all diagnoses are partial; since they are partial, they are dictated by the biases of the diagnostician; these biases, when stated explicitly, represent the theoretical framework or model used by the diagnostician. Chapter One includes a brief description of the primary concepts of the theoretical framework, as well as the diagnosis of the living system of the newspaper. Chapter Two describes some consequences of the living system.

Part Two presents the intervention activities. After a brief introduction to the theory of intervention used, the sequence of intervention activities is described. First is the feedback of the diagnoses of the top officials (Chapter Three). Next is a description of the planning for the initial change activities (Chapter Four). Chapter Five describes the first learning seminar, and the next six chapters (Chapters Six through Eleven) describe the consequences of the seminar. Chapter Twelve describes the views and evaluations of the program offered by the top executives.

In Part Three the implications of the findings for effective self-examination (Chapter Twelve) and for effective intervention (Chapter Thirteen) are discussed.

I should like to thank Lee Bolman, Ithiel de Sola Pool, and William Torbert for their many valuable suggestions. I owe Fritz Steele a special debt of gratitude for helping to design and manage the key learning seminars. I am also deeply grateful to the people at *The Daily Planet* who gave fully of themselves in order that I might learn and hopefully be of help to them. I wish that I could identify some of them by name, but to do so would identify the organization. Priscilla Turner and Richard Yoder provided helpful secretarial and editorial help.

CHRIS ARGYRIS

Cambridge, Massachusetts
February 1974

Contents

BEHIND THE FRONT PAGE

Organizational Self-Renewal
in a Metropolitan Newspaper

The Living System

Organizations are designed and partially managed in accordance with espoused theories of management. These theories state various principles—for example, that power should be centralized at the top, that information should follow the flow of power, and that work should be specialized. It is the application of such principles that creates the pyramidal hierarchical structures in organizations. An organization chart is like an x-ray of the hierarchical structure within an organization.

I am not going to describe the organization chart of this particular newspaper, which I shall call *The Daily Planet,* nor report its age, size, location, or number of employees. For one thing, I do not want to jeopardize its anonymity. A more important reason, however, is that these details are not directly relevant to the main purpose of this study, which is to examine an organization's capacity for self-scrutiny and self-renewal. This capacity must be inferred from how people actually behave in the organization, not from how they say they behave. An espoused theory may be highly reliable (different people will repeat it in the same context), but recent research suggest that it will not tend to predict accurately what really goes on in an organization (Argyris 1968, Argyris and Schön 1974).

Nor will I describe the task of the reporter, the copy editor, the news editor, and so on up the hierarchy. Again, for the purposes of describing this study, they are not important. Had the change program been designed to reach the lower levels, these descriptions would have been necessary; but that was not the case.

What I will try to describe in this chapter are the relationships that occur at the highest levels of editorial, news, and administrative activity. First, I will try to present a perspective on the human environment or "living system" within which the top forty executives live and work. I will be less concerned with what they say is their management strategy, than with how they actually deal with each other—in two's, three's, small groups, and intergroups—as they try to accomplish their different organizational tasks. My focus will be on their theory-in-use, the theory that actually explains and predicts how they behave.

Diagnosing people's theories-in-use is difficult because the actors tend not to be aware of them. Most participants in organizations tend to be aware of their espoused theories, but not of their theories-in-use (Argyris 1968, Argyris and Schön 1974). This is another reason why we must focus on how people actually behave while they get on with their daily work.

But if we are to learn about the capacity of a system to scrutinize and renew itself, we need to observe the participants consciously struggling to consider changing their system, and (ideally) we need to watch them experimenting with actual changes. We shall report on our observation of these efforts later, in Chapters Five through Eleven.

It is easy to say that one should observe behavior in the places where it naturally occurs; it is not at all easy to accomplish. One difficulty is assessing the possible effect of the observer and his ever-present tape recorder. To date, our experiences have shown that the observer and tape recorder have a minimal effect on behavior under two conditions: *if* the people observed are in sessions that are highly important (budget sessions, for example), and *if* they believe that the study may produce results which will increase their effectiveness (Argyris 1962, 1965, 1970, 1971).

Since one could spend a lifetime studying the various behaviors recorded during only a few group sessions, another problem is to select one particular behavior for studying. *This study focuses on human behavior that makes a difference in the problem-solving effectiveness of a system.* Problem-solving processes are judged effective to the extent that they fill three requirements: (1) The participants are aware of the factors relevant to the problem being solved (which implies that the members also understand the factors). (2) The problems are solved in such a way that they remain solved (which implies that the problems were solved within the constraints of time and other resources). (3) The first two requirements were met without reducing or deteriorating the present level of problem-solving effectiveness.

One of the most important variables that makes a difference in problem-solving effectiveness is quality of information; unless a system has valid information, it cannot begin to solve problems effectively. But to say whether information is valid, one must be able to describe or assess two factors: first, the level of professional competence displayed in producing the information needed to achieve tasks (to report, to write stories, or to edit); and second, the quality of the human relationships within which problem-solving behavior occurs, as well as the nature of the system's norms that support particular behavior. As for professional or technical competence, I am not an expert in the newspaper business and can make no judgments of my own about it; I have simply chosen to believe that this competence was high because the *Planet* is considered, by the profession and by the Twentieth Century Fund to be an elite newspaper. (I wish I could provide more objective data on the technical competence of the professionals. Such studies are urgently needed not only for enhancing self-scrutiny but for educating and re-educating professionals.) As for human relationships which involve problem-solving, and for norms of the system, they will be identified and assessed throughout this study, as we look at how people actually deal with each other: what they say and how they say it, how candid and open they are, and how they cooperate with each other in achieving the goals of the newspaper.

But we want to go beyond identifying these behaviors. It is important to discover if and how they interact with each other. For example, competitiveness, win-lose dynamics, low trust, helplessness, and "brittleness" were found to exist throughout the top-level management of the *Planet*. How are these factors interrelated to create a self-maintaining pattern or equilibrium? In our language, we must seek to understand these factors as they exist in the "living system."

The methodology. A self-maintaining system, from an analytical view, is a system with built-in circularity. Built-in circularity means that every factor ultimately influences all the other factors. It also means that we can begin the description of the living system at any point within the system because we will evenutally return to the point where we began. The task is to make certain that all the relevant factors are included and that their patterning is made explicit.

The two primary methods used to diagnose the living system were personal observations and semi-structured interviews. I was assigned an office in which all of the interviews were held (so that the executives and editors would have to leave their own offices and thereby be more available to me and less likely to be interrupted by others). Every interview was, with the permission of the individual, tape-recorded.* The interviews usually took about two hours; the shortest was half an hour, most took two to four hours, and several took over four hours.

The more important diagnostic method was to observe in person actual task-oriented encounters and meetings. I was given permission to attend any meeting I considered relevant. My clients were to have the right to throw me out of any meeting, and if that happened I was to have the right to confront them with the meaning of this behavior. All but two respondents cooperated enthusiastically. Many scheduled their meetings to fit

---

* For a detailed description of the strategy used to interview individuals and obtain permission for tape-recording, see my *Intervention Theory and Method* (1971).

my travel plans. Others tape-recorded important meetings that I could not attend, and still others kept notes of important episodes that I was unable to observe. In several important cases where no records were kept and no tapes made, I was able to interview the participants to obtain a picture of what had happened.

The categories used to observe behavior, the way the data were analyzed, the observer's reliability, and the predictive validity of the scheme have been discussed in detail elsewhere (Argyris 1965, 1970, 1971). The point to be emphasized here is that the scheme of categories purports to focus on 36 variables that enhance or detract from individual interpersonal competence, that facilitate or inhibit effective group dynamics or intergroup relationships, and that result in organizational norms that increase or impede effectiveness.

The observational categories used in this research are summarized in Figure 1. The categories above the zero line are hypothesized to facilitate interpersonal relationships, those below the line to inhibit interpersonal relationships. Each category has an idea component (i) and a feeling component (f). The categories closest to the zero line are the easiest to perform, and

Figure 1.

Categories used to score the tapes

Level I				*Level II*	
Individual		*Interpersonal*		*Norms*	
Experimenting	i	help others to	i	trust	i
	f	experiment	f		f
openness	i	help others to	i	concern	i
	f	be open	f		f
owning	i	help others to	i	individuality	i
	f	own	f		f
Zero ———————————————————————————————————					
not owning	i	not help others	i	conformity	i
	f	to own	f		f
not open	i	not help others	i	antagonism	i
	f	to be open	f		f
rejecting	i	not help others	i	mistrust	i
experimenting	f	to experiment	f		f

those farthest away are most difficult. For example, it is easier to own up to one's ideas or feelings (to express one's views or feelings) than it is to experiment with ideas or feelings (to discuss ideas or feelings which, if wrong, would jeopardize one's self-acceptance). There are two levels of analysis. Level I represents the individual and interpersonal. Level II represents norms of the group. Every unit of behavior is scored on both levels.

Every statement by an individual, no matter how long, is considered to be one unit of behavior so long as the statement falls within one category. If the individual changes behavior during the statement, then another unit is used. For example, if I were stating the previous two sentences, it would be scored as owning up to my ideas (*own i*) and as contributing to the norm of individuality (*indiv i*). As long as I continued describing my ideas it would be one unit at Level I (*own i*) and one unit at Level II (*indiv i*). However, if I stopped and asked, "Am I communicating?" that would be scored as *open i* (I am open to information) and *concern i*. The response (assuming it was affirmative) would be scored as *own i, concern i* (the individual owned up to his idea in a way that showed concern for my question). If I then returned to lecturing, a new unit would be assigned to me (*own i, indiv i*). Here are some sample statements and scores:

I believe we should reject the ideas, even though we are told not to.	*own i, indiv i*
I feel tense.	*own f, indiv f*
Would you please tell me more about your theory?	*open i, concern i*
This is not easy for me to talk about. I feel as if my whole life has been a shambles. I feel frightened and bewildered.	*exper f, trust f*

Table 1 (Appendix A, p. 293) presents an analysis of ten news and editorial meetings scored by this system. The results are representative of the findings obtained from the observations of the fifty meetings. Also, based upon the research to date, the results of the ten meetings would represent a valid picture of one thousand and fifty meetings. There is little variance in group

behavior within this organization, which is the case in all other complex systems studied to date (Argyris 1965, 1968, 1970, and 1971). There are several reasons for this lack of variance in human behavior:

(1) People are educated, beginning early in life, to emphasize certain values while they are problem-solving, decision-making, and implementing decisions. The values are: (a) to emphasize accomplishing the task at hand; (b) to focus on rationality and de-emphasize the expression of feelings; (c) to control others through rewards and penalties; and (d) to expect loyalty to the organizational goals and to those individuals who have formal power. Adhering to these values, as we shall see below, produces a clear-cut and narrow band of acceptable behavior.

(2) People will express the acceptable behavior when they are behaving in real (non-contrived) situations for real stakes. If they are going to win or lose, they want to show that they have played the game according to the rules.

(3) People are rewarded for staying within the acceptable limits of what is, organizationally speaking, "civilized behavior" in two ways. First, others understand them, play the game with them, and therefore actions are produced. Second, if the actions are successful, the top management rewards those who designed, created, or managed them.

(4) As we shall see below (and as we have found in all other studies), executives (indeed most individuals) do not have competences to behave in ways that vary significantly from the pattern we shall describe. Indeed, adherence to the pattern is so strong that when executives have decided to change their behavior, they have been unable to do so (Argyris 1970). People may be different; they may be unique; they may have individualized personalities. But when they behave in groups to accomplish tasks, they appear to coalesce around limited patterns of behavior.

The results of my scoring procedure tell us about the way people actually behaved in meetings. They do not tell us how the same persons felt, nor how they might behave if they were observed under different conditions. These results address themselves to the behavior that creates the living system, and not to individual personalities of the executives.

The most frequently observed behavior was people owning up to or describing their points of view; the group meetings were full of articulate people telling others their respective points of view. The next most frequent behavior, being open to new ideas, occurred far less often. Whereas the frequency of speaking one's mind ranged from 55 to 77 percent, openess to ideas ranged from 8 to 24 percent. Furthermore, content analysis of the actual tapes showed that in the meetings where the openness figures were high, it was because people were primarily asking questions of the superior at the meeting, trying to find out what the superior wanted and what he was going to do.

The least frequently observed behavior—indeed, it was not reported even once—was a person expressing his own feelings or being open to other people's feelings. This does not mean that the managers of the *Planet* had no feelings; they did, and in the crucial meetings, their feelings were strong. What it does mean is that they considered it effective behavior to suppress feelings, because people become incompetent when feelings are discussed. Our results would support this view. Whenever feelings did erupt—and on the rare occasions when they did, people either denied it or felt guilty about it—the effectiveness scores did decrease. However, as we shall show, this consequence may be a self-fulfilling prophecy: people who avoid the discomfort of expressing their feelings will not develop skill in dealing with feelings. Working in settings and in a living system in which the expression of feelings is not encouraged will indeed influence people to behave less effectively when feelings erupt.

This may be one reason why I observed no experimenting or taking risks with his own ideas or feelings; if one learns to be careful not to rock the boat, then one learns to think twice about taking risks. In addition, there was no behavior observed in which a person overtly attempted to help someone else express, be open to, or experiment with his or her own ideas or feelings. The scores for *not* helping others, on the other hand, were some of the highest that I have ever recorded in all my studies. These scores indicate that persons were cutting each other off in order to seize scarce "air time" in any meeting.

If air time is scarce, if one feels alone, if the name of the game is to get your ideas across, then the tendency to listen to the substantive views of others in order to understand them thoroughly will tend to be low. Listening, when it occurs, will tend to be aimed at detecting signs that the speaker is about ready to stop, or that he is saying something the listener can use to build his own case.

A living system based on high competition and low trust. If the reader is beginning to infer that the behavior in group meetings tended to be competitive, he would be correct; the results support this inference. Conformity to ideas was the most frequently observed norm; concern for ideas was next. In the few meetings where the concern scores were higher than the conform scores, it was because a presentation was being made and there was little opportunity for discussion. This may be one reason why openness to ideas was higher during these meetings: every contribution from someone other than the speaker was aimed at finding out what the speaker meant by what he was saying. In other words, although people spoke their minds, they did so, especially when there was a discussion of important issues, in a way which reinforced conformity and competitiveness. The instances in which individuals spoke and reinforced the norm of individuality were rare.

In addition, no behavior was observed that contributed to the norm of trust. Under these conditions, persons tended not to behave in ways that would risk their sense of self-esteem and their feelings of self-acceptance and self-regard. The scores for mistrust were also very low—but this is not an unusual finding. These scores represent actual behavior, not attitudes or feelings. It is possible to feel mistrust but not express it, because that would violate the norm that loyal employees do no overtly express feelings of mistrust. Such behavior would be seen as "uncivilized" or "immature," in the words of a senior editor and a senior executive. As we shall see, many participants did in fact harbor feelings of mistrust.

Turning from observed behavior to the interview data, we note that they support the observed system-characteristic of high competitiveness: 75 percent of the administrative people reported competition to be high in their areas; 100 percent of the news people described their colleagues as very competitive, and nearly 90 percent went on to say that competitiveness is a good quality in news people. (All percentages were computed with an N of 37 except where otherwise note.) Here are a few typical statements: "They're competitive as the devil, they're competitive for a sandwich, they're jealous of each other. They love each other personally, but there is unexpressed jealousy." "I don't think there is much competition. But if there were, it would be a good thing." "You should know it by now, newspaper people are a combination of competitiveness and paranoia. They'll fight for visibility and they'll scream that a plot is being perpetrated against them if they don't get the best assignments continually."

A: Newspaper people are the most competitive people in the
    world, and they have gall.
Q: Would you say a little more about gall?
A: Gall, all-out gall. A shy person or an introvert is not going
    to make it.
Q: Would gall include either competitiveness or aggressive-
    ness?
A: Yes, somebody defined a good newspaper man as being
    like a kid who murders his parents and then pleads
    sympathy from the court because he is an orphan.

We noted from the observations that persons who spoke up during meetings expressed their ideas in a way that contributed primarily to the norm of conformity,and secondarily to the norm of concern for ideas. They spoke up, in other words, in a persuasive or selling manner. So we asked in the interviews whether this meant that individuals conformed to the views of others, that they were "sold" by others. Most participants (72 percent) replied No. I would reply Yes and No: No, they probably did not conform to others' views; Yes, they unintentionally created conditions for conformity by their spontaneous behavior. The persons involved are highly intelligent and articulate, are focused more on winning intellectual challenges than on being aware of their impact on others. Indeed, the individuals perceived themselves as being very intelligent and articulate (72 percent).

They enjoyed intellectual challenges and liked—indeed needed—jobs that required them to overcome challenges (84 percent). Important intellectual problems were always seen as posing a personal challenge (84 percent). The need for intellectual challenge was so great that people sought jobs to perform which were intellectually challenging and absorbing (94 percent).

Win-lose dynamics. Competitive individuals tended to concentrate their energies more on winning than on cooperating with or developing others. Thus whenever important and intellectually challenging issues arose, someone had to win and someone had to lose: 71 percent of the administrators and 88 percent of the news people reported the existence of win-lose interactions. The news respondents more frequently saw them as "fun" and said in effect "That's the name of the game." Here are three illustrations: (1) Individual contributions during meetings tended to be opinionated. For example: "The question is . . . What you are really saying is . . . That issue was not analyzed properly . . . The most interesting piece today was . . . Let's go ahead with the piece on . . . Whatever way that you decide, only (then defines how the subordinate should do the story)." (2) Q: "If someone (during a group meeting) told you something that was helpful to your position, if he added something to your argument, how would you react?" A: "Why didn't I think of it?" (3) Some individuals reported that they were cautious about expressing their ideas publicly lest a competing department claim it was doing a similar story, or that it should get the story as part of its mission.

Under win-lose conditions, the group may become a forum for "outshining" others, and for gaining visibility with the leader: 67 percent noted that one of the major problems of groups was that many people "spoke just to hear themselves speak" and "to impress their boss." If the primary activities during group meetings were win-lose, competitive, and controlling, how could one person use other group members as resources for ideas without losing something? One way, suggested by an executive, is "brain-picking"—asking questions in order to clarify one's own thoughts, but asking them (because of the win-lose dynamics) without seeming to need the information. Thus, particularly in news meetings, participants were often busy interviewing, questioning and confronting each other in order to develop their own views. Ideas were rarely created and or tested in group meetings, and others were seldom helped to explore their own views or significantly change them.

   Evaluation and control rather than diagnosis and innovation. The win-lose dynamics and "brain-picking" led to further competition, which encouraged evaluative comments, discouraged innovation, and decreased the opportunities for a superior to learn much about the quality of a subordinate's thinking and performance. In group meetings I heard statements like those on the left instead of those on the right:

I don't see what's new about that!	What is it about the article that leads you to evaluate it as new?
Joe's story was first-rate.	How did you evaluate Joe's story?
We can't debate that forever.	I believe the discussion is no longer productive. How do the rest of you see it?
This is a terrific story! Very important. We ought to (defines what ought to be done).	(Asking the relevant editor) How do you evaluate the importance of that story? What are your plans for covering it?
We must get more at the causes (of this news story). Or, obviously we must send someone down to interview. . . .	Looking at this story, how would you (editor) handle it?
What you're talking about is really peripheral to my point.	How does your point relate to mine?
All you can do with this is assign it to Bill.	To whom do you plan to assign this story?

   Resistances to exploring risky issues and new ideas. Seventy-four percent of my respondents said that groups were poor places in which to explore new ideas and think out loud; they felt that groups thoroughly discussed only unimportant issues. I was not able to observe a single instance in which a group member openly explored an issue that was ambiguous to him and perhaps to others. When such qeustions were raised (and I observed this to occur ten times), the group members immediately replied in ways that resolved or denied the ambiguity and put an end to exploration.

For example, one superior reported that he preferred to ask questions at meetings, in order to generate a dialogue of exploration for himself and others. One day he was observed to ask, "I need your help on this problem. I've really been struggling with it. Are we unbalancing the picture by (giving a certain sort of coverage)." He received several immediate and definitive answers as to how to solve the problem. No discussion ensued and no new ideas were developed. Subordinates seemed to interpret the invitation for exploration and thinking out loud as an opportunity to speak and shine. One executive referred to these people as "quick studies." He said, "You can throw them anything and they'll have the answer. The rest of us need time. The quick studies go on and verbalize and it all sounds very plausible until you get out of the room. Then you realize all the holes. But by then it's too late."

Another executive, at another meeting, asked, "This problem is related to a basic policy issue that I believe we never have worked through. What *is* our policy on. . . ?" Several people nodded approvingly, indicating agreement, but the discussion returned immediately to the problem at hand rather than to the question about underlying policy. The executive asked again, and again there was no reply.

Little additiveness in problem-solving. Since members of group meetings focused most of their energies on gaining air time, being persuasive, and winning, there tended to be very little genuine listening to others' views. As a result there was little additiveness or coherence to the discussions. It also meant that individuals would not tend to be influenced significantly by others to change their minds (when the issue was a critical one).

Did the persons who tended not to be persuasive (those who were more withdrawn) listen? Could they be influenced? Other group members could not answer these qeustions because the more withdrawn individuals rarely expressed their views. Indeed, their withdrawal might be the best overt indicator of feelings of ineffectiveness in the group. However, from the interviews we learned that these withdrawn or quiet individuals tended to have definite views and often held to them with tenacity. When we asked why they didn't speak more often, they all responded with views illustrated by these quotations: "By the time I'm ready to talk, the subject has changed." "Most of the talk is not very thoughtful; why add to the pain?" "I find the best way to disagree is to remain quiet and deal with the issue outside the group meeting."

Aggressive individuals therefore spoke up but rarely influenced the discussion because of the ways in which they expressed their views; the withdrawn individuals rarely spoke up, and therefore they also rarely influenced the discussion. Group conformity resulted in the sense that the unique capacities of the individuals were not brought into use. These group dynamics created tended to cancel out possibilities for integrated problem-solving.

The competitive, win-lose dynamics tended to encourage a pervasive mode of "selling." "Selling" tended to make the speaker feel that he was being articulate and intellectually powerful. However, this very power could act to reduce the probabilities that the "customer" would buy. The customer might sense that the speaker's power was more emotional than rational, yet notice that the speaker was insisting that he was being rational and was asking others to be the same (let's look at the facts). The listener could then mistrust the "sales pitch." He could decide that the speaker was mainly trying to win him over to protect his own departmental interests, not trying to help create a climate where the best solutions could be found or a new idea could be created.

Under these conditions, participants at meetings tended to immunize themselves against infection by the enthusiasm of the seller. They would try to deflate him or cut off his speech; or tune him out and then silently begin to prepare their own sales pitches; or listen only to find weaknesses in his expressed position. Upon perceiving any of these reactions, the original seller would feel less effective. He would react by selling harder and by evaluating the others as somewhat stubborn for defending a "narrow departmental or personal view."

Thus there was a recycling which tended to increase the selling and competitiveness. This made individuals feel they were rarely heard or understood, which in turn led them to be very careful and articulate in verbalizing their thoughts. They concentrated more on preparing their contributions than on listening to others. Moreover, once they began speaking they continued until all of their accumulated ideas had been heard. One result was that the time available to be "on the air" was scarce.

A second result was the creation of diplomatic ways to "relate" non-relatable items to speaker's previous comments. For example, "I agree with Bill, and I'd like to add a few more points." Or, "I agree with Joe, but (and then disagree)." This becomes a conscious deception of others. But if a person secretly deceives others, how does he know that this is not being done to him? Moreover, in this kind of a living system, how could he find out?

Group meetings viewed as a waste of time. The infrequent helping of one another to own up to, be open to, and experiment with new ideas, the predominantly competitive stance, and the lack of additiveness in group discussion were explained by respondents as caused by *other* persons who did not speak to the point, or who tended to speak simply to be heard or to protect their departmental positions. All this led to feelings that group meetings were a waste of time, and that what was needed in group meetings was a good strong leader! It is understandable that most respondents (82 percent) spoke of groups in a derogatory manner. For example:

A: If I had my way, I'd cancel all group meetings.
Q: Why?
A: They're a big waste of time.
Q: Can they be made more effective?
A: I doubt it. You get people who come prepared to talk about their position all day; who repeat, repeat, and repeat—to impress the boss, I guess—and who are unbelievably stupid.

And another example: "I don't like the group meetings myself. Group discussion tends to bring out the hidden positions of individuals or it puts people into conflict over their territorial responsibilities. So that, generally speaking, you get your best solutions, I believe, through one-to-one or any three people talking together. You don't run the risk of exacerbating these particular personal problems. I think this is not a unique attack; this is true in any organization."

Q: If you did get this kind of territorial conflict, how would it be resolved?

A: It probably wouldn't be resolved here. That is to say, the meeting would nullify the thing. You'll find that nothing will come out of the meeting if everybody defends his own position, and in the end it will be a valueless meeting. Or it will come out at the lowest common denominator.

Q: That's even worse?

A: That's even worse, yes. The bane of the committee system.

And another example:

Q: Let me go back to an early answer. You felt that if one isn't careful, the group can reduce the discussion to the lowest common denominator. You said that that is also possible here?

A: Oh, sure.

Q: Now if you have live individual contributors who cancel out each other, unintentionally, what causes it? How come competent people can cancel out each other in a group?

A: Just the same way they do anywhere. Their own particular interests are involved. If you have a city editor and a national editor and a foreign editor engaged in a general discussion of some particular problem, while each one of them is a very competent newspaperman and they may all have the same idea of how a problem should be handled, if the question arises how much personnel should be devoted to a particular project, one of these follows is going to have that project; it will be his

project and he is going to have the manpower and the
space and so on, and the other two aren't. And regardless of how much they are devoted to the paper
and devoted to each other, this personal feeling of participation or non-participation comes in and each of
them says, "I've got Joe Doakes, my star reporter. I
could send him up to Toronto to get this good story;
instead of that, he is going to be off in Texas doing
something for [another editor]. I'd rather have him do
this story, but that's the way it goes."

Q: So in a sense, it stems from the fact that each of these
   men has his own goals and own interests?

A: Exactly.

Q: I infer from your comments that you don't think there's
   much anyone can do about that. It's human nature. Is
   that correct?

A: Exactly.

And that leads to the next characteristic of the living system.

*Deep pessimism about changing human nature and in-
creasing organizational effectiveness.* Notice that these responses
share three qualities: an implicit pessimism about changing
human behavior; an implicit assumption that it is the *other*
person who comes to talk and to impress or who is not effective;
and an assumption that narrow departmental interests create intergroup conflicts. Add to these another assumption held by most
respondents—that organizations necessarily inhibit individual
contributions and innovation—and we may predict the following.

Pessimism about human nature and organizational effectiveness is easily validated because it is found in experience. But
the reason it is found may be a self-fulfilling prophecy. People
develop meanings for their world and then create the world according to these meanings; the world then feeds back experiences
that reinforce their meanings and a self-sealing process is generated. Self-fulfilling prophecies become compulsive, repetitive
processes because there is no way to publicly test them or alter
them. Processes that are repetitive and compulsive are soon
experienced as being beyond the control of the participants. They

may become, therefore, major causes of organizational ineffectiveness.

There is another characteristic of the living system that
flows from this analysis but which is difficult for respondents to
be aware of and acknowledge: the living system may be composed
of people who are pessimistic or fearful about their own change.
How do we infer the probable existence of this characteristic?

We begin by noting several frequently observed behaviors. First, individuals were openly pessimistic about others
changing. Second, the pessimism about individuals and groups
was never tested publicly. When persons were asked why they
did not test their pessimism publicly, the most frequent responses
were (a) that it might hurt others; and (b) since it was never
done, no one would trust their motivations. If one then suggested that the respondents could begin the experiment by
acknowledging openly that it might be misinterpreted since such
behavior was rare and not sanctioned by the norms of the living
system, the respondents turned to the fear of hurting others. But
if the fear of hurting others is the very fear to be tested, then they
cannot use that as a reason. Confronted with this, the respondents
usually began to acknowledge that part of the problem was that
they did not wish to hurt themselves.

How could they hurt themselves? The answer they gave
is that they would hurt themselves by hurting others! But we asked
them to assume that the test would be done publicly and competently. The responses then were (a) it could be done competently, but no matter how it were done, it would still hurt
others; or (b) *I* don't know how to do it competently. The first
response is another defense against experimenting and a further
attribution of pessimism to the other. The second makes possible
an exploration of a person's reasons for being incompetent.
Typically, the system is blamed first because it does not permit
such candid behavior. However, when one asks the respondent
to imagine a system in which such candor is possible and then to
provide a scenario in which he tests his feelings in action, the
result is discouraging: not only does he not know how to attempt
this testing competently, but the only strategies he can imagine
partake of the competitive win-lose dynamics of the living system.

This result is not surprising since the living system does mold behavior and limit learning within its constraints; indeed this very acculturation to the living system makes it unnecessary for individuals to explore their personal resistance to change.

Avoiding interpersonal, group, and intergroup conflict. The low risk-taking, the norms against expressing feelings, and the suppression of issues that may threaten individuals led to ineffective coping with conflict at all levels. From the interviews we learned that most people preferred that conflict be managed "diplomatically" or covertly. Thus 91 percent said that when interpersonal conflict arises, an effective leader "tells a joke to cool things off" or "gets back to the facts" or "stops the meetings and talks to the individuals." And 74 percent said they disliked personal confrontations on issues that involved personal feelings. For example: "I have a horror of confrontation except under the direst circumstances. I think others have the same horror of confrontation. So if you have this feeling, it seems to me what you do, as I do, is idle around the thing, and only go to confrontation when it is the last desperate resort." "If our superiors are unable to confront issues, if they do not like issues that are loaded with conflict, personal conflict, then they must behave in ways to smother them." In fact, 91 percent of the respondents reported that interpersonal, group, and intergroup conflicts were not dealt with openly. "Bury it" or "hide it" were phrases commonly used to describe how to handle a conflict. Some typical comments: "We don't resolve conflicts. If we talk about them, they get solved at the lowest common denominator." "We talk out issues and if at the end disagreement exists, the superior wins." "Conflict resolution is conflict suppression. Now you see it, now you don't." Here is how one executive described the way he would handle a conflict issue:

A: If I thought a man was better at A than B, I would assign him type A stories.

Q: Would you tell him that you have evaluated him as being strongest with type A stories?

A: Yes, but not directly. I'd tell him in a backhanded way [such as] "You handle spot news well." If he says, "I'd

like to do other things," I reply, "Yes, you can and
you will." I can say that because just by the nature of
job assignments, he is bound to be assigned a few B
jobs.

Withholding information that may be threatening. An
understandable consequence of not confronting conflict was the
withholding of information. This happened in group settings as
well as in organizational practices. Here are a few examples from
group settings.

In one meeting one man said: "S's story was perfect
illustration, don't you think (looking at the entire group), of how
a story should be written on this." Several nodded their heads,
several said "yes," several did not speak. One man raised his eye-
brows, implying that he disagreed, but said yes. Five minutes
later he was asked to do something which assumed that he had
agreed with the statement above. He replied, "I think S's story was
good, but he let us down a little bit," and he then continued to
describe the weakness of the story.

When the question "Could you conceive of a group situation where these rivalries and hurt feelings could be discussed
openly with the other men involved?" was put to the individuals
who brought these up—and they were the majority—all but two
replied no. Many added, "Nor do I think it would be a good
idea."

In another instance, a person said, "Mr. Jones came to
this organization with the reputation of being an open, trusting
manager. Well, he tried it. Now he realizes that he can't be open
in an organization as large as this one. He has retreated and become more political. The system is swallowing him up."

One news executive created a periodic news meeting to
keep his subordinates informed of each other's efforts and to encourage creativity and innovation. During the interviews, ten
persons who participated in those meetings noted that they had
wandered from their original objectives. "The news meetings
were a good idea when they were first begun. Now they've de-
generated into—you know, slice the legs out from under every
body except your own people." "People use these meetings to get

themselves known. Visibility is important and they know it."
"Many see the news meetings as a waste of time. They have
nothing to do with work."

Another important example of the way information was
withheld may be found in the area of demotion. The executives
and editors expressed ambivalent feelings about the demotion
processes. Most felt that "the organization takes care of its
people," yet said that the impact on the individual and on others
was "devastating." "There's no such thing as a demotion. We
ease out the person and put him on the shelf. I question this. If
you are going to ease out people, it should be done more
honestly." "It has a salutary effect. The company is seen as
human. This is not a brutal organization." "This is a devastating
problem. I face it every day. In order to help them I had to
give them important assignments once in a while. They do a poor
job, and then I really have to edit them. That gets them and me
in more difficulty." "We don't demote a person around here.
He doesn't get a demotion on the chart. In fact, it may show up
as a promotion. This company is known for cushioning the
shock." Yet the same man later said: "Certainly these pseudo-
promotions hurt the individual. You lower his self-esteem. You
can't convince him that he has a promotion, that he is equal to
his peers. He knows it isn't so."

A: In our organization, as a rule, no one gets demoted. A
   guy is eased out. One day he was doing something important; the next day, not so.
Q: What impact, if any, is there on the individual?
A: The individual is hit hard; his spirit may be broken. Of
   course, it is never discussed. I guess partially because
   he is *glad* to have a job.

What is the impact upon others in the organization? Most
respondents reported a sense of ambivalence. On the one hand,
they agreed that if the organization was going to keep its position,
it had to get rid of dead wood. On the other hand, they knew it
could be cruel to permit a person to stay but act as if he had not
been demoted. A few wondered if they *really* cared what hap-

pened to the next person. This last reaction would fit with the competitive climate in the living system. As one young newsman said: "That's an interesting question. If we're honest, I'd have to say that we're so competitive that our reaction is . . . who cares about the old guys, just so long as it isn't me." A more concerned young newsman added, "I don't expect to stay here long enough to face up to these qeustions. I'm successful here but I'll probably move along."

Secrecy in management decisions. The lack of open discussion of difficult issues, the tendency to make secret decisions about promotions, and the policy of handling demotions "indirectly" operated to give subordinates the view that the organization was managed more by conspiracy than by openness. Thus 70 percent of the respondents reported instances when they wondered why a particular organizational or personnel decision had been made and said that in these cases they thought that a conspiracy may have been a reason. Some comments were: "This is a management by secrets and conspiracies." "Our management wants to do something without saying so, it's the hallmark of our style." "And people gossip! Nothing is kept secret very long; like, say, five minutes. But there are other cases that are conspiracies. I'm not aware of the conspiracies being big ones . . . just small ones; of course, I don't sit at the highest levels."

A: A guy (last week) should have been informed of what was going on, but I couldn't say anything because I was told the move was secret. So I proceeded to do it in secrecy —but there is a limit to secrecy.

Q: Is this a quality of the organization? Some people imply that secrecy and conspiracy are common. How do you see this?

A: This example was secrecy as distinguished from conspiracy. Conspiracy is another subject. This was not to put anything over on anybody. I was told that this must be done quietly. The order came from Adam. It was a flat "nobody but you and Joe is to know about this." It is so palpably foolish that we should try to be secret about this!

Before leaving this topic, it should be noted that the majority of respondents reported that although *interdepartmental* conflicts still existed, they had been resolved more effectively during the last several years, largely due to the initiative of the new president (94 percent). Conflicts were now being talked out much more openly, whereas several years ago the departments were like little kingdoms rarely communicating to each other (94 percent). If the discussions at a given level did not resolve the conflicts, the individuals tended to feel free to take them up to the next level for resolution (94 percent).

The freedom individuals felt to discuss departmental issues openly and to take them up to their superiors was found to be a strength in the system. However, as we shall see, there were forces operating within the system to motivate individuals "pass the buck" upward without making a thorough attempt to solve the problem and reach a resolution at the lower level.

Commitments to decisions may be illusive. Since individuals were familiar with the norm that group meetings were a waste of time, and since the executives tended to be impatient, there was little feeling of freedom to explore all issues thoroughly at meetings. Consequently subordinates found themselves agreeing to decisions even though they were not in full agreement. This reticence occurred even with superiors who wished to encourage a more open confrontation of issues. For example, I referred previously to the news meetings, whose purpose was to generate new ideas and explore long-range planning. The majority of the participants saw these weekly meetings as focused on the chairman and thought this was appropriate. The chairman, however, wanted to have the focus on all the participants. He wanted to act as a facilitator of discussion rather than a controller. The participants felt that the meetings were focused too much on the chairman and wished that some changes could be made. They felt that the meetings could lead to a further centralization of power. "N does dominate it, but not in a harsh way. From the very beginning he opens it up with his ideas and he has ten ideas for every one that anybody else has." "Another respect in which it has not worked is cross-fertilization. A few of the very top people talk beyond their fields. But I have never heard Able talk outside his field, nor for that matter Baker or Charlie. I would say the majority stay within their responsibilities." When asked if these men had raised these issues with the group, all responded negatively, and all but one said that it would be "out of place" to do such a thing in the group meetings.

A second example came from a participant in a news meeting.

A: I didn't find the comments on the airline strike story very
   useful because I have a good rundown on what is in all
   the newspapers, especially in my field.
Q: I observed the meeting today; why didn't you say so?
A: Oh, I don't know. Maybe it is easier to let them to say
   their piece than raise the issue.

Another illustration came from a meeting in which A, B, and C were supposed to present their point of view about a certain decision. They presented their views, but it happened that their views were tentatively rejected. They were upset, and expressed feelings the meeting was loaded against them. The chairman, who learned of their reaction from Mr. S, reported genuine surprise, implying that anyone would know that the meeting was not loaded.

I questioned these three men. They felt that the decision was the wrong decision, and said that a memo had been written before the meeting (to someone not at the meeting) turning down the idea.

Q: [to A, B, or C]: If you felt these things, why didn't you
   raise these issues during the meeting?
A: It would have been viewed as discourteous. By the way,
   this is not over yet. Not by a long shot!

The "courteous" reply actually covered up the subordinates' anger and their determination to find a new way to win. When the next confrontation occurred, their strategy was to introduce the issue as a new problem arising from new evidence. The superior felt a sense of frustration that old issues keep coming up in new packages.

And another example. It sometimes happens that a group meeting is held and a decision is made; later, the superior learns that no action has been taken, or that a different action has been taken, or that the commitment to the decision was not as strong as he had been led to believe. I asked a *Planet* executive to tell me if this ever happened to him.

A: Absolutely. . . . I mean agreements are made, people think they've got this decided, this is now being done. But nothing happens.

Q: Why?

A: Breaks down?

Q: Yes.

A: Combination of things. The debate or discussion is usually aimed at perfection. Even if no one says so, the group usually takes an idea that M or N have, and comes up with a plan they think is the absolutely perfect projection of this idea. It loses something immediately if it is filtered down one level to a group of editors, who will discuss it on their own. It loses considerably more by the time it gets down to the operating group. And then if there's been any resistance to the idea anywhere along the line, it will get diluted even further. Someone can say, that guy doesn't really believe in this anyway, but all right, he wants this, we'll give him a bit of this. Bit by bit that beautiful thing up here, which starts off at a hundred percent, comes out at 60 percent or 40 percent, or may be only 20 percent by the time the rewrite man finishes with the thing. People at the top say, "But I asked for it this way!" And they can never understand why it hasn't come out that way.

The tendency to centralize decision-making. Given the win-lose dynamics, the absence of risk-taking, the lack of effective conflict resolution, the secrecy and at times conspiracy, and the top management's desire to run a "humane" organization, subordinates at all levels will tend to play it safe and pass on decisions that tend to threaten themselves or others. Eventually the buck will land at the superior's office. He will tend to make decisions with no more new information than the protagonists had before the meeting was held. Also the dynamics of the meetings will be such that the subordinates will present their views persuasively, argue down the other side, and then wait for the ruling from on high.

For example, several qualities impressed me about the decision-making processes involved in two decisions that were taken up to the President. (1) Each side (at a meeting prior to the one with the President) presented its views to its own superior in a way that asked him to agree with them and to place the other departments involved in difficulty. As one person described it, "We're in the process of throwing the dead cat over in the other guy's yard." Issues were presented in a win-lose manner. (2) As the superior became convinced that his subordinates had a valid case he focused on finding ways to strengthen their case and begain to make contacts with the "rival" peer or with the superior, indirectly alerting him that his group had reached certain conclusions which, if accepted by higher authority, would mean that someone would win and someone would lose. In the vernacular of the system, this is "lighting a fire," being gracious to alert the other team leader. (3) When the decision was one which threatened some sub-group it was viewed as involving a major policy and therefore had to be passed on to the top. (4) In neither case was any new information added at the top-level meeting. The function of the meeting seemed to be to pass the problem to the top. The top seemed to accept it, and indeed enjoyed making the decision.

The result of these processes was to help centralize important decision-making at the top and help the lower levels "get off the hook," especially if they lost. It also tended to make some people heroes and others losers. These are not uncommon results (Blake, Shepard, and Mouton 1965).

There is another set of forces that leads to increasing centralization. Persons who are very competitive also tend to "over-respect" authority. The superior represents to them an individual who has won, and who, because of his power, can continue to win. With time, "over-respect" becomes the acceptable psychological stance for subordinates toward their superior. This may mean that the subordinates who are over-respecting their superior will tend to expect their own subordinates to behave in the same manner. Under these conditions, attempts to create meetings for activities other than to inform, to control, and to direct others will unwittingly be changed into meetings where those activities become ends in themselves.

A certain series of news meetings, for example, had been created in order to encourage subordinates to think innovatively and in more long range terms about their work. However, 71 percent of the subordinates saw the meetings as a place for the chairman to set forth his own ideas. For example: "Basically it's his meeting. It gives him the chance to make his own impact on the paper." "The meeting is basically to allow him to ask questions that interest him and to generate ideas." "The purpose of the meeting is to bring everyone together and get them on the same wave length. Participation is tricky in that meeting. The more you say the more work may be assigned to you."

The tendency to make the superior's needs the center of attention continues in the interaction the members of news planning have with their subordinates. They may, unintentionally, use the "authority" of the meeting to explain why certain tasks must be done. Six respondents, for example, reported that the news planning meetings were being turned into sources for new orders to give to the "troops out in the field." For example: "There's a tendency for some people to walk out of that room thinking they heard an order and then to pass it down as a command, when in fact the intention most of the time is to raise a question." "The meetings began with the idea of getting a more effective intellectual shaping of the newspaper. Now it's become more like a brainstorming session where the name of the game is one-upmanship. What concerns me more is that the ideas become lists of proposals that get sent out to the field as orders. "

A: This has happened to several of us. I got an assignment which I thought was foolish. I went to talk with H. He refused to listen. He told me that Mr. J had

asked for the story and that was that. I was angry—
mad! I know Mr. J and he was too good a reporter
to make such assignments.

Q: What did you do?

A: Nothing. What can you do? You have to pick and choose
the case on which to make your stand.

Finally, respondents reported that comments and ideas of
the top editors became orders for those below. For example, at
various times, "microcosm" and "color" were used as criteria
for effective stories; then "people got on that kick and it was
overdone." It is not easy to confront superiors about overdone
"kicks," especially when middle management refuses to listen
and defends its rigidity by saying, as one man put it, "S ordered
this and that's it. Now don't ask me again."

News planning meetings will tend to be seen by people
down the lines as an important source of orders. Since they are
so far removed from these meetings they will tend to feel less
optimistic about influencing the news planning and eventually
they will become less motivated to contribute. This attitude soon
feeds back to become an important force for the centralization of
authority and control.

Under these conditions, if top management insists that it
wants increased involvement from all participants, the statement
will, if believed, place the good men in a bind. They may say
to themselves, "They want me to think and contribute, yet they do
it all." The uninvolved or ineffective men may feel confirmed.
The uninvolved will see the incongruity between management's
words and its behavior as proof of duplicity, and thus feel reinforced in their intention to remain uninvolved. The incompetent
men may see the increasing centralization as the cause of their
inability to contribute.

*The belief that effective leadership is directive, con-
trolling, and focuses on tasks and ignores feelings.* Given the
competitiveness, low trust, avoidance of conflict, managerial
secrecy, and centralization of decision-making, it is not surprising that most of the *Planet* men I interviewed assumed that

effective leadership is strong, directive, believes in competitiveness, and confronts interpersonal conflicts covertly. For example: Groups are effective when they have strong leaders who run disciplined meetings, and who in most cases know what the decision should be before they come to the meeting, although they do not act as if they do (94 percent). Serious blocks to progress occur when people speak only to be heard, or to make an impression and the leader doesn't shut them up (70 percent). Also, 69 percent of the respondents described the majority of the top leadership as directive and controlling; a few executives were seen as more passive and less aggressive. Here are some remarks by those who saw the leadership as primarily aggressive: "Most of the top people are brilliant, insecure, emotional, with a need to dominate. You wouldn't understand this need but it is there." "Take V, for instance. He probably doesn't even realize he has made up his mind, but when he does he has to have his way. We know it, and that stops the discussion. It's a brutalizing conversation afterward—do it my way! And mind you, I love the guy. He's not doing this out of selfishness; he is doing it out of an incredible desire for professional perfection." "Most of the executives really want participation until we disagree with them." Turning to comments about the more passive leaders: "Z is a quiet, thoughtful executive with thousands of ideas. Without realizing it, many times, he controls the meetings in a very subtle way." An executive who described himself as being less aggressive added, "I believe that my job should be to leave these people alone and draw them out rather than try to tell them what to do. I love to see a team operate. I love to participate in what a man is doing vicariously. Manipulating people, getting people in a great human organization to do what you want them to do and also to determine what you want to do by dealing with them—that's my way of leading."

Thus two kinds of leadership style emerged. The predominant one was a directive, controlling style; the other was its polar opposite, namely one of withdrawal and passivity. The directive style was associated with "emotionality," "harshness," and "anger"; the passive style was associated with "coldness and distance." Both were associated with brilliance and manipulation.

The aggressive leadership causes conformity, dependence, submissiveness, and inhibits innovation and internal commitment. The passive leadership "cops out" and encourages the more aggressive leadership to predominate. Thus both styles feed back to reinforce the difficulties of the system.

There is another quality common to both types of leadership: 64 percent of the respondents believed that news executives and managers (of either variety) consciously planned to have several good men competing for stories. They were seen as believing that competition was important in motivating news people. One respondent, who apparently knew some of the management literature, commented that, "We have our own rabble hypothesis where people are pitted against each other." Two respondents cited a letter, by the President saying in effect that a good staff is a restless staff and that the company is not an old age home.

There are at least two difficulties involved in the effective execution of these policies. First, these policies help to reinforce the win-lose dynamics we have already described. This in turn increases the subordinates' mistrust of each other and their dependence on the superior. Second, it becomes difficult for the superior to learn when the unmanageable point has been reached, because the persons involved in the competition will tend not to inform the leader. It is likely that the superior will not learn about a problem until it can no longer be contained, or becomes a crisis.

The majority of the leaders in the system did not view their behavior as conforming to the competitive authoritarian qualities of the living system (even though they reported that these were the qualities that the living system sanctioned). For example, they rated themselves (N-37) on encouraging the expression of others' views and on openness to new ideas.

	High	Moderate	Low
Encouraging the expression of views different from their own	75%	18%	07%
Openness to new ideas and taking risks	79%	18%	03%

Some of their illustrative comments were: "I am trying to get people to be open. This is unusual in our business. I know when I was a reporter I would rarely be open." "You can't order people around in a creative organization." [Yet later in the same interview] "Every morning I assign them their work." [And still later] "The thing that fascinates me most about my job is teaching. Take in some kid and make him, mold him into a finished newsman!" "The best way to manage news people is to give them their own heads." [Yet later in the interview] "If there is editing to be done, I call him in and say, 'Here's what I've done to your story.' I'm careful to explain why. The next time I expect him to have learned." "I try to be gentle with them. I try to avoid being authoritarian. Of course, it is up to me to show them the way to do the job. I've got to assume that the way I do it is correct."

The incongruity between the view of leadership style and the actual behavior leads to an interesting irony. Many of the executives believed that groups and organizations tend to smother human beings, yet these same executives created as much, or more, conformity and dependence by their behavior as could be attributed to the groups or the organization. Moreover, this conformity and dependence was more difficult for their subordinates to overcome than the kind created by the groups and organization, for several reasons: (a) the executives were seen, by their subordinates, as being unaware of when they were creating conformity and dependence; however, (b) the subordinates also knew that their superiors believed deeply in individual autonomy and development; thus (c) for the subordinates to tell their superior that his behavior caused the very conditions that he abhorred would run the risk of upsetting the superior; and since (d) the living system contained a strong norm that one should not discuss such issues openly, the subordinates felt little freedom to discuss the dilemma.

The subordinates were therefore in a bind. They would be damned if they did (by others) and damned if they didn't (by themselves). One way to adapt was to act as if one were open and confronting, while at the same time actually withholding many feelings. The subordinates learned to be "controlled rebels," to deviate carefully, and if they were to deviate to do it effectively and rarely. For example: "There is a lifestyle of being a renegade. Not a renegade; a controlled rebel. To know how far you can push. I think this is something everybody looks upon as good. It isn't being the 'yes man' but a kind of 'yes man' who argues here and gives there." "I used to be a good little boy and do my work. Do everything that was asked of me and do it well and figure somebody would notice me. That's not necessarily so." "I've thought about this a lot. The go-getter who advances his career is going to get ahead. Talent isn't the only thing. It would be great if it were. But there is a balance and you have to be very careful in creating the balance." "You have to be especially careful with these fellows. The initial reputation is the important one. People tend to get typed early because they're so harried." "A willingness to speak up and make yourself known; not to be hesistant, not to sit back, to push a little bit, but to know just how far to push."

The leaders of a newspaper have a difficult job. They are faced with systems that resist change, and with individuals who condemn the system but would be threatened by change, and they are of served and monitored by craft unions and by an increasingly disgruntled citizenry. It is understandable that an editor said, "After a while, you wonder if this is all worth it. What the hell is life all about? Is this what I should be doing? Maybe I should go back to my typewriter." It is no fun to be boss, to be condemned if you act to produce change, and to be condemned if you do not produce the change—and, if you have some sensitivity, to react to this double bind with a feeling of helplessness.

To summarize, the living system may be characterized as competitive and low in trust, and as operating within win-lose dynamics. Evaluation and control are more important than inquiry and innovation; risky issues and innovations tend not to be discussed; additiveness and coherence in problem-solving activities are low; group discussions are ineffective and group meetings are considered a waste of time; and there is deep pessimism about changing human nature or increasing the effectiveness of the system.

Conflicts between individuals, and conflicts within and between groups, are avoided; information relevant to any decision-making that might be threatening is withheld; management operates secretly; commitments to decisions seem illusive; decision-making is centralized; and the directive, competitive leadership styles that predominate in the system act to reinforce the competitiveness, low trust, ineffectiveness of groups, and lack of individual initiative and risk-taking.

It seems fair to suggest that in this living system, the factors supporting ineffectiveness in problem-solving, decision-making, and implementation will tend to be greater than the factors supporting effectiveness. (For a note on determining the validity of this diagnosis, see Appendix A.) The diagnosis would support predictions like these:

(1) It will tend to be difficult for participants to provide the valid information needed for solving important problems. Any search for alternatives will tend to be narrow in scope, any exploration of alternatives will tend to be brief, and any choice will tend to be influenced significantly by incomplete and distorted information.

(2) Problems will not tend to be solved in such a way that they remain solved. It should be possible to observe frequently that decisions which were described as having solved a problem later led to a recurrence of the problem.

(3) The trust level within the system and the confidence of the members in the problem-solving, decision-making, and implementation activities should tend to be low.

Long-Term Consequences
for the Organization

I f an organization is to develop a capacity for self-renewal, the pessimistic assumptions, the pent-up feelings, and the frustrations should be expressed and dealt with *when and where they are occurring*. If they are not confronted *in their "natural" settings,* they will spread out to other settings, become unmanageable, and eventually exist almost compulsively. Once this occurs, they become uninfluenceable.

The roots of organizational dry rot: ineffective activities become compulsive and uncorrectable. An illustration may be what was commonly described at *The Daily Planet* as "the morale problem on the fifth floor." Some 87 percent of the respondents (N-31) reported that a morale problem did exist on the fifth floor; 13 percent of these did not see it as an important problem. Those who believed the morale problem to be important mentioned the following factors as causes of the problem (total is more than 100 percent because respondents gave more than one answer).

(1) The generation problem (71 percent). "There is a gap between the oldtimers and the younger men. Those with long seniority see younger men getting the best stories earlier, receiving higher salaries, and writing stories with by-lines much sooner."

(2) Low salaries or infrequent raises (60 percent). "I can't give a merit increase for more than a minority of my employees each year."

(3) Superior's behavior (51 percent). "Many of these executives are sticklers for excellence. But the human debris they leave behind is high. Yet they're sensitive human beings."

(4) Lower status of copy editors (32 percent). "The desk people believe they are second-rate. Most top positions are now filled by reporters. Desk people used to have a chance at being editor. Also they're paid less."

(5) Demotions and the resulting multiplicity of bosses (37 percent). "It is really embarrassing, frustrating. I find that I must clear with two or three people before I make a decision. I have too many bosses."

(6) Reorganization and upgrading of standards. There was a smaller group which agreed that people spoke of a morale problem but doubted the validity of this view. For example: "I think, at the moment, we are probably too concerned with the morale problem. Morale is much better than it used to be. The new top team is trying to cement and build." "There has been a morale problem on the fifth floor. It's in the nature of the beast." Nineteen percent, however, believed that morale was high: "There is no real morale problem. There may be some groaning but once they have a job to do, they all get in there and work." "How can you get out a paper like this one with bad morale? There are a bunch of mustangs and thoroughbreds here. That's what you're dealing with. If you can't stand that, you better get out of the kitchen."

If one analyzes the comments of those who believe there is a morale problem, one finds that the majority of the factors have so far been placed by the respondents in the category of "not changeable by management." Thus the generation gap, superiors' behavior, lower status of copy editors, and demotions were seen as inevitable. However, salaries and the organization chart were viewed as changeable; the upgrading of performance standards was also seen as changeable, but less so. If the respondents begin to feel a need to alter morale, they will focus on the factors they see as changeable. Thus requests will be heard that salaries be increased, reorganizations be stopped, and the pace of upgrading performance standards be reduced. One of the problems with reducing these factors is that they do not get at the causes. If action is taken on them, they will help to alleviate immediate frustrations and give the subordinates the feeling that they have influenced a not-too-influenceable system. However, the problems will surface again, and this will frustrate the subordinates even more.

Those who doubted that the morale problem was serious and those who believed there was no morale problem at all suggested that the issue be dropped and said in effect "Let's get on with the work. A busy crew is a happy crew." The result of doing this would be that the morale problem would continue to exist, expressing itself every day and thus becoming even more embedded in the living system.

Another example of uninfluenceable organizational activities was the executive committee. The majority of the committee's permanent members saw it as an ineffective group. They would agree with this comment: "It's not a very effective group. Something must be done about it. I am not sure how to go about changing it. I hate to say that because I participate in it. First of all, by and large the executive committee has not dealt with important issues, and has tended to deal with minor matters. Secondly, it is highly indecisive. Thirdly, there is little evidence of trust and there have been very few indications of past successes on which we could build. There is very little data brought to bear, and decisions, when they are taken, all too frequently are taken by default; we don't take any action, but that in effect is making a decision. In other cases we are in a crisis situation and time has run out and something has to be done. And we just walk out on it and somebody says, "Why don't you do thus-and-so?' "

So we have a group of the majority whose members saw it as being ineffective, yet they were unable to do much that was constructive, including raising the issue itself.

Incidentally, those who visited the executive committee to make presentations and those who heard about the dynamics of the sessions from their superiors also concluded that the executive committee was not very effective. This brings to mind two questions: (1) What effect does this have upon their willingness to be open and take risks when they make a presentation or get a presentation ready for the executive committee? (2) What kind of lessons are subordinates learning about the living system of the newspaper?

Innovation and individual development will be decreasingly associated with factors internal to the organization. This first prediction is a direct extrapolation from the analysis above. I am simply predicting that individuals will continue *not* to see the living system as the context within which innovation and individual development will tend to occur. In this connection it should be pointed out that 51 percent of the respondents reported that they were unable to do creative thinking and writing while at work. The mornings, some lunches, and evenings were most frequently selected as moments for creative thinking and writing. It does not follow, however, that innovation and self-development will not occur. The prediction is simply that these activities will not emanate from within.

One danger is that the managers, at all levels, may begin to feel a sense of helplessness and eventually a lack of responsibility about designing and executing activities that may enhance innovation and individual enjoyment. This could lead young men with innovative ideas to withhold them or to be frustrated in their attempts to get them considered by managers (who by this time may have given up). A corollary prediction is that some persons may come to see the newspaper as their home, the source of a minimum guaranteed income, and as a base from which to innovate and develop in cooperation with outsiders in contexts external to *The Daily Planet*.

Corrective actions become deviant activities. If conflict resolution continues to be ineffective, if groups continue to be viewed as unproductive, and if decision-making seems arbitrary, then strong forces will be operating to inhibit basic changes in the living system. Changes will be only cosmetic or superficial; or they will occur only periodically, when a "czar" is appointed to reshape policy and practice. The actions of czar will probably give people the reason they need to resist openly; the making of superficial changes will reinforce the view that major changes are not possible.

This will tend to preserve the status quo, as described above, and make individuals even more cynical. "People," said one respondent, "are so suspicious. They always think that someone is pulling strings." "This organizational paranoia," added another, "is in the nature of the newspaper business." As these views become norms they will also act to make corrective actions more difficult to consider and to implement.

The relationship between the reporters and the copy editors provides an example. This problem is not unique to the newspaper business; it is built into the nature of the work. As we shall see, the reporters tended to experience the writing of an article as not very challenging. What added some degree of challenge was that articles had to be greatly compressed and written in short periods of time; the sense of satisfaction therefore came from producing a story to fit a limited space under pressure of a deadline.

Finished stories were rarely considered perfect by their writers; most were the result of what one reporter described as a "creative compromise" among a host of factors. In the eyes of the reporter, the copy editor attacks the creative compromise, the reporter's last remaining stronghold for satisfaction. "The essential problem is that a reporter sits down and writes. He usually puts a tremendous amount of effort into putting words together. When an editor then rearranges this masterpiece, he is rearranging your creation and that gets in the way of your ego."

"The problem of the copy editor is that if he were to be given freedom, he reduces our freedom. But I can see their problem. This used to be a copy editors' newspaper. Editor Black was the king of the copy reader movement. His altar was that there was a single truth and we tell it. Now, with the new editors, the reporters have more to say. The copy editors feel that they are treated as mechanics; do this, do that, insert this, no imagination."

The way management has dealt with this problem fits the norms of the living system and guarantees that the problem will persist: rules were developed whereby reporters are not permitted to talk to copy editors directly (although a few do) and vice versa. Communication goes through channels.

Now if a reporter believes that he has difficulties with the copy editors, if he believes that they are understandably defensive, if he believes in the unchangeability of human behavior in organizations, and if there are rules against talking with the people involved, then the norms of the living system are strengthened while the chances for genuine problem-solving and learning from each other are greatly diminished. The rules help to create self-sealing processes, because both sides come to believe that the other is irrational and that management does not want to deal with the issues openly. Witness these two statements by reporters: "We can't go directly to the copy editor. We're not supposed to. The idea is to complain to our editor. He then initiates a strawberry investigation. Well, all this does is to create additional hostility between the reporters and the copy desk because the copy editor feels that we squealed on him. You would rather go directly—but there is no machinery for this." "After a while the tension is so great that there is no sense in going to the copy editors. They're in no mood to listen. All they'll do is explain to you their reasons and defend themselves."

To break through the norms and rules of the living system would not only make the individual appear to behave deviantly—as one reporter put it, "like a damn fool." If you ever tried to deal with the issues openly and directly, he said, everyone would ask "What the hell does he think he's doing?" The bewilderment is caused not only by the existence of rules against open and genuine problem-solving or by the knowledge that both sides are uptight. It is also caused by the common assumption expressed by one oldtimer, "Hell it's like tilting with windmills to think you can change anything in this place."

The living system will magnify conflict and fear; executives will fear making changes. Since it is difficult to express tension, frustration, and dissatisfaction, these feelings may be suppressed or sublimated. To the extent that they are suppressed, persons will spend much energy building up and maintaining personal defenses against blowing up. To the extent that they are sublimated, persons may become "carriers" of low morale and seek to infect others; they may work very hard and take out their aggression in the kinds of stories they write (and write best); or they may work long, hard hours (regardless of whether their performance is effective or ineffective) in order to prove their loyalty. This last alternative is especially troublesome for the individual because it forces him to admit not only that he is unable to leave but also that he cannot even express his anger openly.

Under these conditions the "human atmosphere" will become a *magnifier* of conflict and fear. Every molehill may become a mountain. Given the norm against open confrontation, the management may find itself increasingly reacting to assure people that the newspaper, as an organization, is kindly and humane. In selecting executives to supervise situations in which performance is relatively effective, management seeks executives who can be "diplomatic" and "help the situation de-fuse." If organizational performance in one area becomes highly ineffective, then they seek more aggressive executives, who are charged with "cleaning up the mess" and yet warned to "go easy lest there be union difficulties or someone hurt." This charge places the executive in a double bind. He is asked to make changes, which are intrinsically upsetting, in a system that magnifies the upset, without upsetting anyone! There is also the implied threat that if he does upset the system he will not be supported.

For example: When twenty-two persons made comments about a major organizational change carried out several years ago, their statements were congruent with this one. "I think that somebody's got to do it. What I admired S for most, when he took over he had to get rid of the old layers and he did. In doing that, my own opinion, S committed suicide on this paper. It is too bad in many ways. That was the mission that descended upon him and I admire him for having done it. At the same time I admire him in the abstract, particularly admired him in the personal, I don't want to do it myself. . . It would give me a great personal anguish as I'm sure it gave him."

Is it any wonder that individuals who have had to make these kinds of changes begin to wonder "Who is with me?" and that they may have reacted by becoming more conservative in their managerial actions? As one *Planet* man said, "You know, the funny thing is, the guy who came in to revolutionize [that department] is now the defender of the status quo."

Both the request and implied threat may cause tension and fear. The manager may feel that he should become very cautious in how he makes changes, especially those that involve people. This caution can result in much time and effort being spent in "setting up" people for change. As one executive put it, "You have to start a long way in advance, say three or six months and longer. You have to plant seeds in people's minds. "

But what is the process of "planting seeds?" Do people know when this is being done to them? If they do, will they not tend to feel surprise and irritation at being manipulated? How about the individual who "plants seeds?" Will he wonder when this process may be tried on him? If so, is it possible that individuals may become increasingly sensitive to manipulating and being manipulated? This may be a cause of the view that management manages by secrecy and conspiracy.

Being cautious had reached the point where some key executives felt forced to use subterfuge to manage change. Here is an example. Executive Able wanted to institute a change in his area. He checked it out carefully and it was assessed as an excellent idea. Able feared that manager Baker would resent the idea and be hurt. He therefore asked manager Charlie to schedule a luncheon with Able and Baker where he Charlie suggested the idea. Able acted as if he were not too sure of the idea and kept asking Baker his opinion. Baker bought the idea from Charlie, and Able kept saying, "Well, if Baker agrees, I'll go along." Baker reported in an interview that he knew the luncheon was rigged to get him to accept the change. However, he was not aware that Able had initiated the meeting. He thought Charlie was the initiator who asked Able to assist him. The "fact" that Able had colluded with Charlie (a manager in another department) "against him" infuriated Baker.

News executives may find that the best way to deal with persons who are easily hurt is to make certain that the top stories are assigned to the best men and leave the assigning of all other stories, plus their editing and inclusion, to lower-level news managers. These lower-level managers, however, may be forced to take into account more than objective factors in deciding what news goes in, and the length of stories. This may be a partial explanation for the views of four senior executives who shared this opinion: "I don't think our editors make enough hard judgments about the kind of thing we put in the paper. There's entirely too much stuff that doesn't really belong there in this kind of newspaper. A lot of stories are too long; a lot of stories shouldn't be written at all."

Demands for benefits and wages, as payments for dissatisfaction, will increase. Employees will also react by increased requests that will help reduce the tension by getting rid of obvious inequities. These demands will be more on "hygiene" factors (e.g. more money, overtime, people, and expense accounts, better offices, better living arrangements) rather than on factors that influence creativity and high-level of performance. Those, for example who can compare their present lot with the more "lush" foreign assignments will focus on these comparisons partially because they provide a rational reason to raise these issues.

What keeps the system operating to produce a high-quality product? Why, given the analysis above, does *The Daily Planet* have such a fine reputation? Why has it been judged by the Twentieth Century Fund and others in the field to be an excellent newspaper? There are, I think, three reasons.

(1) People do not expect a living system to be different. The qualities described above are not unique or peculiar to the *Planet;* all the complex organizations that I have studied have living systems that are similar. People who have worked in organizations for a while soon learn that this is the case. Consequently, they also learn to lower their level of aspiration about the quality of life to expect while working; they raise their tension and frustration tolerance, and then get to work. Human beings, especially those at the upper levels, seem to be willing to take a lot of psychological punishment without reducing their commitment to work, their sense of responsibility, and their sense of constructive intent. This generalization represents one of the most optimistic findings that can be reported. It also represents, I believe, one of the more unfortunate findings, because I do not believe that work life has to be as painful as it usually is.

Yet the *Planet* executives, and many others we have studied, willingly accepted this low quality of life. For them it was as natural as love, as inevitable as taxes, and as unchangeable as death. This Calvinistic-masochistic view of life may actually encourage people to continue working and producing even though life, to put it mildly, is not much fun. This socially condoned stiff upper lip is therefore the first reason that participants can function productively in this living system.

A second reason flows from the first. If pain and suffering are inevitable, it is difficult to blame anyone in particular. It is difficult to point to a superior and say, "You are creating this suffering to make life miserable for me," since it is also painfully clear that the superior appears as helpless and as tense as others in the system. Many participants therefore take the living system as inevitable because no one, so far, has seemed to know how to design or manage a system more effectively. If the system is so obviously arbitrary and unfair, and produces tension and frustration, then one has a valid reason to fight it, undercut it, condemn it, bypass it, short-change it, and hate it without generating too much personal guilt. The opportunity to hate and condemn with minimal guilt may be an extremely important one for employees oriented around the American version of the Protestant ethic.

It is also important to remember that the living system is an abstract construct designed to conceptualize the degree of interdependence of a certain number of characteristics of the organization. The living system therefore does not represent everything that may be true about the organization. It attempts to capture only the most important characteristics of life within it. There may well be some degree of openness, fairness, cooperation, concern, anh warmth operating within this living system. What is being asserted is that these are not qualities that the living system promotes, sanctions, and protects.

Finally, the qualities or characteristics of the living system vary in importance. For example, on the *Planet* there was more competitiveness than win-lose dynamics, and more of both than of hypocrisy. Moreover, the potency of these factors will tend to vary in different situations and with different individuals.

(2) The nature of reporting and editing fulfills needs of the participants. A high percentage of executives on the *Planet* had personal needs that were consonant with the requirements of the organization. The most obvious case was the need for intellectual challenge: 80 percent of the respondents reported that their work was intellectually challenging and meaningful. Moreover, 84 percent believed that their effectiveness was measured by the degree to which they performed their tasks well, and 84 percent believed that being task-oriented, working hard, and producing were qualities that led to promotions. Finally, 71 percent reported experiential evidence that their hard work and performance were related to financial rewards. (However, many predicted that this positive relationship between rewards and performance would decrease as one went down the line.) Clearly, the nature of the work was a major factor in keeping the living system productive. People were working hard and enjoyed doing so.

Two other needs were very strong in many news people. The first was a need for confirmation, from significant others, that one was, professionally speaking, above average to tops. The very fact that they worked for *The Daily Planet* meant, to some, that they had received a degree of confirmation. Moreover, as the individual grew in stature, the number of significant others who knew of him increased significantly. He received confirmation that he was valued by an audience that he valued. Some people needed confirmation frequently; some needed it less frequently. Because the *Planet* is well known, it provided almost limitless opportunities for this type of confirmation. The frequent positive confirmation also increased the individuals' feelings of responsibility to produce a high quality product. Also, "stars" are valued because the audience values them, and increasing audience confirmation would increase the chances that they would be valued by the newspaper. As one newsman put it, "This place appreciates you when others do."

A closely related need was the feeling of being essential to the success of the newspaper. This need, too, was fulfilled primarily as a function of how good one was (technically speaking), except in the case of younger men. They tended to believe that personality factors played an important role in advancement. They based their judgment on their observations that men who were as good or better than they were not promoted as rapidly unless they were also "optimally" brash and aggressive.

Working for the *Planet* also provided an opportunity available in only a few organizations—the opportunity to feel that one works for an organization that is essential to the nation. This kind of "essentiality" reinforced feelings of responsibility "to do a first-rate job." The feeling of essentiality also acted to cause disappointment and bewilderment (especially for the younger men) if their assignments were not challenging and important. "One cannot feel essential to the world at large and do the weather column."

Finally, news people (especially) wanted to work with an institution that would back them up when in difficulty with the public if the job was well done. The overwhelming majority felt that the *Planet* did back up its reporters and columnists, and this gave them a deep sense of security. As we shall see, news executives did not tend to feel the same sense of security when given a difficult managerial assignment (for example, to upgrade performance).

(3) The system permits a range of conceptions of reporting. Because of resistance from the upper levels of the news management (Chapter Eleven), I was unable to study the work

of reporters intensively.* I did interview, however, a group of twenty younger reporters and copy editors (ranging from average to star reputation) in order to get some feel for the problems at the lower level.

Although I was unable to develop a systematic picture of what the reporters actually did when they were working, I was able to obtain data about the meaning their work had for them, the needs that they consciously tried to fulfill at work, and in a few cases, the needs that I thought they tried to fulfill even though they did not seem to be aware of them.

By needs, I mean the predispositions they attempted to express while at work, or the contributions they expected the work to make to them personally. I am not focusing on needs as psychological components of personality, which people are said to carry around with them throughout life, attempting to fulfill them in various settings. People may indeed have such needs, but my methodology would be unable to identify them. Moreover, my personal bias is that most social-psychological needs are influenced by the environment and the setting. Therefore these are needs that are influenced as much by the situation and the living system as they are by the individuals.

---

* As we shall see in Chapter Eleven, although some of the news superiors invited me to interview and observe their people, when I followed up their request, they resisted by placing the blame on their sub-editors. They stated that the sub-editors were worried that the reporters would become upset by such research. I did not pursue the matter because of the involvement and difficulties that I was having at the upper levels. I did not wish to study reporters, perhaps raise their hopes about possible changes, and then have the project discontinued. This would hurt the reporters and the management. Moreover, if I had negotiated such a study, I would have had to do it knowing full well that genuine progress was doubtful. I would have had to convey this evaluation to every reporter. I doubted that they would be highly motivated to cooperate, and I feared that such candor might be divisive. If there were reporters that would be willing to cooperate, two problems would exist. The first would be related to the motives these reporters might have for participating under such conditions, and the impact they might have on the data that I would obtain through interviews or be permitted to observe. The second problem would be that too often top management encourages such studies in order to learn more about what is going on at the lower levels, and to defuse temporarily the anger and frustration of some subordinates, since the research could be interpreted by them as a sign that management cared.

The reporters' conceptions of their jobs may be categorized into three roles: the Traditional Reporter, the Reporter-Researcher, and the Reporter-Activist. These conceptions build upon each other to some extent. The second role requires the skills of the first but not of the third; the third requires the skills of the first and the second; and the first does not require the skills of the second or third.

The Traditional Reporter. The reporter's first commandment is to be objective and get the facts. The facts are the four W's: what, where, when, and why. Skilled reporters are able to compress them into an opening sentence or brief paragraph, usually called a lead. The remainder of the story is shaped into the form of an inverted pyramid. The facts are given in descending order of importance, a process that gradually makes clear, through revealing detail or quotation or both, the outline of what happened. The paragraphs are separate building blocks.*

Reporting, according to most of my repondents, is a craft, composed mostly of "common sense." It seems very difficult and challenging at the outset, but the basic skills become routine during the first year of work.

The reporters who adhere to this conception strive to present the news as objectively as possible. They work hard at developing the inverted pyramid to its highest quality. However, many of the younger reporters, especially those with a college education, have mixed feelings about strict adherence to the inverted pyramid. They prefer much more color in their writing, yet they admire those stars who are masters of the inverted-pyramid. "I think that now we're much more into show business. I think the younger reporters realize this. That's the fun in the business of saying something well. Z is the greatest reporter I have ever met, only because he can tell things so accurately, and so carefully, and with such a conscience. He is the only one I know who does. As a result, some of his stories read like mortgages." The same reporters soon tire of the established conception of reporting: "Basically journalism, despite the attempts to

* I am heavily indebted to Herbert Brucker's discussion of this issue in his book *Communication is Power* (1973).

elevate it, to give it stature, is a fairly elementary craft. It relies more on instinctual things than an acquired body of knowledge."

Once the craft is learned, the satisfaction and challenges come from applying it under pressure and with news that is of great import to the nation, and more preferably, to the world. Learning to write a story in the form of an inverted pyramid may be easy for some, but even the most experienced are challenged by the fact that they have to take a complex episode and reduce it to a few paragraphs without distorting the underlying themes. Moreover, few reporters have as much time as they would like to write and rewrite their pieces. For example, I observed a two-hour meeting of the key executives of the paper. The transcript was approximately 75 double-spaced pages. If I were assigned to report on the meeting, I would have about one hour to reduce the story to less than one page.

The conscientious reporter realizes that much is lost in the process of reducing the story. However, much can be gained if the major themes are identified and highlighted. This would appear, to a social scientist, to be a very challenging task. How do the conscientious reporters overcome their fear of presenting the wrong themes or developing the wrong emphasis? No reporter, senior or junior, reported that he or she had overcome these fears. Indeed, the fear of being wrong haunted many of the star reporters. Nothing would be more humiliating than to be proven wrong by succeeding events—or worse yet, by a competing newspaper. The psychological defenses developed by reporters to cope with these fears appears to be a subject worthy of study. As two of them said: "I have a highly developed fear of being proven wrong and being humiliated. The only time I see us become very emotional and close to runnning out of control was when there is a fear of being personally embarrassed." "We hate to be wrong. God, it hurts, especially in this paper with its high standards. Reporters break down when face is involved."

A good reporter has a very high sense of curiosity. "He wants to know every single thing about everything." "No bit of information is assumed to be too small to follow up." Along with a high degree of curiosity comes "a solid chunk of distrust." Early in their careers, reporters learn that respondents may have attempted to use them for personal purposes, or may have lied to them, or may have kept information from them. A good reporter comes to expect that others may attempt to deceive him.

A good reporter may also deceive his respondents in order to get a story. Many reporters freely described how they "laid it on thick" to Mr. So-and-So in order to get a story, or acted as if they respected the individual when in reality they did not, or promised to get something in print when they knew that the entire story would probably not be published.

Finally, reporters said that they liked the fact that most of their jobs had a short time perspective. Once the story was written, it was published quickly (if published at all) and the writer could receive feedback from others immediately. They reported that they liked the sense of immediate closure and getting on to the next job. The preference for immediate closure may be one of the defenses developed against possible error. If news dies quickly, then the need to confront a reporter may also die quickly.

This is related to a need most reporters stated that they brought with them to the job and which was reinforced by it— namely, the need for recognition. "If your name appears in the paper a lot then your ego is massaged a lot. If it doesn't appear very much you get jittery." "Two days passed without my getting a story in the paper and I began to wonder. To make it worse one of my friends called and said, "What's the matter? Have they fired you?" "Reporters are an irrational bunch. And the ego is high. You need to hear you're doing well." "We are in the ego business and it's a treacherous business. We tell ourselves, 'Never believe your notices, no matter how good they are.' "

Yet limits must be imposed on the need for recognition because the reporter may be seduced by clever actual or potential subjects. One said: "It [the desire to feel needed and accepted] goes with the profession. It seems to me that if you have a desire to be needed and recognized, and if you are close to public officials, if you bask in the reflected glory of the invitation to the White House, you shouldn't be in the business. This is the curse of the business." Another added, "I think the best ones resist this."

Another need brought to the job (and reinforced by it) is being competitive. Indeed, competition along with intellectual challenge were the two most frequently mentioned needs reporters attributed to each other. "If you have a good story, you've got to be careful someone doesn't steal it from you." "There is no teamwork in this business. The name of the game is competition." "The job is a very individual one. Reporters generally don't cooperate with each other. The notion of interdependence is a foreign one except for a very few guys like Zeke. But that may be because he is very secure. He doesn't have to fight for the stories." "Even if I have a good idea for a story that I'm unable to do, I'm afraid to tell it to the desk. They'll assign it to someone and my name will be on the memo. They'll just hand the memo to another reporter and that guy will resent me for having done it."

Q: If I understand you, you dislike what your own com-
     petitiveness can do to others, yet you remain strongly
     competitive.
A: Yes. I am always out for hurting people. I don't feel good
     about that as a human being, but I still seem to do it.

The Reporter-Researcher. All reporters that I interviewed began with the traditional conception of reporting described above; all reported that a highly developed sense of curiosity and distrust, or as one put it, "functional paranoia," was important; and all identified as important the needs of being recognized, of competitiveness, and of the need for immediate closure and feedback.

However, some reporters described themselves as having all these skills, values, and needs but as having moved beyond them. These reporters no longer found inverted-pyramid news coverage challenging even under time pressures. They sought to do more interpretive news. They wanted to dig beneath the surface of events to find the critical but half-hidden forces that were shaping events. (For example, one reporter did a thorough analysis of societal trends and pressures for urbanization and pressures creating dry rot in our cities. From this analysis, he could predict which sectors of our society will be in the news in the future.) The process of digging into complex events was differentiated, by these reporters, from discovering a chain of simple events—the detective activity that is characteristic of high quality investigative journalism. They enjoyed this sort of work, but so did most of the Traditional Reporters. They wanted to go beyond the story uncovered by keen detective work to write the story that based on analytical and conceptual skills. These men emphasized scholarship, and came the closest to being identified with the academic game. They represent some empirical evidence to question Kristol's assertion that journalists are not competent analytically (Pool 1972).

The Reporter-Researcher therefore was attempting to find the news in stories that exposed some of the critical processes society was going through. They were going beyond the four W's; or to put it another way, they dug below the immediately given, to develop an analytical model of forces, which, if valid, would be the basis for important news. These reporters were imposing their analytical abilities and their conceptual models upon reality to give it deeper meaning.

There is a thrust, in this conception of reporting, that goes beyond describing the immediately given. Yet the reporters are not interested in imposing their views on the reader. Their objective is to make clear a pattern of forces that may be affecting the reader although he is unaware of it.

In addition to satisfying the need to use their analytical and conceptual skills, reporters also get the satisfaction of knowing that their analyses "may be contributing to the well-being of the country, perhaps even to the way decisions are made in the operation of the democratic system." Or as another stated it, "Part of the job of the newspaper is to create pressures in our society, and along with investigative reporting, the reporting of real but sub-surface events may create pressures for good." The key to success in this type of reporting is to create the pressures, not by imposing personal views but by compelling the reader to belief through tight analytical thinking.

These reporters believe that they are constantly teetering "at the edge of influencing events, not in the narrow petty sense of coloring their stories, but of saying, 'this will show them, now maybe something will get done in this country.' It is always a problem to make sure you don't go over the edge." Another put it, "We've got to do more than just report what is immediately evident. Hell, TV does that well. It's our job to put the truth in the story; to explain the meanings not so immediately evident. The world we present is never the real world; so we must be especially careful to make the case compelling through the logic of the story."

The Reporter-Activist. "Well, that's the trouble with us. We want to be observers or analysts and not participants. We have this godlike role where we can function professionally as a god. And we make our own psychological deal with ourselves to cop out when it affects us personally. Maybe this is all bullshit."

This comment goes to the heart of the Reporter-Activist role—the wish to use journalism to change or shake up the world. These reporters understand the other two roles but believe that they are outmoded and cannot help serving the established order. For example: "The ethos of this paper should be to rock the superstructure. Rock is a bad word. Sweep away the cobwebs, push it, make the damn thing rattle a bit; report when the emperor has no clothes on and say it good and loud. It is not the function of a newspaper to feel sorry because someone has tremendous pressure." "Very often I find J's columns like pablum. They say everything's going all right. I think that is writing down the middle. I don't think that is how change is effected. I think the way change is effected is when extremes are created . . . and that's our job, to produce change!"

Another illustration of the thinking and psychological set of the activist comes from an interview of Geraldo Rivera (*Penthouse* Interview, 1973). When asked if he might not be taking too much responsibility into his hands and overstepping professional bounds, Rivera replied: "No, I don't give a damn about the other side of that story. All you really have to do is to be honest. If you see something wrong, you say it. And as long as I have nothing to lose or gain by saying one thing or the other, then I, the newsman, should be the one to make the judgment." This statement shows little awareness that the speaker may have personal psychological gains or losses involved, and that the truth does not come automatically and accurately to persons who believe that they are supporting the proper cause.

The Reporter-Activists seem more like "angry young men." They are more critical than constructive, a bias that Pool and Shulman (1959) have shown may be a bias in the psychology of some newsmen. Their need to dig beneath everything is much stronger, and their paranoia is exceeded only by their deep disappointment that the men they had revered in public life are human to a fault. They gave me the impression that they had felt let down by the senators, governors, and presidents they had met. They were great cynics. I began to feel that they were almost saying to me that these public figures had no right to be so full of human foibles. "I think cynicism among newspapermen is largely a defensive act on their part. They have known many of the mighty that not only have an Achilles heel but are basically not as good as they are thought to be, or are weak." "Cynicism is not a fiction among us. We do it to protect ourselves from disappointment." Several of the reporters were so storng in their anger toward anyone in the establishment that they admitted enjoying finding stories that they knew would be embarrassing. "There's really a fine sense of satisfaction when we really find out something that even embarrasses people." "I had a story two days ago that embarrassed the hell out of N. I wrote it with relish. I knew that he would be embarrassed and he *was* embarrassed. I just hope I haven't lost a news source."

These reporters go beyond the Reporter-Researcher in that they do not mind imposing their views on others. "Instead of describing what the President said about the Vietnam bombing and then comparing it with what North Vietnamese said, we should state the facts directly, and say the President lied." Their concept of "facts" is very close to their perception of the world. When asked whether this is not a dangerous conception of facts, they reply, "Of course, but aren't all our stories simply our perceptions of the world?" They would not believe, in the bombing example, that it is desirable to give the reader only the directly observable data (the statements by the President and the North Vietnamese) and let him decide for himself who is lying, or more important whether the response need be made in terms of lying at all.

Where does this anger and impatience come from? Part of it, psychologists would say, is related to personality themes developed early in life. Another part may have been formed by the reporters' experience of growing up during the past turbulent decade and finding that they were faced with monumental legacies of human failure—war, racism, poverty, pollution, organizational dry rot—which their parents ignored in order not to upset the establishment. Still another part may have been created by working in a living system full of conspiracies, inconsistencies, pressures, conformity, and antagonisms.

All of these causes continue to exist, not only in our society in general but in the living system of the newspaper in particular. They feed upon and reinforce each other to make the problems seem more entrenched, more unsolvable, more insurmountable. Living in such a world takes courage and a willingness to act. And if my preliminary data are valid, most of these reporters have somewhat suppressed doubts about their courage, and especially about their capacity to take action. We have caught glimpses of these doubts in Chapter One, when the reporters spoke disparagingly of being "just observers" or "analysts" and backing off just before action is called for. Several reporters were more direct about these issues: "Most of us like to rattle things around—but what the hell would we do if it were our job to resolve them?" "I wonder if basically I'm not afraid to be a person who has to take action." "In the process of doing it [an article on housing], I came to the point of thinking, 'Boy, I'm really glad that I don't have to do anything about it. I can sit back and put all the arguments together and analyze and recommend but I don't have to try to solve the problems.' It's chickening out in a way." "It's difficult to be emotionally committed to a story. You observe and then you write and that's supposed to be it. It's down on paper; there is nothing more you should do." "I think that's the hardest thing I have to do. I know that I have political ideas but I can't join a club; something keeps me from joining a club and participating." "We've taken vows and we are sort of pristine —we're clean. This presumably gets us off the hook so we don't have to make any active commitment, but we're constantly in the area where commitment is."

We now begin to see the possibility that these men who are impatient, if not angry, at the limitations of others, have limits of their own (similar results are reported in Swanson 1956, 1957). These men who resent others for not being strong and facing reality also "chicken out" when they are faced with similar problems. If we add to this the already mentioned fear of being wrong in collecting the facts, not to mention the fear of being wrong in carrying out some action, we begin to develop further insight into the degree of disenchantment with themselves that these reporters may feel. It is possible, for example, that they have written themselves the cowardice they see in others, and that if faced with the imperative to act they might disappoint their society just as others have done.

(4) The system permits semiconscious forms of adaptation. How does one live with such a possibility? One strategy is to suppress it. Another is to locate the evil in the environment and condemn it; this is called projection.* The reporter condemns the world for his own limitations and thereby unconsciously punishes himself. But since it is unconscious, the reporter is not aware of his own motivation and his condemnations do not reduce "his" weakness. The individual therefore develops a strong and persistent need to expose cowardice and express disappointment with human limitations in the world. This may be *one* source for the energy behind investigative reporting, and *one* source for the enjoyment in proclaiming publicly that the emperor has no clothes. It may be *one* source for the energy to polarize and magnify differences between the ideal and the real.

Another way to live with the possibility is to seek out a living system that has these undesirable qualities and to condemn them while working within the system. But this strategy has a risk. It is harder to excuse oneself for not taking action against

---

* I am using the concept of projection as does Brown (1940), to mean the activity of attributing to environmental objects or other persons characteristics of one's own personality which are unacceptable to the ego. In at least semiconscious form, projection is the tendency in all of us to seek our faults in others (p. 175).

inequalties when the inequalities flourish in one's own back yard, instead of in the outside world. Some reporters may realize the hypocrisy of not struggling to change what they condemn in their own living system, and may decide to take action. It is unlikely that they will settle for partial reform. If the living system is really as bad as they have come to believe it is, then there is no choice but to change it totally. But this is not possible, according to their view of the establishment, and most of their superiors represent the establishment. This leaves only one answer: the reporters must take over, they must run the living system. Here we have *one* source of energy for the takeover attempts made at *The Daily Planet*.

Although our prediction is that it would be Reporter-Activists who would probably conceive and instigate internal revolutions, this does not mean that they would be alone. They might be followed by reporters of the other two types who had been frustrated for a long time. For example, in the *Planet,* there have been more reporters than stories. The reporters have therefore been placed in severe competition with each other, or ignored and shelved, or given stories that have covertly been assigned to several people, or pulled into participating in the managerial secrecy, covert demotions, and hypocrisy identified as part of the living system.

If this analysis is correct, it can also be predicted that if these reporters were to take over, they would tend to create a living system of precisely the kind that they so vehemently condemn.

Another strategy for justifying inaction within one's living system is to withdraw from involvement in it. This strategy is especially popular among star reporters, who can use their extra time to write books, make speeches, and accept visiting lectureships at universities. The strategy again prevents going to the underlying causes; it leads to the withdrawal from the system of key individuals; it reinforces the probabilities that change in the living system will not occur, and it guarantees that the stars will direct much of their energy into activities not directly related to the newspaper.

Yet another strategy is to develop a firm conviction that human behavior is unchangeable. We have noted that pessimism about human change was felt by many of the reporters, and was especially deep in the Reporter-Activists. This pessimism has a basis in reality, of course: we have described a living system that would be very difficult to change. The part of the reality that the reporters may be less aware of is their own personal inability to change.

There are several strategies which are more periodic in nature. One is to attend the get-togethers at local bars where people seem to blow off steam and get close to each other. "Everyone feels being part of something during those drinking sessions. You feel close—yet you are not close." "Most reporters, after they have two or three drinks, will sit around and talk about what great guys we all are. They talk in terms of contempt of anyone who does anything else." "There is a good deal of socializing among reporters. I generally don't enjoy these evenings." "You have enforced socializing. When the *Planet* throws a party, it's a big farce." There is also the action of just blowing up at oneself or at one's boss (opportunities to do the latter, in person, are rare indeed). "Once in a while you'll see a guy scream and guys will clap. It's like the breaking of a seal. You get the monkey off your back, and you can yell and shout." "There is one editor who has many faults, but one of his saving traits is that he lets you shout at him. And he takes it and doesn't go any further. It's a very good safety valve."

All of these strategies are unsuccessful: they are ineffective, in that they do not get at causes of problems; they are self-sealing, in that they reinforce the living system; and they are self-maintaining, in that they are responsible for the creation of two styles of leadership which also reinforce the system.

(5) Individual semiconscious adaptation. V is a famous reporter who attacks the establishment. Indeed, the attacks are so frequent that they have become almost predictable. He is a supporter of the new left and a hero to many of the younger activists. He has written several pieces condemning the hypocrisy of people who maintain they are loyal to the Constitution yet do not want to grant the rights and privileges of the Constitution to minorities. In one article he condemned certain Southern police officials for being bigots. He stated that the time was ripe for people to remove

hypocrisy from American life. He questioned those who spoke one way and behaved another.

I would like to examine not the substance of the positions taken by V, but the hostility he expresses in his articles toward the Southern "hypocrites" and "cowards." Why this anger? Also, if V means to help bring about change, where did he learn to believe that people can be moved to change their behavior by hearing it condemned (even justifiably)? Whenever others try to condemn his ideas and point to his hypocrisy, he tends to become defensive; he resists considering ideas that would lead him to become aware of his own inconsistencies.

V exhibits a high degree of personal hypocrisy in his dealings with people. Three examples: (1) He made a speech at a university in which he criticized listeners who might have idolized him, saying that such hero-worship would make them blind to human limitations and foibles; yet he himself seems blind as any idolater to his own limitations. (2) He dislikes supervising others because he considers himself a coward (to use his word) when handling such tasks as confronting reporters with poor work or transferring them to stories he knows they will not like. (3) He states that one of his great skills is to be hypocritical about his own values when trying to get story material from someone who represents values and points of view that he condemns. "I've always found it's much better to get a good easy-flowing conversation rather than be blunt with people. Take (a man whose views he has condemned in his articles). He and I are about as opposite as two people can get. I established a good easy relationship with him and he talked and I got what I wanted out of him. I did it by *sheer hypocrisy*. It has *always* been my style. I'm not particularly proud of it. That's the way I am."

If V is not proud of his behavior but has found that it leads to success, one way for him to live with possible guilt feelings is to admit intellectually that he is a hypocrite (it goes with the newspaper business) while not accepting it emotionally. An emotional acceptance would include, by definition, an ability to express genuine empathy for other hypocrites and to speak in an understanding tone about their psychological needs, even though one does not approve of them. (An example that comes to mind:

an AA worker who is capable of being empathetic with an alcoholic without approving of his behavior.)

V's hypocrisy is high whenever he is in a face-to-face relationship. "I almost never say what is on my mind, particularly if it is going to lead to an unpleasant exchange." And later, "One thing that I learned being a boss over others; I had a yellow streak when it came to doing the difficult things a boss is supposed to do." Consequently, he developed a leadership style epitomized by what he called the "flannel technique." "The flannel technique. You gotta give people assignments so that by the time they've walked out of the office they think their new assignment is the greatest one ever created, one created particularly for them."

During an interview, I had questioned V about an article in which he described someone's behavior as "a bad idea, intellectually shabby." He said that he hadn't written what he felt, namely, that the person had behaved like a stupid ass. "To me," he explained, "this is quite different. Maybe that is a distinction without a difference, but to me it is a real one." The differences between telling someone he behaved in ways that could be categorized as "intellectually shabby" or "a stupid ass" is, according to V, to be judged by him. He does not feel obliged to find how the other person feels about this distinction.

Yet V has been observed to explode and threaten to resign when someone decides for him what the meaning of a situation should be. For example, once he was invited to a hurriedly called meeting to discuss with a small group of other key officials the possible hiring of Mr. Y. The President of the *Planet* was not only interested in obtaining their views privately; he wanted to have a meeting with his key editors in order to get various views explored thoroughly. V's reaction was this: "I was absolutely outraged that he would throw that question [about Y] in my face in a public meeting." Here the President unilaterally decided that such a question should be discussed openly among key officials, and V was outraged because he found that embarrassing. Yet it is not unfair to say that V has been the cause of the embarrassment of many people, and has done so in a much more public way through his writing.

V described himself as angry at large organizations that are impersonal, yet his own leadership style is impersonal. If he ever managed reporters he would leave them alone and provide them with the resources they needed. Why the inconsistency? If V leaves the reporters alone then he cannot be held personally responsible for what they do, nor be blamed by them for being a meddler. But this protection would be only temporary, because as their superior he would be responsible. Moreover, his job would be made more difficult because he would have to take action after the fact.

Here we see the struggle: to keep away from face-to-face relationships where negative feelings—anger, rejection, the urge to dominate—may come into play. Such a strategy is difficult to carry out because feelings tend to be central to the role of administering others, especially talented professionals. Yet if V confronted in himself feelings like anger, rejection, and the urge to use power to dominate, he would risk having to face the very same feelings that had been carefully repressed or run the risk of blowing up or breaking down, neither of them enjoyable alternatives.

Interestingly enough, V argued that it would be dangerous to institutionalize self-scrutiny in a press council, and that self-examination is properly an internal task for every newspaper. In his case, however, the living system would guarantee the failure of self-scrutiny. Perhaps V needed to guarantee this failure, because successful self-scrutiny would inevitably lead to himself, and eventually to those practices that he had dissociated from himself through denial and projection. It is not surprising that V advocated an even more vigorous and aggressive press. In making this point, I am not, at this time, making judgments about the validity of V's substantive views. The point being made is that he consistently designs a world and consistently writes articles with predictable tone and thrust.

(6) The star system. V is a star, and the stars, regardless of their need fulfillments while at work, produce effectively, thereby helping to confirm and maintain the excellent reputation of *The Daily Planet*. However, the quality of the commitment of the "stars," "near stars," or "up-and-coming stars" does not

include being concerned about the health of the organization. As one star said: "You've got to create the conditions under which they are encouraged to do their best work. Now, what does that mean? I'm not clear what it means and since I don't have the responsibility for it, I'm not really forced to think about what it means."

Since they are very effective, the stars will tend to be left alone by the top management. Few demands will be made of them to get involved in maintaining and increasing the effectiveness of the newspaper as an organization. As one executive put it, "Good management and good organization begin with people who are tops, and in my opinion it practically ends there." This philosophy pleases the stars and confirms their view of their value to the newspaper. However, it also makes the organization increasingly dependent upon the stars, near stars, and up-and-coming stars. The resulting dependence will lead the management to leave these people alone. The major managerial relationship will be one of seeing to it that they are paid well, get the best stories, have opportunities to write, make speeches, and be professionally productive.

The resulting emphasis upon the stars may make the remaining news people feel like second-class citizens. One of the younger newsmen described the star system as follows: "As I rate that newsroom, there is a spectrum. At one end there are maybe four, five superlative writers with great insights. At the other end, there are a very few that are not particularly good. The rest of it is a gray, interchangeable mass. That's the beginning of the problem. These guys compete but what can you do with people who are not very good?" This feeling, coupled with the dynamics of resignation and hopelessness about change, may give the mass of the workers a feeling of alienation. As one respondent put it: "We're the faceless people. You've got to shout and scream to make yourself known, to become a face person."

Since exerting pressure to make oneself known is a painful process for the great mass in the middle, they may find it easier to accept the fact that they will not move up and concentrate on other demands. They may pressure management for higher salaries, better assignments, and other benefits, which will do three things: (1) it will cause management to respond positively and selectively to these individual pressures; (2) this, in turn, will anger those who have hesitated to make demands; and (3) it will cause the great majority to wonder about the kinds of "deals" that have been made to keep certain individuals satisfied. All these factors will, in turn, increase the pressure on management, whose response will be to seek even more stars and to satisfy the "hygiene demands" of the non-stars as the gap between the stars and non-stars becomes increasingly bigger. It will make the stars even more desirable, less reachable, and more enviable.

　　The persons who are affected by the living system and who experience these consequences most negatively are the young men and the older men who are average or below-average contributors. They are the ones most upset with what is going on. The first-rate reporters leave, either permanently or psychologically. Examples of psychological leave-taking are writing books and making speeches. As for quitting the *Planet,* many younger stars spoke openly about the possibility of leaving in five or ten years. In their view, they would leave *not* because of internal dissatisfactions, but rather because the excitment of their present jobs had worn off, or the creativity in their jobs in themselves had dropped, or they had grown "tired of it all." Such weariness can have several sources, which are worth noting: there is physical pressure from the work itself; there is the pressure the individual puts on himself to meet his level of aspiration and satisfy his most respected public; and there is the weariness that may come from working in a competitive, secrecy-oriented, and at times conspiratorial environment. Management can of course alter the environment, and intervene to reduce the chances of long-range exhaustion in its stars; but in so doing it is likely to be caught up in another circular process. If it hires or develops stars who do not become deeply involved in the health of the system, but who are paid well and given the best possible benefits, these stars may leave early, especially if they grow tired—a probability that is quite high, given the living system of the newspaper.

　　(7) The realization that others cannot perform more effectively. The persons who are not managers now know that they would not be able to behave more effectively if they were

the managers. Indeed, many believe that if they were managing, they would make the situation worse. An example of this phenomenon occurred during a meeting in which I met with ten reporters and copy editors. After I outlined for them the study I wanted to undertake, they began to discuss the issues. Most behaved in an articulate, opinionated, and competitive manner. There was little additiveness, the "air time" was scarce, and helping others was nonexistent. After forty minutes had passed, I interrupted the discussion to say just that; the reaction was immediate and unanimous: "You hit it on the head. That's pretty perceptive. That's the trouble with this place. We're always at each other." "As one of the less aggressive guys around here, I can surely back up what you say. I have always wondered what makes us so competitive."

I then added that I was able to make the observation only by shouting and taking charge. This meant to me that I had to become authoritarian to get some semblance of coordination in the discussion. Yet they complained about authoritarian leadership. Could it be possible that the dynamics of their group meetings required such leadership? "Oh sure," one of them replied, "The boss has to show tight control and it's our job to complain about his control." All but one nodded approvingly.

Some further support for the conclusion that subordinates would be as authoritarian as their superiors (if they became superiors) came from their responses to the incomplete sentences on effective leadership: 93 percent responded that an effective leader is one who (a) leads, (b) knows exactly what he wants from the group, and (c) keeps everybody on the right track. Also, 86 percent described themselves as highly competitive with each other, 7 percent as mildly competitive, and 7 percent as slightly competitive. Here is an illustration of the thinking of those in the highly competitive category:

A: First of all, there is the genuine competition for stories. There is the big game of making points. You made points with a story or you lost points with a story. Obviously much of this carries over to later recriminations and hostilities. . . .

Q: Would people even sit down and openly discuss if this
    is the kind of work life they wanted?
A: No, it's much more Machiavellian than that. It's always
    done with a stiletto and a knife in the dark, undercover,
    using intermediaries.
Q: Doesn't this lead to feelings of secrecy and conspiracy?
A: Absolutely.

Thus the subordinates have little idea how to manage the news activities differently. They may not like the situation, but they may also admit that they see no way to correct it. This would lead to feelings that the problems are unavoidable. Such feelings may reduce the motivation to act aggressively against management, but they would not reduce the pressures to receive more rewards from management.

Summary. The living system produces consequences that will tend to make it increasingly ineffective. They are: (1) its activities become compulsive and uncorrectable; (2) managerial innovation will come to be seen as deviant activity and will be inhibited; and (3) conflict and fear will be magnified.

The living system also encourages behaviors that help to make the newspaper a first-class product. They are: (1) it encourages journalistic and editorial excellence; (2) it fulfills important needs, such as feelings of being important and essential to the nation; (3) it permits the expression of semiconscious ways of blowing off steam and reducing tension; and (4) it rewards excellence through the star system. These same factors, however, may blunt the participants' needs to reexamine their system and attack the causes of its ineffectiveness.

Feedback of the Results

In addition to serving as a partial test for self-examination, the feedback session had several other objectives. The first objective was to communicate the results of the diagnosis to the executives. The second objective was to learn, in more depth, about the dynamics of the top group. How do they react to the results? Are they open to learning from the data and from each other, or do they spend their time ignoring each other and the data? If they believe the diagnosis is valid, what action steps do they consider? If they believe the diagnosis is invalid, how do they test their beliefs? Do they confront the diagnostician openly and constructively?

The third objective of the meeting was to use it as a test of the previous diagnosis. As the executives listen to the results, upon which do they choose to focus? With which of the results do they agree and disagree? Do they modify the results? How congruent are their views with those presented in the diagnosis? Is there any behavior during the feedback meeting that varies significantly from what would have been predicted by the previous diagnosis? For example, one would predict that such behavior as expressing feelings, helping each other, and exhibiting trust should be rarely observed, while owning up to ideas and not

65

helping others should be relatively high, with the norms of conformity and concern ranking next in that order (since the group is competitive). The next step—after interviewing, of serving, and drawing up a diagnosis of the living system—was to present the diagnosis to the clients in an extended feedback session.* The design of the session was influenced by the purposes of the feedback. First, I hoped that a presentation of the results could begin to free the top people to consider changing the living system, so that they could manage it rather than having it manage them. Beyond that, I hoped that it would prompt them to begin changing the system so that genuine organizational self-examination would become possible. A third objective was to use their reaction to the diagnosis as a potential validity check on the analysis of the living system.

A self-regulating system has the capacity to diagnose itself accurately and alter itself effectively. Accurate diagnosis depends upon valid information. Valid information, as pointed out in Chapter One, is not easy to obtain in any organization; it is especially difficult to obtain when a primary function of the living system is to distort any information that may be threatening to individuals. Moreover, in the living system, it is possible that the needs of individuals (such as those of reporters) and the requirements of reporting (as reporters conceive them) fit so well that reporters may be unaware of some of the needs they are fulfilling at work and how these needs influence their reporting. Finally, some participants may be projecting their own problems onto the system, so that the validity of the data they may give about themselves and the living system may be unintentionally distorted.

Having the diagnosis conducted by an outsider may have helped minimize these distortions; besides the fact that I was not responsible for what went on in the living system, I brought to it some pre-validated interview and observation technologies and skills to assist in obtaining valid information. But these skills, though helpful in obtaining a valid diagnosis, could also work against helping the organization become self-regulating. The par-

* For a discusson of the feedback session as a validity check of the living system, see Appendix B.

ticipants could develop a dependency relationship with the interventionist by accepting his diagnosis and encouraging, if not demanding from him, a set of action recommendations. Or they could develop a counterdependency relationship in which they criticize him and induce him to fight them, thereby leading him down the primrose path of eventual rejection. If the interventionist accedes to either demand he will have prevented the members from becoming responsible for their own diagnosis and action recommendations, which is the first step toward becoming self-scrutinizing.

Conducting the diagnosis unilaterally, as I did, would not tend to promote client autonomy and capacity for self-examination. But I saw no other choice, because when I entered the organization the participants expressed little need for the diagnosis. The challenge was now clear. If progress was to be made, a different strategy would be needed.

Elsewhere I have tried to show that for individuals or systems to become self-examining, they require, as a minimum, conditions that encourage valid information, free and informed choice, and internal commitment to the choice (Argyris 1970). If valid information is to be generated, especially about important and threatening issues, the participants must feel some sense of concern about their own effectiveness and the organization's effectiveness. Thus the first use of the diagnosis is to see whether the members will confirm it, and if they do, whether they will respond by asking for help to overcome the problems. If they do choose to seek help, then the second condition for effective intervention—free and informed choice—will be activated.

Free and informed choice is a complex state of affairs, with four defining or necessary conditions: (1) the clients define their own goals; (2) the goals present a realistic and meaningful challenge to the clients' abilities; (3) the clients define and design the paths they will take to achieve the goals; and (4) the goals are meaningful and potent to the clients. I tried to design every step that I took as an interventionist so that it filled each of these four conditions to a high degree. For example, if I were meeting with five executives to discuss working with them, I tried to help them make explicit their goals, their level of aspiration, and the paths to the goals. When two high-ranking editors asked me to help them develop more effective communications between them, the sessions were designed in such a way that they were in control as to what topics they would discuss, how deep the discussion would go, and when the discussion should be ended. This strategy was an ideal state toward which I aspired; I did not achieve it completely, but I used it as a guide for every action, from answering a reporter's question to planning a three-day learning seminar.

In addition to providing for valid information and free choice, effective intervention helps the clients implement their choices and then monitor them to see how effectively they are being carried out. Accepting the responsibility of monitoring their own actions will tend to increase their desire to give valid information and make correct choices. Therefore, monitoring activities will reinforce the probability of generating valid information and seeking free and informed choice.

The primary processes of the intervention activity are therefore generating valid information, free and informed choice, and internal commitment to the choice, so that the implementation will be genuine and the monitoring continuous. I submit that an organization that can perform these activities effectively is an organization that will be able to examine and regulate itself.

Self-regulating intervention. An organization that can (1) generate valid information about any problem, (2) define the problems it wishes to solve, (3) design the paths to solving them, (4) monitor the solutions as they are being implemented, and (5) make any necessary corrections is an organization that is showing a capacity for self-examination. The intervention processes could therefore be used as a test of the organization's capacity for self-examination.

This test would be credible to the extent that the interventionist has been able to adhere to the theory of intervention, but that is not an easy task. As we shall see, there was strong resistance to self-examination when it meant openly confronting issues that involved particular individuals and intervening in interpersonal relationships that had been long established in the organization. For example, the editorial and news officials had significantly different views about each others' effectiveness. The members of the *Planet* organization would have gladly taken bets that these issues would never be discussed by the parties involved, because such discussions would get hopelessly bogged down in deep personal feelings, long-standing interdepartmental barriers, and a predisposition, by each of the parties involved, not to trust the other's willingness to listen to proposals for change.

Another difficulty was the defenses people used to protect themselves and the system. For example, each group maintained that the other was so emotionally involved in its work that it would not listen to reason. At the same time, members of each maintained that they kept their personalities out of their jobs and were able to separate their feelings from the rational requirements of the work.

Moreover, there were system-wide defenses available to anyone the moment genuine self-examination threatened to uncover "difficult" issues. For example, executives expressed concern about becoming more open because things could become so easily magnified out of proportion, because relationships were so brittle, and because the proper solution was for the chief executive officer to design more effective structures. These conditions are defenses because they help to prevent diagnoses, learning, and change. A condition that is confrontable and influenceable will rarely become a defense; a condition that is not confrontable and not influenceable will almost always be one.

My implementation of the intervention strategy may appear annoyingly slow to some readers. The patience shown in being willing to deal repeatedly with expressions of the same fears may, in fact, make the reader impatient. If this sense of impatience develops, the reader might keep in mind that he or she is being managed by defenses of the very kind that controlled the executives of the *Planet.*

If the participants could make the interventionist impatient, and if he were to act on that impatience (a feeling which *they* had created within him), they would have succeeded in passing the buck to him, just as they pass the buck to the President. This would make the interventionist a part of the system, and confirm to his clients that he could not help them change because he is vulnerable to the same pressures they are, the pressures that support their living system.

We should not forget that the management of *The Daily Planet* believes in self-examination. To use our language, there is a discrepancy between their espoused theory and their theory-in-use. They are blind to the magnitude of the discrepancy because their living system creates conditions in which such blindness is not noticed.

The news exectives responsible for the stated policy were not lying or making political hay. True, they have some feelings that self-examination will be difficult, but they also believe that these difficulties can be overcome, especially if the stimulus for self-examination comes from the "artillery of the public." There is some validity to this position, because then the public (or whoever is doing the confronting) may be seen as the enemy and the need to resist enemy attack may cause greater internal cohesion. Even if some of the systemic defenses were reduced or ignored under such stress, and an effective response were developed (neither possibility seems probable), this could not be the long-run solution. For one thing, the *Planet* is now being managed in response to the anxieties of outsiders. For another, the strategy is reactive; it does not focus on preventive solutions.

The first step in effective intervention is not for the outsider to induce, persuade, manipulate, or coerce the insiders into more self-examination. The first step is to help the clients to see the real depth of their resistance to self-examination, the causes of the resistance, and the degree to which they are responsible for creating or maintaining the causes.

The feedback meeting was held in a hotel, in the same city in which the *Planet*'s offices are situated, but at some distance. The choice to remain near their offices could have become a problem for the participants if their subordinates had interrupted them to cope with questions and crises. However, there were no interruptions. The executives apparently adhered to the request that they not permit themselves to be interrupted. The fact that this request was honored over a period of a day and a half shows that even in a group whose decision-making was highly centralized, the executives could leave without disrupting the pattern. The fear executives have about leaving their organizations may be grounded more in the realization that their absence could be proof that the organization can be managed without them than vice versa.

The top fifteen news, editorial, and administrative executives attended the meeting. Each was given a written analysis of the living system (substantially the same as presented in Chapter One). The diagnostician stated the primary results of the report orally, and read from the report only verbatim comments that illustrated the findings. The executives interrupted whenever they wanted to make comments, to ask questions, or to discuss the results with each other.

Primary themes of discussion during the meeting. It is difficult to provide a brief account of this day-and-a-half meeting that does justice to the level of involvement and inquiry that was reached. The executives took the session very seriously and worked hard at understanding the diagnosis and confronting it constructively. Indeed, the degree of constructiveness surprised me, both because of the implications of the findings and because at least half of the key executives present (mostly from the news and editorial departments) had expressed genuine doubt about the ultimate validity and usefulness of the behavioral sciences. Most of these men saw themselves as humanists and regarded the behavioral sciences as mechanistic and blind to the uniqueness of the individual. Several, during feedback episodes, also expressed annoyance and despair about the poor writing skills of behavioral scientists in general, and about my own writing in particular. I accepted the criticism of my own writing abilities quickly. I responded to the view that the behavioral sciences are mechanistic and anti-individuals, whenever it was expressed, by agreeing that some behavioral science research is mechanistically oriented, but that some of it, including mine, is not. I also reminded them that they were responsible for a living system that had created a low quality of life for many of their colleagues, a system in which the uniqueness of individuals—their humanness

—was constrained and suppressed. How could they believe in the qualities that they mentioned, yet create a living system that acted to suppress them?

The strategy throughout the session was to be forthright and direct in answering all questions they asked me about the nature of the findings, the methodology used, or the validity of the results. In responding, I tried to stick as closely as I could to actual results and actual methods. I would lean heavily on directly observable data and stood ready to play back any tape that was relevant to a question. For example, if an executive believed that there had been more risk-taking or more expressions of feeling in certain situations, I would ask him to describe an incident that would illustrate his position, or invite him to identify a meeting that had been tape-recorded so that we could listen to an episode that illustrated his point.

I always tried to relate discussions to actual behavior rather than to abstract descriptions of behavior. There is little value in discussing abstractions if there is no agreement on the specific behavior from which the abstractions are inferred. If the executive and I disagree about the degree of trust that exists in a group, the first step is to see if we can agree on a description of behavior that expresses trust. If, for example, both of us experience an episode and he describes it as indicative of trust and I disagree, then this is the first problem to be discussed.

This heavy emphasis is placed on using directly observable data because people tend to hold espoused theories about their managerial styles and group effectiveness which do not influence their actual behavior (their theory-in-use), and because they tend to be blind to this discrepancy. Change will not occur until they become aware of it, and they cannot become aware of it without focusing on the directly observable data from which the theory-in-use is inferred. Once the theory-in-use is made explicit, it can be compared with the espoused theory.

This strategy also has pedagogical value. By revealing discrepancies between a client's behavior and his espoused theories, it may help generate some of the constructive tension and energy needed for change. It is important to remember that these discrepancies are created entirely by the clients, and not imposed upon their behavior by the consultant (as would be the case in the use of most psychological tests, or group diagnostic instruments).

If the clients find the living results of these discrepancies believable and valid, then the primary thrust of their questions tends to be whether the results are desirable for the health of the system. I try not to answer directly the question of desirability unless the clients connect it with their own criteria about organizational health. I am able to be specific, for example, about the consequences of win-lose dynamics, but I cannot say whether the clients should evaluate the consequences as desirable or undesirable. The purposes of this strategy are to inhibit attempts to make the outsider (in this case, me) responsible for the actions to be taken, to increase the quality of the discussion that the clients must generate in order to arrive at a decision, to increase, their internal commitment to the action strategies, and to force them to maintain their independence in relation to the intervenionist.

For further examples, let us turn to an examination of nine themes or issues that arose during the feedback session. (The issues are ordered in terms of time spent discussing them during the feedback process.)

(1) How desirable or undesirable were the findings? For example, how desirable were competitiveness, win-lose dynamics, secrecy in management, lack of experimenting, and so on? Could a deadline-oriented business like this one be administered in any other way? Further, if ideas are the materials to be worked with, one would naturally expect executives to engage in brain-picking. ("How else would you run our business? You have to sit down and ask, 'O.K., what ideas have you got?' Isn't this standard?".)

The desirability or necessity for competitiveness was dependent upon the quality of life the participants wanted in the living system. I can indicate the consequences of competitiveness and win-lose dynamics upon decision-making, implementation, morale, and the level of trust. Deciding whether these qualities are desirable was up to the participants.

If, as in the case above (where the executives stated that brain-picking was standard), the client responds with an assertion that a practice was common, my task was not to evaluate it but to point out the dilemmas relevant to the issue. For example, "brain-picking is standard but the persons I interviewed tended to resent it." Exposing the dilemmas led one senior editor to state: "This is important. Sometimes I think that we pick brains in order to find ways to implant ideas in their minds about news stories. We want to avoid giving orders." Another added, "And according to these results, they see right through the strategy and accept the question as an order."

(2) How did these findings compare with other systems? As the clients began to realize that I resisted making judgments about desirability or undersirability, they turned to asking questions that attempted to compare their living system with those of other organizations. The answer to these questions depended upon the motivation for asking them. Sometimes people asked for comparisons because they were hoping that I would say that their organization was unique, or hoping they could build such a case from my answer. Others asked the same question for the opposite reason. They wanted to show that their living system was not significantly different from those of other organizations. In both cases, the intention appeared to be to defend the present organization and to resist exposing dilemmas. If their living system is unique, then they should be cautious about changing; if it is typical, then what sense does it make to change?

My response was to be willing to share results from other systems (without identifying individual systems). First, I attempted to understand the motivation behind the question. For example, "I should be glad to compare these findings with others that we have obtained. It would help me to select properly and to be specific if I knew what information you are looking for and what is prompting you to ask the question."

Another strategy some clients used to obtain similar information was to ask one of the interventionists (X or Y) for his reactions to the data. Again my response was to attempt to uncover the motivation behind the question. For example:

A: Are you surprised with what you found?
X: I'm not sure I understand. Surprised in what sense? These

results do not surprise me because they are based on my diagnosis. Are you asking me if I am worried about my findings, or how I would evaluate them?

A: No, were you surprised?

B: Did you find something different than what you expected to find?

X: I didn't start the project with preconceptions about what I should find. But I would be glad to discuss the long-term implications of these findings for the effectiveness of your organization.

A: I'd like to do that. Perhaps you should finish your report first.

(3) The third most frequently asked set of questions concerned the technical details of the analysis—such as the meaning of certain statistical analyses, the categories used, the graphs presented, the tables included, the sample developed, and so on. All these were answered directly by the interventionist.

(4) A fourth set of questions sought clarification of the results, and was usually motivated by disbelief. For example, "Are you suggesting that you rarely observed us helping each other?" My answer was yes. "Then, could you give us some examples of what would be scored as helping others?" Several examples of the usual response were then given and compared with the responses that would have been scored as helpful. Another example:

A: Do you have any way of judging the validity of the subordinates' judgments?

X: Yes, there are several. One is to see if there are patterns in the client system: do the majority of subordinates agree on the problem? Another is to examine the internal consistency within each interview; we look at all the related answers as well as the lack of answers. Also, you may recall, there was a separate set of interviews of reporters and editors at the lower levels. We compared these data with those found in the separate interviews. Finally, we can test the validity by seeing if we can make predictions based upon the subordinates' responses that are eventually confirmed.

(5) The fifth set of questions contained requests for the explanation of a concept, such as the concepts of double bind, trust, openness, and risk-taking. In all cases I tried to respond by giving examples from the data and then providing a definition. My aim was to provide with each definition some directly verifiable examples, to make it easier for the clients to question the concepts themselves if they so desired.

(6) A sixth set of questions represented attempts to understand the points being made in the diagnosis. For example, "Are you saying that people leave our editorial meetings with the idea that the questions we ask represent covert orders for stories to be written?"

X: Yes, this what many reported.
A: Then we haven't conveyed the sense of our meetings, have we?
X: How do others of you react?

Included in this category were comments I felt that I should make in order to prevent the results from being misunderstood. For example, immediately after the question above, one executive began this exchange:

C: Hell, people below may think that, but that is not our intention [said with anger].
X: I'm not trying to attribute a particular motivation to you. I'm suggesting that there may be a gap between how you see the situation and how your subordinates experience it.
C: [Still with anger] I'm just setting the record straight.
A: Why don't we go on? We don't mean to fight you, you know.
X: There will be times when people *will* mean to fight me. I welcome it. It's important to express all our views. I'll express mine!
D: These are all new ideas and sometimes they're not easy to accept.
X: I understand how you feel. I have similar feelings when I get the same type of feedback about my own behavior or about the organization I work in.

Another example:

A: I thought those meetings were one of the most valuable innovations we had.
X: Some people would agree with you.
A: I thought they were well conducted and very productive. Are you saying I'm worng about all that?
X: I'm not saying that you're wrong. I'm saying that almost none of the people I interviewed would agree with you.
A: [Laughter] That's a perfectly valid answer.
B: What's happened to that idea? What is causing that meeting to lose its effectiveness?
X: One reason that was reported was related to the way the meetings were led.
B: That astonished me.
X: That raises an interesting question. [Looking at several people] Why weren't any of you aware of this information? What does it mean about your relationship with these people?
B: Yes, I see your point.

(7) The next set of questions were those which challenged the validity of the research methods used by the interventionist. For example, one person said that I had attended "too few meetings." I responded by describing the number attended, the sampling theory behind the selection, and my experiences in other organizations. Then I said, "Sometimes when people question my sample, they mean to question the results. Would you be willing to tell me if there are any results that you find hard to believe, that is, that do not square with your experience?"

A: I can't believe there isn't any risk-taking in our meetings.
X: May I suggest several ways of tackling this issue? One is for us to go to the data on the meetings in which you were involved. Perhaps you can give examples of risk-taking. Another is to ask others to give us their views. A third is to listen to parts of the tape recordings [which I have brought with me].

Whenever the executives recalled a particular meeting, they had difficulty recalling what they and others had said, and if they could recall, they could seldom agree on one description of a particular behavior—whether, for example, one man's statement was an example of risk-taking. Whenever possible, I urged listening to the tape recording. But even the most vociferous doubters would not agree to playing back portions of the tape. I would not press them to do so.

(8) The next type of question—asked frequently at the beginning of the meeting but only rarely after that—was a request that I identify one or more of the persons whose behavior was being discussed, in order to help participants test the results of the diagnosis in more detail. As the interventionist I refused to give the names of any persons who were not in the room, but said I was willing to identify comments made by groups about the executives in the room, if those executives requested that they be identified. It is often difficult to make this offer and at the same time give a convincing guarantee that individuals really feel free to reject it. I said this openly and invited the clients to help create a climate and a set of group norms that could assure maximum freedom to those who did not wish to be identified.

Clients at times expressed disappointment at being misunderstood by their subordinates, and soon developed needs to express their disappointment and anger. I used these questions to help the clients confront their behavior or their policies, because it was important for the clients to explore the degree of their own responsibility for these problems. I tried to be especially alert during these discussions because they provided insights into the willingness of the executives to explore their own behavior. These insights were important in helping to judge what kind of a change program might be of help to the client. It was also important to help the clients express and work through these feelings so that they would not make life difficult for their subordinates when they returned to the organization. Here is an extended example of this type of question:

A: Everything you say is true. Do they realize the pressure
    that we're under?
C: That's true—all of us are under pressure. Sometimes we

get so preoccupied with a deadline that we don't look at the human problems.

A: Are we sidetracking your presentation?

X: I think we should discuss these feelings as they come up. We've scheduled plenty of time so that issues like these can be fully explored.

A: Well, do they want us to ask if the elevators should be painted blue, or do they want us to tell them to do it?

X: As I understand their views they are as follows: On unimportant issues, like the color of the elevators, tell them. On important, long-range policy issues, many want to be more involved. Also, if you want to be directive and not involve them, they will go along with this policy, but they question the validity of all the talk about increasing their participation in decision-making. Finally, I'd like to emphasize that they *are* aware that all of you are under pressures. They sympathize with you, and this is one reason that they rarely discuss these issues with you.

Still later:

A: I suspect that [in discussions] he cuts off the dumb ones and encourages the bright ones. It seems to me that you're suggesting that everyone, dumb or bright, should be encouraged.

X: I'm asking, how do you know they are "dumb"? Could this be a self-fulfilling prophecy? Also, why do you invite the "dumb" ones to the meetings?

A: You can't afford to exclude them.

X: That's not their view. If they are going to be treated as machines, many prefer to be excluded. Maybe it's time that they were helped to see exactly how their superiors evaluate them.

C: He's right. We rarely tell people about these evaluations.

Still later:

X: What would you predict as their view of that news meeting?

C: I think they think it is practically useless.

X: You're correct, and they don't know why you continue
        them.
C: Well, it's a kind of nostalgia.
X: That's their feeling about it—that they're being used to
        serve nostalgia.
C: Not *my* nostalgia.
X: That's their view.
C: I must say that they're wrong.
X: Let's check it out with others around the table.
D: [The interventionist] is correct. These have been your
        meetings for years.
C: Well, hell, let's drop them!

And finally:

X: I gave an example where, in order to save face, manage-
        ment created two bosses for a particular group.
P: Yes, we did that and it was wrong.
X: But as far as I can see, you're still doing it.
P: Yes, you're right. It won't be easy to change.
E: But why is this wrong? Doesn't it show that our organiza-
        tion has a heart?
F: Well, I can give you several examples of how this has
        harmed us, especially with our better younger people.
        They believe we prefer to reward dead wood.
D: Frankly, I feel we also destroy the people we think we're
        helping. They know that their jobs are meaningless.
E: I think a certain amount of subterfuge works because
        people like it.
X: If it does, I would say that could be a sign of sickness in
        the system.

(9) As the meetings developed, some of the clients began to test hypotheses that they were developing. For example,
two executives asked if the men were not finding it terribly ex-
pensive to live in a very large city. They had wondered recently
if they should not pay some allowances for people living in the
city, especially those with large families.

I replied that I had heard comments about the high cost

of living, but I also warned against believing that management could solve the morale and commitment problems with fringe benefits. To be sure, the employees would appreciate a cost-of-living bonus, but that would not overcome the morale problems caused by other factors mentioned in the report.

In another example, I reported, as interventionist, that the professionals who were administrators did not seem to value their jobs.

A: You know, I've been thinking about this lately. I hope we can explore it someday. I never think of myself as an administrator.

X: Perhaps that's part of the problem.

B: I think you're an able administrator.

A: Maybe so, but I don't like to think of it.

X: Perhaps we should examine the sources and impact of this anti-administrative bias among the professionals.

Finally:

A: Let's suppose that we now all agree with the essentials of this report. I know I do. What do we do? One of the implications is that we should become more open. A lot of us have found that not being candid works well.

B: Yes, I have difficulty with the same question.

C: But we may think it works well, because a lot of information is kept from us.

X: These are critical questions. I have some suggestions on how to experiment with candor. However, nothing that I have to offer will work unless you are willing to make a genuine test of the value of using more candor.

What action should be taken, given the feedback? The discussion about the next steps was long and involved individual executives more than any of the other phases of the program. To their credit, some of the executives openly questioned the advisability of continuing with the program. I valued that type of confrontation for several reasons. I wanted to do my best to create a climate of free and informed choice, in which people who chose to continue did so because they wanted to, and not because they believed that the President wanted the program and therefore they had to agree.

If a client confronts and rejects the concepts that he believes I value, he can provide a valuable living test for the client group: how well can I behave according to my values, especially under conditions of stress? Finally, if individuals confront each other openly in the meeting, they will have begun to behave in ways that are not typical in their regular sessions. Even though the experimenting with confrontation might have begun with the interventionist (who may be seen as more competent to deal with such behavior, or as having the advantage of being an outsider), it can elicit open and risk-taking responses from members who disagree. Thus individuals begin to experiment with the types of behavior that a change program would focus upon. This experimenting may help provide them with experimental data upon which to make a more informed choice about the next steps.

The dialogue that took place during this part of the session illustrates so clearly many of the genuine questions and issues that the clients developed that I should like to quote from it at length. My purpose in doing so is to provide some directly observable data about what issues are raised, how they are raised, and how the interventionist might respond.

A: Is there some training technique that you would suggest? Or are these problems due to personality issues, or the history of this organization, which makes it difficult to change?

B: Perhaps this calls for a sort of rededication to being very honest instead of dishonest.

X: I do have some suggestions. Before I do, I'd like to say that if people are behaving dishonestly, and I would place that in quotes, they do so because they genuinely believe that is the way to help someone and to survive in the system. They're trying to get a job done. Most individuals do not prefer to behave dishonestly.

C: They're well-intentioned.

D: As you have said before, our motives are clean; it is just our ability to lead effectively which is in question.

X: Yes, I would question the interpersonal competence of the members, not your motivations.

I then gave my first suggestion, which was to hold periodic half-day meetings, in which half of the time would be spent discussing substantive issues and half would be devoted to diagnosing the behavior of the group members.

E: Are you suggesting that we need practice in telling the truth? [laughter]

X: Speaking of practice, I believe that the group will have to do more than focus on increasing its openness and trust. The members will have to practice a new set of skills. The world of trust requires a set of skills that you do not possess. As we said before, one reason that ineffective behavior does not have as great a negative impact as it might is that many of you discount the other person's ineffectiveness, without telling him so.

B: Let's assume that we began with a good hot subject. So we let fly at each other and everybody is open. If everybody gets to a position where they are not talking to each other, that's no good. How do you control this?

X: What you have just said is a first step toward self-control. Your caution makes it possible for the group members to discuss this issue, explore their fears, and establish norms and controls to prevent something from becoming destructive. Another point is that openness exists when both people can be open. If I let fly at you, I doubt if I have helped create conditions in which you can be open. It will be my task, at the outset, to help the group explore behavior that may be destructive. Eventually, the control must be developed in the group and should be based more on competence and less on restrictive rules.

C: Do we have to let fly and scream first?

X: I'd put it this way. It is important for you to be your natural selves. Only if you expose your natural behavior and attitudes can we help you explore your impact on others and on the group.

G: Isn't there a danger of destroying our group?

X: I, for one, would work hard to prevent the members from

destroying each other. But more important, as I look back on this meeting and others, I have seen people struggle to be helpful and constructive. If we discover that being open means being destructive, then I should think we should alter that behavior or stop the program. I must emphasize, however, that things will not be easy at the outset. Changing behavior is like learning a new way to walk. The first steps will be awkward, ineffective, and exaggerated.

B: If I think someone in this room is a shit, I don't have to say that, do I?

X: First, no one has to say anything. As I have said many times, there must be as much free choice as possible for each individual. Second, to say to someone that he is a shit is not very helpful. Evaluative comments tend not to be helpful. Indeed, such comments may say as much about the speaker's defensiveness as they do about the recipient's ineffectiveness. Thus one important task for the speaker is to find out what the recipient *does* that renders the speaker unable to respond except by condemning the recipient. In our jargon, we call this learning how to give minimally evaluative feedback.

F: Would you suggest that we try to attempt your technique at our next meeting?

X: I don't see that anyone has learned any new behavior yet. If you tried to be more open during the next meetings, I doubt if you would behave much differently. Perhaps the first few minutes might be different, but the members would soon revert to their genuine behavior. The new behavior is going to be difficult to learn and it requires some help from a professional.

A: You're saying, then, that the way for us to learn is to have an active experience—expose our behavior—and then critique ourselves.

X: Yes, I see this as an important first step. There is also the need to practice the new behavior.

Some members began to propose issues that might be discussed at the meetings. After several minutes they were interrupted by Mr. A:

A: Before we discuss organizational problems, shouldn't we discuss some of our feelings, our fears, the question of how far we want to go, of how can we express our trust of each other?

X: How do others of you react to this question?

C: I think this could be quite dangerous and destructive. We can get to more openness by beginning outside ourselves.

D: If we start the way A suggested, we're dead. It could become destructive.

A: Maybe you think we're going to be more destructive than we really would be.

X: How do others feel?

G: Maybe we should take an hour or so and try it out right now and see how it goes. [no response]

B: If we are going to talk about leadership, we're going to have to discuss the President's leadership. Do we really want to do this?

P: If I didn't want to involve myself in all this, I certainly would not have agreed in the beginning when we talked with [the interventionist].

A: Obviously, we'll have to talk about the President. But we won't stop there.

B: I don't think this group is ready to be honest enough or open enough to discuss these issues. We never have been. I don't think that overnight we are going to be open about the President.

D: Is it necessary to zero in on the President?

E: I'll volunteer to ask the group to start with my leadership style.

F: I just question the desirability of having a sort of group therapeutic self-examination.

G: Are the consequences of self-examination good or bad? Do we have to become specific?

P: I don't think we can discuss things in a vague way.

X: I have two observations. If we experiment with examining leadership styles and find it destructive, what is to prevent us from stopping it? Second, I for one would work to prevent destructiveness and I assume that many of you would do likewise. If not, then we need to reexamine the suggestion. I guess I have a third

observation. It should be up to each individual whether
he wants to have his leadership style discussed.

Toward the end of the meeting, in order to communicate
the meaning of the analysis, I made two predictions based on the
assumption that the participants would decide not to continue
with some useful organizational change activities. They were:

One. About a year ago, many of the group members were
involved in the problem of assigning certain editors to certain
positions. Because the impending shifts were surrounded with
personal and interpersonal issues, they were planned and made
with much secrecy and manipulative activity. The result was what
they called "the great fiasco" in which some people resigned,
several became extremely angry, and several withdrew psychologically although they remained within the organization. I predicted
that such fiascos were natural consequences of the living system
and that they would tend to occur again.

Two. As the newspaper hired younger, brighter, more
autonomously oriented reporters, they would not tend to accept
the living system, as did the old timers, with patience and
magnanimity. I predicted that unless changes were made, the
younger, better, and more aggressive reporters would revolt and
even ask for significant influence in managerial activities.

Both predictions surprised most of the participants, some
to such extent that they felt they were unreal and inappropriate.
Some months later, the conditions for testing the first prediction
became available. The results were as predicted. After this
occurred, I received at least three telephone calls telling me about
the second fiasco. One executive said: "It was a weird feeling to
realize that I was living through the same fiasco with the same
people, and it was an even weirder feeling to realize that it had
been predicted."

The test of the second prediction occurred when a small
group of aggressive younger reporters did hold several meetings
to consider the possibility of taking greater control over the management of the newspaper. By that time, the senior editor (who
had learned more than the other executives during the first change
session) was able to hold long meetings with the reporters. Ap-

parently he convinced them that they could work through the existing structure to obtain satisfaction of their demands.

Summarizing the major questions explored. As may be inferred from the transcript, the group members identified several key areas of concern. All of the issues were important, which shows that the group members do have the capacity to identify important issues and present them for discussion. To summarize, these key issues evolved around six questions.

(1) Can the group members hurt each other and the group's effectiveness by becoming more "open"?

(2) Is it realistic to consider talking openly about our leadership patterns, especially the one exhibited by the President?

(3) Can human behavior be altered to become more effective without basic personality changes? Aren't basic personality patterns beyond alteration?

(4) How do we learn to become more honest with each other if we have found "dishonesty" to be useful and necessary?

(5) Is it possible to transfer the new skills that might be learned during a conference to the back home setting?

(6) How is this process kept under our control, so that it would not become destructive?

I stated that there was much ambivalence in the group about designing and participating in a change program. I also felt, from the behavior during the feedback session (and from the previous diagnosis), that *if* the members genuinely wanted to correct some of the problems identified, they could do so. I suggested that each member think further about his possible participation in a change program. I also recommended that the group hold a meeting, without the interventionist present, to decide whether to undertake a change program.

Three weeks later, I met with the President. He reported that the group had decided to go ahead. One person had voted against the program, and the President said he was going to do his best to make certain that this person felt free not to attend the conference and would not be harmed, organizationally speaking, because he preferred not to attend. The President said that the strong vote to continue represented, in his opinion, an expression of trust in the interventionist, an awareness by the members that they had a responsibility to take some constructive action, and a realization that the design and implementation of the program were under their control—they could decide, as a group, to stop the program at any time.

The President then asked me if I could plan a learning experience in which promotions, demotions, and the importance of the jobs of each top executive would not be discussed. The President was planning certain changes and did not want to have these jobs discussed. He also felt that some of the men who might have questions about their jobs would be terribly threatened by an injunction to talk openly. He asked me to guarantee that such subjects would be ruled out of order.

I responded that I could not do this for at least two reasons. First, I was a consultant to the entire group, and such a decision would require that it be discussed by the entire group. Second, if free choice is to be developed, I could not collude with the chief executive officer to prevent certain topics from being discussed. I could promise to do everything I could to prevent someone from being hurt, but I could not agree to censor certain topics myself, ahead of time or in group meetings.

I suggested to the President that he think carefully about continuing my employment, and said that I would do the same. The implications of the management philosophy that I believed in led to practices that were in direct contrast to the secrecy and non-involvement he had just proposed. I said that if he still planned to operate that way, I preferred to discuss the matter with the entire group or leave.

The President thought about the issues for several weeks. He then decided to make one final round of changes in the top management without consulting the members of the group I had been working with. He promised that this would be the final such round and that if a learning session were designed, he would not require any constraints. I agreed to return two months after the changes were made if he could tell my group the reasons why the program had been postponed. The President agreed.

4

Planning the Next Step

Although I was told that near-unanimous agreement was reached about taking the next step, I was concerned about the degree of freedom people had to reject taking further actions. The executives' vote seemed to be too optimistic. I agreed to move ahead, however, because I knew there would be other opportunities to test the degree of commitment of the participants. The next opportunity would come when they would be asked to participate in designing and approving the first seminar away from the office.

Two months later the President telephoned me to set a date for the planning meeting. During the telephone call he asked how long the meeting might take. He doubted whether they would be willing or able to leave for five full days and nights, as I had requested, and suggested a long weekend instead. I responded that I could not recommend such a short period, but if they insisted, I would try to design a program to fit it. We agreed to discuss the matter further with the entire group.

The meeting was held at the corporate headquarters. The President opened the meeting by saying that the objective was

89

to discuss various designs for a conference away from the office. He ended his introduction by saying, "I'm sure you will have questions to raise with [the interventionist], to get more precise information about what may happen at these kinds of meetings, and about how far you really want to let your hair down, and then we can make up our minds if we want to proceed."

I proceeded to make a short presentation. The conference, I said, would focus on increasing our effectiveness in dealing with human relationships, group dynamics, and intergroup relations. We would also explore different ways of using power effectively, as well as our own leadership styles. The springboard for discussing these issues would be a list of real-life organizational problems. I would interview each individual to obtain subjects and would then present the array at the beginning of the conference in the form of a brief written and oral report. Our main purpose would be to explore actual behavior. Turning to the transcript of the meeting:

> Why look at our behavior? Well, last July I presented a report which I think provided a partial explanation for some of the kinds of problems that we've seen here. For example, I talked about the competitiveness, the lack of openness, the lack of hearing people the way they intended to be heard, and so on. These kinds of findings, plus others, I suggested, could help explain what happened in what has been called the first fiasco. I also predicted that if the living system did not change, the fiasco could be repeated. At that time, I had no idea that an opportunity to test this prediction would arise. We all know now that the incident was completely duplicated, two months after the report was discussed, by several of you who were most supportive of the validity of the report. I think this illustrates that people don't easily change their behavior, and that intellectual understanding and even agreement will not guarantee any type of behavior change.
>
> Why wouldn't it? Well, it's a very complicated set of reasons, and especially difficult to discuss within a two- or three-minute period, but let me mention just one. People tend to read a report like the one you

received and recognize the validity for *other* persons in that report. If they recognize their own behavior, they usually defend themselves by saying that, in their case, they *have* to behave that way.

In order for us to change our behavior, we need to behave spontaneously and encourage others to let us know our impact on them. Why do we need others to tell us our impact? One reason is that we tend to be blind to the impact of our behavior, especially the ineffective behavior. Why should we be blind? One reason is that others rarely tell us when we are behaving ineffectively; it's a carefully guarded secret at times. Other times, when people are told about their behavior, it is done in such a way that it doesn't encourage change; it probably produces defensiveness. Finally, we have defenses to prevent us from seeing what we do to others. If we didn't have those defenses, we'd go around being completely overconcerned about everybody else, and if we did that, we'd not get a job done.

I am suggesting in this seminar that we go on location with a slow-motion camera and put it on us as a group. Then we look at the movie, pretty much the way a football team does when it looks at last week's game, and ask how did we behave and how can we do it more effectively the next time.

Let me emphasize, I'm not asking us to become amateur psychologists to start digging in to people's psyches or trying to start finding out why so-and-so behaves as he does. I am suggesting, for example, that we take a look at how we actually behave toward one another.

How long would it take? I would recommend a week. Now, this may sound like a long time; frankly, I've never been in a group that didn't feel it was a long time, and if you didn't think it would be a long time, I would be worried. I can also say that I think this amount of time is minimal.

The discussion that followed began with such items as the probable schedule for a typical day, where the conference might be held, and problems of transportation. Soon someone asked the question that was asked during the previous session: "How do you know a conference like this might not make interpersonal conflict even worse?" I responded that I could not guarantee that no one would be hurt, but said I could guarantee that I would work hard to prevent anyone from being hurt. I also suggested that the best guarantee would come from the group; they could commit themselves not to strive to hurt anyone.

X: There are some people here who are hurt not because they are expressing something, but because they have been hiding something, if you will, suppressing it for years, and who are kind of fed up with suppressing it. One reason they tend to suppress it is that they assume being more open would upset others. My experience is if these individuals learned to say these things effectively, it would not upset the other fellow; in fact, he would probably say, "You're not telling me anything new; I knew you felt that way all the time." There is then a great sense of relief and an increased sense of trust in the competence and the confidence among people. Am I getting at your question, A?

E: You have certainly gotten to A's question, but my own question is, I have to tell you frankly that I don't see the value of it at all. I see the value to you as a sociologist to analyze an interesting group of people acting and interacting. I can't see the value of it to us, as a way that it would actually affect our future actions as executives of the organization. Perhaps as a catharsis, a one-week psychoanalysis or something like that, maybe it will relieve people of feelings. I can't see it myself, but that doesn't mean that I won't give it a try.

X: Well, first I can tell you what I infer about this place, and I can tell you what's happened to other places. I believe that it can be of help to your organization to help it reduce the compulsive, repetitive ineffectiveness. For example, the second fiasco. People were well-meaning and well-intentioned, but the communication was so bad that the very thing that they didn't want to

occur occurred again. Second, if this group feels that
what it is going through is ineffective, not useful and so
on, there is the freedom to stop it. This group must be
in control of the choice to participate and to continue
to do so. No one is saying that we can't stop it at any
point. I value your comments and I hope that we can
create conditions for people to feel free not to attend.

E: Nothing personal in my remarks.

X: I think there may be something personal in them, and I'm
not uncomfortable about it. I think what you are doing,
E, is raising a terribly important question. If the group
members honestly feel hesitant and fearful, then I think
the program could fail. There is no magic to this
process. The most important single variable in the
process is the quality and depth of commitment you
make. There is no magic that behavioral scientists have
that can take uncommitted people and put them
through something that can make them effective.

G: You're not suggesting, are you, from your answer, that
in one week together we will solve all our problems?

X: Oh, no, no. All the conference will have done is to begin
the process, that's all.

B: Then what we do from then on will be something else.

X: Right, this is only a beginning. If you indeed can confirm the usefulness of it, then it's going to be easier for
you to ask other people in your organization to try it.
If this organization gets seeded with more and more
people who understand what this is all about, then I
think behavior will begin to change.

Someone then asked if real decisions could be made during the discussions of actual business problems. I said yes. Someone then said, "If we try to make decisions, then we'd better re-
serve this place for a month."

The discussion turned again to the likelihood that behavior would change. Someone said he doubted that the group
members' behavior would change because human beings don't
change that easily. I agreed that the probability of behavioral
change at the end of a week was not very high. The realistic
aspiration was to see if a process for development could be begun.

Several news editors then gave examples of the interpersonal and intergroup problems that had to be resolved if the paper was to become more effective. As more individuals contributed examples of problems they wanted to solve during the conference, desire to participate in it spread contagiously within the group.

One of the executives who had serious reservations agreed that all the problems mentioned were important but said, "We should be able to solve them without going through the exercises." Someone responded, "I agree with you that we ought to be able to solve these problems, but the facts are that we never have."

The discussion then turned to whether the important problems were caused by interpersonal issues or by poor structure and policies. The group was divided on this issue. I commented that both were resopnsible; that from my interviews, I had learned that the members had many ideas about structure and policies that they were not sharing; and that the key would be to create a living system in which the participants could redesign their structure or policies as they wished.

The meeting ended again with a commitment for holding the conference. I agreed and said that I would interview each executive to get his recommendations for topics. I planned, during the interviews, to check once more on each person's desire to attend. This was agreed to unanimously.

To summarize, the major issues raised and the responses given were as follows:

Issues Raised by the Group	*Interventionist's Response*
(1) Questions about the design of such an experience. For example, how long should it be; how many should attend; what would be a typical schedule; how could topics be found that were of equal involvement to all.	(1) The conference should be at least five days; the entire top group should be invited (but not required to attend); the day and evening would include short periods of relaxation; and people could practice skills in diagnosing group dynamics when they were not involved in substantive issues.

Issues Raised by the Group	*Interventionist's Response*
(2) Concerns about whether the sessions could accentuate interpersonal difficulties, whether it did not make more sense to discuss new kinds of structures rather than interpersonal relationships.	(2) The interventionist believed and would work very hard to see that no one in this group would get hurt. The key to safety in the seminar was for the members to have genuine concern for each other and to develop ways to alert each other if they are being hurt.
(3) Concerns regarding whether people would be coerced to talk; whether they could choose their own topics; whether they could influence the design of the experience.	(3) The interventionist would work hard to estabilsh group norms that no one be coerced to say or do anything; the agenda be in the control of the group; the group would be encouraged to examine the entire experience to suggest ways to redesign it or to stop it.
(4) A genuine belief, by some, that the sessions would not be worthwhile. A lack of understanding how discussing interpersonal issues would help the organization in its problems.	(4) The interventionist did not share their disbelief but could understand why they would feel this way. He suggested that they experiment continuously to see if the session was worthwhile and that it be stopped whenever there might be agreement that it was not worthwhile.
(5) Is this designed to make management more personality-oriented? Can systems really be managed by focusing on the personal needs of individuals?	(5) The present style of management *is* personality-centered. The difficulty is that it is oriented toward the defenses and anxieties of people and that it tends to be covert about the orientation. All living systems take into account aspects of the personality of their

Issues Raised by the Group	*Interventionist's Response*
	members. Effectiveness depends on making this explicit so that the system can be oriented toward the growth and innovative aspects, and not the defenses and anxieties.

The final pre-seminar interviews. All the participants were interviewed privately in order to ascertain once more their feelings about the seminar. In all cases, the individuals repeated their decision to attend the conference with a genuine commitment to learning. The interviews confirmed that the members felt responsible for helping to make their organization more effective.

Five major clusters of problems were identified as a result of the interviews. They are reproduced here exactly as stated in a memorandum given to each member upon arrival at the seminar location.

(1) The chief executive officer (CEO): His role, his style of leadership, his hopes and aspirations for the organization. The most frequently mentioned cluster of issues were directly or indirectly related to the role of the CEO and to his way of managing the organization. (a) What is the best way to make decisions at the highest levels? What decision-making structure should the CEO develop? Who should be included in this structure? (b) What is the impact of the present practice of violating the lines of authority and responsibility when seeking information or making a decision? (c) Is it legitimate to consider the CEO's style of leadership as something that is subject to change? Can the authority of the CEO's office be undermined by questioning the impact of his style of leadership? (d) How can the long-range problem of succession be analyzed and solutions developed that fit the needs of the CEO and the long-range interests of the *Planet?* If the CEO had to choose a half dozen or so people to work with him, who would be selected?

Note: In addition to being the most frequently mentioned issue, this one also attracted the strongest feelings of ambivalence. Individuals were very concerned that their motives for asking these questions be clearly understood. Their intent was to be constructive; to be supportive of the CEO; to help him increase his involvement in any activity at the *Planet* without inhibiting its effectiveness.

I suspect those who worry that a discussion of these issues might undermine the authority of the CEO or their relationship with him also unknowingly communicate the same message to their subordinates about the advisability of confronting them. Thus part of the concern about how the CEO might react may be due to their own concern about how they would react if their subordinates confronted them. To put this another way, with one exception, the men whom I have seen actually invite confrontations by their subordinates are also the ones who worry least about the impact this discussion might have on the authority of the CEO.

In my experience, the first step toward building an effective team is for the members to explore their relationships with the leader. The second, and equally important, step is to explore their relationships with each other. Almost every problem of leadership style that people have with the CEO they will probably have with some sub-group or other individuals on the executive committee.

(2) The effectiveness of the executive committee. The second most frequently mentioned cluster of issues had to do with the effectiveness of the executive committee. (a) Why is the executive committee unable to take action, to make decisions without undue procrastination? (b) Why does the executive committee get bogged down in trivia and detail? (c) Are all the members of the committee as powerful as their titles suggest they should be? (d) Do the members really understand the problems and issues in each other's world? If not, how can they meet to make policy that affects the entire organization? (e) Why do some members of the executive committee behave (in and out of the meetings) as if they have little patience with, and respect for, the executive committee? (The disrespect is rarely communicated openly. More often, the individuals show it by playing their cards close to the vest.)

(3) The vision of our organization in the future. The third most frequently mentioned cluster of issues has to do with

the long-range development of the organization. Some expressed concern that the CEO might unrealizingly alter the basic course of the organization. Some wonder if the CEO does not have a more parochial view of the objectives of the organization than is appropriate. Some of the specific issues mentioned were: (a) The new feature. (b) Subjective and objective reporting. (c) Is the news being filled with too much "soft stuff"? (d) What is the appropriate decision-making process within the news activities? The roles of some persons at the highest level are not clear. (e) How can the CEO be involved in the news activities, yet not be inhibiting?

(4) The relationships between departments. Relationships between departments have improved, but during the new cost cutting, some interdepartmental strains appeared. Might they get worse in the future if we have on-going cost reduction campaigns (or other campaigns that apply pressure on people to give up scarce financial, human, and time resources)?

(5) The vision of the total organization (including its subsidiaries and future growth).

The clients' anxieties and the interventionist's double bind. The interviews also reinforced the ambivalence of the executives. Many of them expressed a genuine concern about someone else being hurt. Not one expressed worry about himself. Each was worried about the other; each had one or two persons about whom he was particularly concerned. When asked to specify in more detail what concerned them about the others, the respondents were unable to do so. They would simply state that they felt so-and-so was brittle or rigid, that human behavior was difficult to change, and that working in the organization for years has left deep wounds which the seminar could reopen.

The executives also stated that they would do their best not to open up such wounds and to help make the meeting a constructive one. Most of them did not begin citing possible organizational subjects to discuss at the conference until they had drawn from me, indirectly or directly, a promise that I would do my best to make certain that no one was hurt. I, of course, agreed. I had made that commitment on several different occasions.

By the time the interviews were completed, I began to realize that something had changed within myself. I felt more responsible about someone being hurt at the conference than I had when dealing with other clients. I began to wonder if the group members had not subtly succeeded in placing on my shoulders more than my share of the responsibility for the effectiveness of the conference. If so, then the decision to go or not to go was largely in my hands. The centralization of decision-making that is characteristic of the living system had been introduced into my relationship with them.

My concern was not so much with anyone being hurt. I was fairly confident that Dr. Fred Steele (my co-worker during the seminar) and I could handle such a problem before it arose. My confidence was reinforced by the belief that, given the extreme concern these individuals had expressed about hurting someone, they would deliberately be cautious about being open.

If this were true, however, then an important force was operating to minimize the effectiveness of the seminar. The seminar required persons who were motivated to become increasingly more open, to expose their feelings, and to uncover ideas they had covered up.

I began to realize that I was in a double bind. If I acted to keep the group, as they preferred, low-key, the seminar would probably succeed in not running the risk of hurting anyone. However, it could also fail because none of the important issues would be faced. If this occurred, then the entire program could be stopped without the individuals feeling responsible for the failure. If, on the other hand, Steele and I pressed carefully (and competently) for openness on the important issues, and if we succeeded without anyone being hurt, the group members could assign the success of the program to us. Consequently, their dependence upon us would have been reinforced and their internal commitment to organizational change and development would remain low.

Becoming aware of this bind helped me to raise an important question: Given the high degree of participant ambivalence, why was I encouraging the holding of the seminar? The immediate answer was that the group had to run an experiment;

it had to take a swim in a lake that it was afraid to go near, much less swim in. I was confident that the probabilities of anyone being hurt were low. However, I had to admit now that this placed the entire program in a precarious position. If it succeeded it would be because it developed the same kind of dependence dynamics and centralized decision-making that were characteristic of the living system.

Perhaps part of my problem was embedded in the fact that I had selected this organization partially because it was full of executives who genuinely did not believe in the approach that I represented. Thus, if I were pressing for the seminar to prove to myself and to them that I could win them over, then I had placed myself in a dependence posture that was deeper than was helpful for them or for me.

I concluded tentatively that these binds may be inevitable with any system that is "successful" and simultaneously resists personal and organizational learning. My task would be to be open about these issues, to ask the group to explore the territory they know they have to explore, to confront them if they move too slowly or withdraw too quickly, to be sensitive to episodes when anyone might be feeling hurt, and to press openly for the exploration of issues that the participants have agreed are real for them—but at the same time to remain open to being confronted about my own behavior and capable of being influenced to change it.

These are very difficult tasks to accomplish, especially if one has an internal commitment to such values as free choice. There would be moments, I feared, when I might, out of anxiousness to have the seminar succeed, press beyond the line of free choice for the clients. If so, I had to be ready to be confronted, to own up to why I was doing it, and to encourage the group to alter the course I was suggesting they take. As the reader will see, this happened at several key episodes during the seminar.

As a result of becoming aware of my own feelings, ambivalences, and double binds, I tried to write a memorandum that made explicit the thoughts and feelings that I had about the group. I had great difficulty completing the memorandum to my satisfaction. Looking back, I now believe that one reason I had these difficulties may have been that although I knew that I had colluded in generating greater client dependency upon me than was desirable, the acceptance of this incompetent behavior on my part was something that I may not have wanted to face. If I had faced up to that issue more effectively, I believe I would have realized that my incompetence was not the only factor. This was the first time *I* had selected an organization in which to work, and I had picked one that was a challenge. Such an organization would be more resistant, and I would have to face many more episodes in which I walked a tightrope between interventions that encouraged free choice and internal commitment and interventions that did not. What I had not realized was how much I wanted to "win." I wanted to help the clients even though many of them probably did not want that help (despite their realization that they needed it). If I could have acknowledged this more clearly, I might have been able to be more accurate with the clients as to why I was persevering.

Perhaps, again looking backwards, this was a key concern of many of the clients. Perhaps they saw me as a person who was bent on "winning" even at their own expense; they could understandably be worried about my intentionally or unintentionally throwing them into water way over their heads.

I reproduce the memorandum that I wrote to myself (which was completed after the seminar was held) to give the reader a more detailed picture of my concerns and to provide a better basis for understanding some of my behavior during the seminar.

> In preparing myself for the seminar, I was aware that I felt the group was one of the most difficult ones I had ever dealt with. I was aware that the quality and depth of individual involvement in it varied widely. What made me somewhat uneasy was: (1) The seminar was to be a combination of laboratory experience and regular discussions on substantive issues. A highly conflicted group could easily vacillate between the two or retreat to the substantive issues and rarely explore their own behavior. (2) I felt that a certain

amount of positive learning would have to occur early
or the group would vote to disband. Not only did I not
have the week that I had felt was a minimum time; I did
not feel that I had three days [which is what they agreed
to]. My own feelings about the group are:

(1) Forces acting to inhibit group and organizational development. A significant proportion of the
members in this group:

(a) Are uncomfortable or do not believe that
it is necessary to talk about interpersonal issues in
order to have more effective substantive decisions and
more effective groups. They are genuinely afraid to
generate valid information about interpersonal issues
that inhibit the open discussion of substantive issues.
For example, the substantive issue of the design of the
new feature is not going to be solved until the issue of
who controls it is resolved. On the issue of control,
people have important views that are related to trust.
Yet, there is little predisposition to talk about them
openly with the people involved.

(b) Believe that openness about emotions and
interpersonal issues is dangerous;

(c) Are not committed to the idea that an
effective executive committe is necessary to manage the
organization.

(d) Are influenced by a long history that the
publishing and administrative sides should be kept
separate.

(e) Are quite willing to own up to their ideas
with the CEO but feel little need to make a decision.
There is a view that the CEO must resolve any conflicts and make decisions. An effective leader is a
strong leader. A strong leader is one who controls the
group, listens to all sides, and makes his own decisions.
The CEO does not find these views helpful. He experiences his vice-presidents as willing to be advocates who
with practice "legitimate distortion" of the issues in
order for them to win. He is left with the task of guess-
ing what he must discount and how he is to develop an
integrated decision.

(f) Feel a minimal sense of responsibility for

group effectiveness. They believe their responsibility is primarily to be good advocates of their positions.

(g) Believe that the very need for an outside interventionist is a sign of failure.

(h) Believe that human nature is difficult to change and that this is especially true of people in their occupation.

(2) Forces acting to facilitate group or organizational development. A significant proportion of the members in this group:

(a) Are aware of and own up to the fact that the system and its decision-making processes are not effective. They do not retreat from acknowledging that their system has problems.

(b) Manifest a high sense of constructive intent and a deep sense of obligation that they are responsible for the effectiveness of their system.

(c) Are willing to question their managerial competence.

The CEO is in favor of genuinely exploring organizational development. He wants very much to institute some organizational development activities, yet he also wants to provide the officers with all the encouragement they need to question such a desire.

Although the CEO is in favor of organizational development, this does not mean that he is completely clear about its meaning. He experiences much ambiguity regarding the concept. However, he is willing to give the concept meaning by experimenting with different learning experiences.

Nor is the CEO unconflicted about his style of leadership. For example: he wants to develop a strong cohesive executive committee, yet he prefers to work with small sub-groups (sometimes including members not in the executive committee); he wants to help the system rid itself of dead wood and historical legacies, yet he maintains some of the former and creates his share of the latter; he wants people to be candid with him, and he wants to be candid about others, but he tends to be closed about his feelings about himself.

(3) Prediction about how the group will use

the interventions. If the above analysis is valid, then I can expect a range of differences in the way the members will expect me to act during the seminars. The range might be described as a continuum with two extreme points, A and B.

A	B
1. Agree to attend the seminar with the tacit expectation of depending on the interventionist to develop a process and climate which protects them from being harmed; from exposing their behavior; from diagnosing their effectiveness; from experimenting with new skills; from the requirement that they learn from others.	1. Agree to attend the seminar with the tacit expectation of depending on the interventionist only *initially,* and of striving to reduce the dependence. They expect the interventionist and themselves to be responsible for the climate and for being protected. They seek to expose their behavior, to diagnose their effectiveness, and to experiment and to learn from others.
2. They have difficulty in trusting their own and others' ability to give and receive interpersonal feedback and deal with emotions.	2. They have difficulty in dealing with emotions and interpersonal relationships but they trust their own and others' abilities to learn.
3. They will look for subjects and activities that protect them.	3. They will look for subjects and experiences that expose their behavior and lead to learning.

It is difficult to know where all the individuals may be placed on this continuum. It will probably vary with the development of the group, the subject being discussed, and their personal strength. A gross estimate is that, at least, 50 to 60 percent are at the right end with the others in the middle.

It follows that I must be seen, by a large proportion of the members, as inviting them to attend a
seminar that violates many of their group and organizational norms as well as their personal values. One can
expect them therefore—given their constructive intent
and sense of responsibility—to participate to the extent they can hold the interventionist responsible for
their behavior. Examples of comments that occurred
early in the seminar to illustrate this point are: (1)
"Are the rules of the game that *you* want all of us to
respond?" (2) "I'm saying this in the spirit of the
exercise, even though as many of you know, I have
some reservations." (3) "It is your responsibility to tell
us what to do."

Why did the executives take so long to agree to the learning seminar? One cluster of answers to this question may be
derived from the analysis above. If the executives attended the
learning seminar, they knew they would be asked to discuss
openly the issues that they had privately agreed existed, but had
publicly denied were crucial; and they knew that they had created
all sorts of individual, group, and intergroup defenses and policies
in order to maintain the discrepancy between what each privately
knew was true about the public reality yet which publicly many
had worked hard to cover up.

For example, the members were aware of the dependency
of many executives upon the President. As documented in
Chapters Two and Three, the executives questioned the others'
all-too-easily given acquiescence in what the President asked. They
observed their peers, during the executive committee meetings,
disagreeing with the President in a form so mild that it was difficult
to discern the disagreement. If the disagreement was discernable,
it was usually followed by the assurance that the individual, having raised his doubts, would now go along with the President's
decision, even before the President and others had reacted.

Also, many of these professional newsmen had a curiously
difficult love-hate relationship toward administration as a process.
Most of them considered administration second-class work, and
journalism first-class work. They would condemn bureaucratic

rules and subservience to authority, yet become extremely sub-
servient to the President when he appeared at a meeting. Yet, as
we shall see, the dependency was denied when it became a topic
of conversation with the President. Indeed, he even denied it
because, as he told me several times, it was embarrassing to see
so many of his top people so fervently deny their own behavior.

As the project continued, I discovered several other forces
at work, and I shall mention them here even though I was not
fully aware of them until the learning seminar got underway.

The observable consequences of the feeling of helplessness
are that it confirms the sense of helplessness and it produces behavior that reinforces it (such as passivity, lack of risk-taking,
fear of openly discussing threatening issues). Thus, people exist
in a system that provides them with daily evidence that others
feel helpless and behave accordingly.

The same living system induces people to magnify events
out of proportion; encourages over-reaction by individuals; and
produces tensions and responses that seem inappropriate to a
given episode but are predictable given the pent-up feelings of the
actors. What individuals see, in the system, is what they describe
as colleagues who appear to be easily upset and brittle. Note, so
far, that any given individual sees all these behaviors as created
by *others,* and understandably attributes the brittleness to *others.*

There is little attributing of over-reaction to one's self for
two reasons. First, in this system, if Mr. A over-reacts, the others'
responses will be guided by politeness, diplomacy, and tact (or
however one wants to label these defensive behaviors). These
fellow-workers will not inform A that his behavior was experienced as over-reacting or inappropriate. Indeed, I observed countless episodes in which the immediate reaction of others was to
assure the individual that the explosion was understandable,
reasonable, and just. "Joe, I know exactly how you feel," was
a commonly heard response. And it was commonly used because
it was true (the other person may have had similar feelings in
other settings), and because it could serve to reduce the individual's defensiveness.

Moreover, if one believes that his colleagues are defensive
and brittle and one has to work with them, then he will be pre-

disposed to use up his energies in being sensitive toward *others*. Soon, one may come to believe that the others are indeed the cause of the problems. Thus the system induces other-directedness, to use Riesman's concept. It is understandable, therefore, that when I asked the executives to discuss their views about the learning seminar and, more specifically, to discuss issues they believed were critical yet threatening, in order to focus on their fears about others, they hesitated.

One way to account for each executive's immediate denial that he is brittle is to say that the processes of other-directedness had led the executives to project their own brittleness onto others. Projection, as a psychological defense, usually unconscious or semiconscious, leads the individual to project onto others characteristics that he or she also manifests. This analysis may provide illustrative case material of socially functional projections which may have their source in consciously identifiable system characteristics but which, over time, and given the necessity to be concerned about the other, cause the individuals to come to ignore their personal responsibilities in these matters. The result is a group of executives who are able to express a sense of helplessness about changing the system and the others in it, but who simultaneously deny that they exhibit the same brittleness they assign to the system and to others.

What makes it difficult to intervene effectively with such defensive procedures is that the individuals are able to point to innumerable examples, where, indeed, others *are* brittle, and where the system is defensive. If they can prove that point, why do they need to focus on themselves? Is not this adequate evidence that the learning seminar would be dangerous and that their ambivalence and hesitation are rational?

The self-sealing, defensive aspects of this logic are especially difficult to confront effectively if one holds a theory of change that is based upon allowing the clients to choose freely and become internally committed to learning. Under these conditions, the clients can rightly maintain that their resistance is necessary to provide others the freedom to choose *not* to participate, a freedom that I would encourage.

There is a deeper reason for the difficulty in producing

effective learning, a reason that I sensed before the seminar but did not become fully aware of for months. As I re-examined my memorandum, I realized that one of its major themes was that I believed the group was brittle and was feeling a sense of helplessness about being effective. The problem, the reader may recall, was not that Dr. Steele and I were not competent to deal with foreseeable difficulties; the problem was not that I did not have faith in the clients' abilities to grow. The problem was that I did not trust them to trust themselves and others in a growing environment.

In other words, the helplessness-denial processes characteristic of the system were beginning to influence me. I was beginning to become apologetic for my position. For example, I began to wonder, was I "selling" too hard? If so, that would be reducing the choice of the clients.

The paradox was that I was faced with a group of clients who, if given the freedom to choose, would choose to reduce their freedom. Under these conditions, a learning seminar based upon free choice (among other values) was going to be difficult, to say the least.

One way to begin to resolve the paradox was to create a setting in which the individuals could begin to see that their diagnosis of others as brittle was valid, partially because it was self-sealing. Each individual confirmed and reinforced brittleness in others. Therefore, they were creating conditions that they described as personally defensive and organizationally detrimental. Such a learning environment would require that these dilemmas be generated in such a way that they could not be attributable to the interventionists. Thus we worked hard before and during the seminar to produce data that individuals created and had imbedded in them, the dilemmas that could be a source for growth.

The paths for free choice and the generation of data that produce learning where people feel threatened are very difficult to create and to traverse. They require, on the part of the interventionists, at least, the ability to own up to their own anxieties and their own dilemmas. Without accepting these anxieties, they cannot cope with them. They immediately become living examplars of their clients' behavior, which is the last thing the clients need if they are to grow. Moreover, having exposed these feelings, the interventionists must be open to learning and to confrontation by the clients. As we shall see, this occurred several times during the seminar. The result was that the clients were more able to manage the speed of their own learning; which reduced my compulsion to "push" learning; which in turn provided living examples of how to begin to confront the I-am-helpless-because-they-are-brittle defense.

5

The Learning Seminar

In this chapter, I should like to provide the reader with a historical account of the activities that occurred during a three-and-a-half day seminar which the entire top management attended, as well as to provide some evidence for the difficulties the group members had in unfreezing.

In order to give the reader a close experiential feel for the learning processes that were generated, heavy emphasis will be placed on providing excerpts from the tape recordings made of the meetings (with the knowledge and approval of the participants). They will illustrate the frequency, especially during the learning seminar and the other sessions that followed it, of four occurrences: (1) the members generated micro-diagnoses of their system that were confirmed, but they backed away from dealing with the issues because of their threatening implications; (2) the interventionists presented directly observable data on key problems that were confirmed, but the group members pushed them aside; (3) the group members and the interventionists made requests that the group members examine their flights from reality but these requests were translated into topics of even further flight; and (4) on a few precious occasions, social pain and embarrassment were overcome and the participants not only faced the issues but began to change the situation. Regretfully, these small steps taken by a few individuals were so insignificant for the system as a whole that the system (through its agents) reacted as if to say, "You didn't get permission, so you may not move forward." *

The excerpts included represent only a small sample of the available protocols. They have been selected to represent the key moments in the learning seminar. A few of these moments exhibit hard work, in which individuals did struggle to unseal self-sealing processes, to make publicly discussable what had been only privately thinkable, and to find new ways of coping with recurrent problems. I realize, however, that for many readers the examples may become tiresome and annoying; some may even find themselves impatiently flipping past the quoted tran-

---

* The data included in this section came from the tape recordings of the entire seminar. I listened to all the tape recordings, making detailed notes about individuals' participation, including my comments. The analysis included all identifiable themes. The detail with which each theme was described depended upon its centrality to the living system. The behavior of individuals while in the group, the group dynamics, the behavior of the individuals back home that related to here-and-now behavior were all considered central. For example, discussion on the leadership style of any member was noted in great detail. An equally long discussion about management philosophy or organizational history was noted in summary form. The analysis of twelve meetings produced slightly over one hundred pages of notes and comments.

The next step was to review these notes and divide them into episodes. Some episodes had endings; others ended several meetings later; and still others continued after the seminar was over. An example of the first was a discussion of the development of a new product; the second, the leadership style of the chief executive officer (P); the third, the degree of internal commitment, on the part of the executives, to the managerial values implied in the program.

The following crude criteria were used to identify episodes. (1) What is the issue that is being discussed at this moment? Has it been discussed before? If so, had the discussion been completed? Is this a repeat of the same issue but examined from a different viewpoint? (2) Are there other issues interspersed with this discussion? Do the members identify these issues as tangential? If not, would the analyst make such inferences? (3) Are there any flights from the topic? If so, do the members identify them? If not, what evidence does the analyst produce that the discussion is a flight?

script in search of relief. I decided to risk creating these feelings because they are similar to the feelings many of the participants had during the sessions. A few found the sessions full of learning, challenging growth experiences, and rare opportunities to confront major systemic issues; but many began to find them repetitive, tiring, annoying, dull, and frustrating; and many chose to withdraw and ignore these problems. Many hoped that these problems would be overcome by better management procedures, such as budgets and planning. As we shall see, the problems not only remained, but they reappeared woven even more intricately in the fabric of human relationships that were now significantly affected and controlled by the sophisticated techniques of management information systems and planning.

Session I. I began the first session by reiterating the objectives discussed in the previous section (increased self-awareness, competence in interpersonal and group relations, more effective leadership styles, and so forth). Then I asked if there were any questions. The first episode began when several members asked such questions as "How much openness should there be?" "Isn't it possible that there can be too much openness?" "Are we talking about openness at the interpersonal and business levels?" I interpreted these questions as expressing three possible concerns. The first was to obtain the information implicit in the question; however, this was no longer considered the major concern because these questions had been discussed several times in several different meetings with the group. The second was to alert each other to be careful in what they said; this may have been an attempt to define limits within which to operate. The third may have been to attempt to make the interventionists reasonable for defining the limits, or to make them responsible for stopping any discussion that might become harmful.

The interventionist's reply attempted to expose these possibilities and to suggest that such questions would be most effectively answered by the entire group: "Neither Y [Dr. Steele, co-interventionist] nor I can define the limits. They will vary with the subject, the stage of group development, the individuals, and so on. Our task is to learn how much openness can be constructively created. Y and I will work hard to help create that degree of openness that encourages further openness and learning. Neither of us is interested in openness that may be harmful to individuals.

"Finally, yes, one of our goals is to help develop openness on the interpersonal level that facilitates more effective decision-making and more growth for the individuals involved. We have no tricks to push you into any more openness than you wish. It will be our task to help you be in constant control of your activities.

"By the way, one of the conclusions that I came to from the interviews (held just before coming to these sessions) is that most of you seem to be pessimistic about *others'* potential for openness and optimistic about your own." [laughter]

The next episode consisted of attempts by the group to define which topics they wished to discuss. Each member had a copy of the pre-meeting agenda. Consequently, most of the discussion was limited to the agenda. The group members were ambivalent. On the one hand, they had come expecting to talk about the issues they had identified; on the other hand, many of these issues could easily lead into somewhat threatening discussions of leadership styles and their group process.

I reviewed the five clusters of issues and then asked: "Do any of these five make sense? Do we want to discuss any one or a combination of them? If not, what do we want to discuss? Dr. Steele and I are committed to helping you define the answers to these questions."

P (the President) identified topics (1) and (2)—the chief executive officer's style of leadership, including his hopes and aspirations for the system, and the effectiveness of the executive committee—as being interrelated. B agreed that they were most important but said, "Is it wise to take on the most difficult first?" "Why not?" asked E, "We can always talk about the easiest ones at home." P again invited a discussion about himself. D suggested that perhaps such a discussion be conducted at a general level and not be too specific.

Several people agreed that it should be general and E suggested that they go to topic (3), the vision of the system in the future. The discussion left the leadership style of P. After further discussion which seemed to have little additiveness, F said, "The question is whether to dissect or not to dissect P. I for one have decided not to try this."

P responded, "I won't mind it. That's why we're here. We can't run this place like it used to be managed years ago." This last phrase triggered a long discussion about the "old days." Finally G asked if the group would like to experiment: "Why not try talking about P or me and see how well it goes?" The suggestion was received with total silence.

H returned the group's attention to topic (3) and another long discussion ensued about the old days. I then interrupted the discussion and asked for an experiment. He asked them to look at the decision-making process that led them to talk again about the old days.

X: How did you feel after you made your suggestion?
G: Not very good—no one picked it up.
E: Look, let's face it. (1) and (2) are the guts of the issue. A lot of us are leery. We're dancing around it. Discussing number (3) gave us an excuse. We're simply postponing the moment of truth.
C: Maybe we need a strong chairman to discipline us.
X: There are at least two ways to get discipline. One is to appoint a chairman. The other one is for each member to develop a strong sense of responsibility for the effectiveness of this group. I think one of the reasons the executive committee back home is ineffective is that there is little of the latter.* Also, if you select a chairman you dump the decisions onto him. You may recall that this was another finding of our diagnosis.†

A discussion followed about the difficulties that this group had in making decisions. E again confronted the group by say-

---

* Almost all the members of the seminar were members of the executive committee.

† If the seminar had been planned to last longer, it might have been advantageous to let the group experiment with appointing a chairman and seeing that this would not help to overcome their difficulties.

ing, "We've danced up to this issue several times. Let's start with (1) and (2). It's getting late!"

E apparently became the "strong" leader the group wanted, and with his prodding, all but one agreed to discuss (1) and (2) during the next session. They all stood up and started to request drinks. The interventionists felt that the decision did not carry much individual commitment, but they doubted if it would be wise to bring the group back to discuss this issue.

Sessions II and III. (These are grouped because the members took a short break and returned to their work, and because the topic was continuous.) The session began next morning with a discussion of three back-home issues. They were "cost cutting"; "the problem with budget people"; and "the ineffectiveness of the executive committee."

Although these issues were clearly not the ones that the group had "decided" to discuss the evening before, the interventionists did not interrupt the discussion. One reason was that they knew all these issues were alive and potent for many of the executives, so that there was a lot of commitment and energy behind the discussion. Another reason was to see if the group would learn to police itself. If the interventionists brought them back to topics (1) and (2), then they could be held responsible for the direction of the discussion. If something then went wrong, they could also be held responsible. If the decision turned out to be a good one, the members could become dependent upon the interventionists.

The discussion of the executive committee (to which most of this group belonged) was the most potent issue for the group. P described the committee as "overly slow and ponderous," and said many of its meetings "serve no useful function for me."

B asked that they examine some of the reasons why the executive committee was ineffective. There was a silence. I decided to intervene and use this suggestion to relate it to P's pattern of leadership. He noted that many of the people in the room had told him that they were annoyed and perplexed by the way P used the executive committee. He seemed to bypass it, to go directly to their subordinates, and to talk with some individuals on the executive committee but ask them not to talk about the issues with other members.

P responded, "That's fair. I've been trying different methods. So far I find that the smaller the group, the more effective it is. Also, if we're going to level, many of my associates around here help to erode the effectiveness of the group. They come to me in a one-to-one manner."

My intervention may have helped the group to focus on P's leadership (a subject they had identified as critical), but it was made in such a way that the interventionist could be held responsible for the change in direction. In other words, this could have begun to build up an expectation or hope, on the part of some group members, that if they waited long enough, X or Y would take the initiative to bring them back to the subject.

This expectation was not inaccurate, as far as I was concerned. On the one hand, I wanted to do my best to make the sessions succeed. On the other hand, I knew that genuine success would come only when the group members felt that they were responsible for their own growth.

As we shall see, I continued to make interventions of this kind. They seemed to generate progress and learning. However, they also permitted those who did not want to commit themselves to remain privately or internally uncommitted. Without conditions that would border on experimental control (such as the introduction of a control group), it is difficult to provide unambiguous explanations. What seems likely is that in groups where commitment to learning is ambivalent and external, it may be necessary for the interventionists to take these initiatives and create the dependence. If they do so, it would also be necessary for them to make their strategy explicit and to invite confrontation whenever members felt the need for it. As shall be seen below, the interventionists did raise this issue with the group members.

Returning to this session, a lively discussion was generated about the way people used P, how they manipulated him to get what they wished. C asked P to deal with them less in a one-to-one manner and to follow more formal processes. P responded that he realized they felt that way, but he disliked formal processes. Several men then responded that the one-to-one relationships, on the part of P, were undermining many formal groups that he had created.

At this point, several people, all of whom belonged to the sub-group that was concerned about the dangers of this process, reminded the group members of the important and instructive changes that P had instituted. They warned the group about becoming too negative. P, they insisted, was doing a first-rate job. A bandwagon effect was created, and many people jumped on board to pay homage to their superior.

X: I'd like to point out a dilemma. During the interviews, many of you expressed hopes that P would change some of his behavior. He was described as a person who, in many cases unrealizingly, rejected people, lashed out, hurt them, and so on. Is the group backing off just as it is getting at one of the critical issues? Am I making a mountain out of a molehill? [Retrospectively, this last question seems defensive; I may have been feeling a need to protect myself.]

E: What you are seeing is the normal expectation of men in their forties and fifties faced with having to be honest with each other and quite rightly being unable to do it.

G: When I hear P's faults being described, I realize a lot of them apply to me. I feel somewhat guilty. I too have the same problems. Possibly this is true of many of us.

P: But we must discuss these issues. As all of you know, there is an issue that we planned to discuss here which has been on and off for four years. Each of you tell me your views and then you leave and nothing happens.

H: After four years of waiting, I think P should make the decision.

D: But how can he? He doesn't really know where we stand.

P: I guess I can make assumptions.

A: Yes, but your assumptions have been wrong.

X: Perhaps you can test your assumptions.

C: Why do we have to focus on P? Why can't we talk about the best decision-making structure? Why do we have to get into this behavioral science crap, if you'll forgive the expression?

P: But will we learn anything?

E: How can we talk about this in the abstract? He is the only P we have.

G: I'm sympathetic. This conversation is focusing increasingly on you as an individual.

P: I want it to.

A: He's asking for it.

P: I want to listen, learn, and come back at you. [laughter]

X: Perhaps this is another fear. If we talk about P, then it makes it more legitimate for him and others to talk about us.

B: Does it make sense to analyze motives? I think we ought to stop this.

X: I agree with you that analyzing motives may be ineffective. However, if my diagnosis is correct, the people in this room—indeed in the entire organization—spend much of their time analyzing motives, never testing their analyses, and then acting on them.

P: Why is it necessary to look at how we operate as a group? Let's take an issue and discuss it.

X: Once in a while, it's important to open up the hood of your car and see if the motor is working effectively.

D: The old P used to say that if you had a car going 50 miles an hour, never open up the hood.

X: This is a choice that we now have to make. Do we want to look at our behavior?

P: I think we have to. We can't go back to the old days. I doubt if that will work. You and others ask for involvement. I am trying to give it. My difficulty is that I try to involve everyone and I get no decision made.

There appears to be a substantial degree of ambivalence and fear in the group. There are a few members who are willing to explore their own behavior. Two of them have quite openly confronted the group's inability to discuss P's leadership pattern. A third has contributed by admitting having guilt feelings during discussions of P's leadership style. The majority of the group, however, is very cautious about the need to focus on the behavior of the individual, even though the individual in question is the P and he has repeatedly requested this feedback.

During lunch, several of the members sat with me and raised serious doubts about the value of the program as it was going. They expressed fear that it could harm relationships and undermine the authority of P. I responded that I did not share their fears, but that I would encourage a discussion of this issue at the beginning of the next session.

Session IV. I began the session by stating that some people had expressed concern, during lunch, about the harm that could come to personal relationships if we continued discussing behavior. G said, "I'm not sure it's fair to bore in on P. But since we're challenged to do so, I will."

My query was never discussed. Although G began as if he was going to continue discussiong P's leadership pattern, he quickly turned to the idea that there ought to be more structure, more group discussion back home. P agreed. He wanted to develop this top group into an effective policy planning group. Some members expressed concern that this might give administrative officers some influence in publishing matters, which would violate long-standing norms. Y then raised the question whether that did not imply a degree of mistrust. Before a response could be made, P said that his biggest worry was that "The group will be open, leave the meeting, and do nothing."

B suggested that the members would have to build new levels of mutual respect, especially between the administrative and the publishing sides. "These are not the only walls," added F; the editorial and news departments have their problems. B added, "If we don't face the fact that there are walls between us, we will fail in these discussions."

A long discussion developed that took the focus away from the issues of mistrust and intergroup rivalries. After nearly one hour, I intervened to attempt to return the discussion to the original question. This intervention failed. G, somewhat annoyed, asked, "What is it that you want to come out of this?" I responded that I wanted to explore why my original question was never discussed. I recalled that in the previous session some members were upset about the dangerous track on which the discussion was proceeding. "I raised the issue," I continued, "and the only response I got was a discussion that had little to do with the issue, but which in effect kept us away from it."

R: I think you are overinterpreting. People talk about hurt feelings. Well, I have them. The news people have for years been against [the new feature].

C: But are you willing to discuss these [hurt feelings]?

R: Of course. As long as any proposal does not threaten the autonomy of [that department].

Q: I agree. We are all influenced by history. When I took my job, I decided to get rid of historical barriers. I have found that there are many people who want to help me out.

The time to end the session arrived. People asked each other what they wished to discuss at the next session. They quickly agreed that the discussion should focus on "the new feature" that was being discussed. They had been discussing this project for nearly four years. P expressed a hope that a solution could be found. The group agreed to return and work hard on the issue. The interventionists decided against attempting to focus on the interpersonal and group issues. The new feature was too hot an issue to be set aside. Also, if the discussion became animated, some of the group and intergroup problems might be brought into the open.

Session V. The session began with the introduction of an agenda developed by H. The agenda began with the underlying concept of the new feature and went on to deal with the mechanics of producing it. After H finished describing the agenda, D suggested that the discussion begin with several "stipulations" with which he felt everyone would agree. No sooner had he finished than several members objected to them.

P then asked D to give his views. D, in line with his preferred manner of thinking about problems, went directly to the mechanics of publishing the new feature. He proposed a compromise plan which he said would satisfy everyone. He kept reminding the group members that they had discussed this for four years; that everyone was ready for a compromise; and that according to his *pre*-meeting soundings, this compromise was closest to all views.

For the next sixty minutes, various members agreed that D's plan was a viable compromise; that they were tired of four years of on and off discussions; that financial constraints made an innovative new feature impossible; and that they would therefore reluctantly go along with D's suggestion as a second-best solution.

After nearly half of the key people had agreed, a news executive said that he saw D's plan "as a brilliant means of evading the issue." He added that D's concept had little vision and less distinction. Then H, an executive on the business side, chided the news executive for being too concerned about financial problems related to producing a first-rate new feature. He said he expected them to develop the best possible concept of the new feature and only afterwards worry about the financial issues.

P agreed that this proposal was a compromise and that he did not want to accept a proposal that most of the creative people were not at all enthusiastic about. One news executive asked what had happened to the news and editorial executives.

Session VI. I opened the meeting by asking if people would like to discuss how they felt about the previous night's session.

Q: It was destructive. I felt that my department was attacked unfairly, and I would like an opportunity to respond.
B: I'm sorry that Q saw it as an attack on him. I didn't. I thought that it was a good meeting.
R: I think a lot of useful things were said. I learned that we on the creative side have to keep our eye on the ball. I might add that nothing was said that has not been said privately.
C: I think because of four years of frustration, we lost sight of our objective and watered it down. We went for an undistinguished compromise.
D: I felt that the compromise was a good one. If the red herring hadn't been raised, I think this group would have come to an agreement.
H: I think that it began as a good meeting, but soon de-

generated. As all of you know, I was concerned about the creative people accepting the lowest common denominator in the interests of economics.

E: It was about as good a session as you will ever get. I still think that the dangers and destructiveness implicit in this whole process are not sufficiently recognized. When you ask people to bare their breasts and talk openly with each other, the normal human hypocritical intercourse is let go and then it is very, very dangerous.

R: Let me say that it was Q's remark that a lot of people were angry at our paper because the part I'm responsible for is run in an unbalanced and distorted way that led me to make my comment.

P: How will we ever talk about an innovation without getting these issues out in the open?

E: Well, I felt that very wounding things were said last night.

F: I agree with E.

R: I was favorably impressed with the [compromise] decision. I'm not sure it's a good idea to shoot for the moon if the money isn't there.

I: I think we can solve the economic issues.

P: [to X] I hear that you listened to the tape. Did you hear R's comments to Q? Were they destructive?

X: I did listen to the tapes and have them marked. No, I felt R's comments were not destructive; they were less aggressive than Q's to R.

Q: Well, it was a criticism of the way my department was run. The criticism was not about me as an individual. I'm not important. I'm not objecting to the criticism; I just want to reply. I felt it was personal in the sense that it was an attack against the management of my part of the paper. I don't think it should have been said.

P: Was it any more personal than your comment to R that there is too little balance in his department?

R: Or, as you said, distorting the news.

Q. I felt he got personal. I do not mean in the sense of whether we like ourselves. It was a direct attack on the way my department was run.

This dialogue illustrates a crucial problem that will be discussed several times during this and other seminars. The professional writers and editors had a deep personal involvement in their work, yet they maintained that they were rational people who do not let personalities affect them. Thus Q kept insisting that the attack was not against him but against the way his department was managed. He did not feel personally attacked, yet he wanted time to respond to the attack. Q's denial of personal involvement, his insistence that he could separate his personal feelings from his work, despite his statement that his whole life was wrapped up in his work—all these were *emotional* responses, not strictly rational ones.

P asked Q if he would have preferred to have R's comments made to P and then transmitted by P to Q. Q responded, "It would have been better if they had not been made in public." X commented that R's statement implied that he did not see this group as one in which some of his most important issues could be discussed. Q agreed. I asked if others felt that way, and said that if they did he doubted whether there could be adequate energy and commitment to make the group an effective one.

P commented that he was somewhat bewildered. If this process did not work, the only other alternative that he could see was dealing with people on a one-to-one basis and making his own decisions. However, he reminded the group that this was precisely the behavior that they did not like. He also admitted that he did not prefer this method.

Y then went on to describe what he had seen the night before as "compromise-group process." It was not problem-solving, in which everyone started with the assumption that there was a better solution to be developed. In problem-solving, all relevant factors must be examined. There were several norms in force which inhibited problem-solving. First, "If you say something, be careful that it does not reflect on someone else's competence." When group members wanted to make a suggestion they first asked themselves, who will it reflect upon? Second, there were taboo areas, and a group cannot solve problems if it is constrained by taboos.

P agreed with this analysis. C added that the same process was going on in the country as a whole. P then reminded the group that they had never discussed the basic philosophy of the new feature page; they went directly to mechanics.

I made several points about this observation. First, the

group never questioned D when he began by taking the discussion directly to mechanics; this was another example of a decision being made by default. Second, D pushed hard for the compromise solution largely to satisfy P. Apparently, P had told him that if they could arrive at a decision on the new feature, the entire seminar would be worth the effort. D therefore had tried to design a compromise solution that would appeal to the majority of the members.

As the analysis of the previous night's discussion continued, Q seemed to alter his position. He now wanted some time to respond, but he also said: "If I can get the floor, as far as I'm concerned, the taboo is off. It is quite true that I did not consider the new feature an appropriate matter for this meeting. I'm quite willing to withdraw that, now, given what has gone on during the last two hours. I will simply say that I am no longer an obstacle to this process. Insofar as I am a taboo area, I'm not anymore."

R: I realize that you mean what you say, but we must not forget that taboo areas are created by the group. We also have a responsibility here.

Q: I'm still not sure that it is wise to dissect P. But if he is willing, I will withdraw my internal reservation.

R: You seem to see this approach as a dissection. A dissection involes a knife.

Q: Those are your words.

R: No, you just used them.

Nearly four hours later, Q replied to my original question. Indeed, he had thought the process was destructive, but as a result of the discussion he was convinced that all this was worth a serious try. This represented the first overt change of commitment, and it came from a very important executive. It helped others feel less anxious about talking about interpersonal issues. Q turned to me and said, "I think you've said that we won't find out unless we try it. How do we get ourselves to try it?"

I responded that members of the group were moving in the direction of experimenting, and that I hoped more of them would be willing to experiment further. When making this statement, I had R and Q in mind. Both showed a willingness to inquire, to test, and to be open to confrontation. It will be useful at this point to chart some of Q's development during the seminar, because he showed movement toward becoming more aware of his feelings and accepting ownership of them. Here are some excerpts from the tape recording that illustrate Q's changing views: "Well, I feel it was very destructive. I didn't like the sessions and I have various reasons for saying this. I feel that it put the thing in the wrong perspective. I feel that maybe some good can come out of it, and I hope that's true. I said last night that I thought we ought to have some files on the subject, which I've since obtained. I think the fact that we didn't have the actual material in the background put a false glitter on the issue of the new feature, particularly for the people in this group who have not been involved in it before. I feel there ought to be some corrections made. This may be part of group therapy; I'm not sure that I think it's such a great idea. We've done it, we're in it, and I'm simply giving you my reactions to it. I do think some progress was made on the new feature page, but I think more could have been made in a group of three or four people."

I then asked other members of the group to state how they felt about the meeting in question. At least half of the members did not believe that the session was destructive. Moreover, three felt that Q's behavior toward R was more destructive than the reverse. This information apparently surprised Q. He wondered why he experienced the situation differently from half of the group, among whom were some men that he especially respected. I commented that I tend to experience reality as more hostile than others do whenever I feel personally attacked. Q again denied that he felt personally attacked. "I don't mean personal perhaps in the sense that you mean it. I mean a basic criticism of the way my department is run. I don't mean me as an individual. I'm not objecting to criticism. I'm saying that I feel that since such criticism was leveled, it is only fair that I reply to it in front of the same group. It is personal in the sense that I am responsible for that feature. I felt it was personal in that sense; I don't mean personal against me as an individual." Later, he added: "It's a little hard to pinpoint. I felt that, yes, we did get into, broadly speaking, the personal in the broad sense. I'm using personal in a little different way perhaps from the way you were using it earlier. It is personal in the sense that I do feel it was a direct attack on the management, and I happen to be the management of that particular aspect of the paper. So I think it was a personal attack on the management of the page, the way the feature is run."

Still later, there was this exchange:

R: When you want to discuss what you call distortion in my department and the general philosophy of the paper, which will include news judgment, you do not consider it destructive, yet when I discuss your responsebilities you consider it destructive.

Q: You won't agree with me. This point was brought in by me as an incidental thing. I felt that you were making it a major issue. I had not made a major issue of what I really feel, which is that the policy you feel is a dangerous policy. I had not made a major issue of that; it's true that I alluded to it particularly. I hadn't made any thing of it particularly.

R: But you intended to make it today.

Q: In a totally different context, that's right.

The discussion continued with most of the speakers expressing disagreement with Q's views.

Q: I don't have any desire to pursue this point because we're here and we're making progress.

Y went on to present an analysis of the previous evening's discussion. He said that three things impressed him: the number of taboo areas that existed within the group; the tacit agreement among members that "if I don't talk about you, you won't talk about me"; and the willingness of members to make decisions they believe are second best.

F asked Q if discussions about his department were taboo.

Q: "There's a real failure of communication here, maybe my fault, but in any case, a failure of communication that I don't want to let go any longer. In the first place, I don't think there is anything sacrosanct. I don't feel that my department is beyond criticism. I felt that a couple of points R made last night (regarding Q's department's work) required an answer. I don't say they should have not been made. My point is that they ought to be answered, and not that they should not have been made." Still later: "I don't believe that these policies can be made by committee. Now again, this is not personal; this is institutional. Any more than I, I don't feel that I have much of a gripe that I'm not on the executive committee. And I don't see why the hell I should be. I don't know enough about the financial operations of the *Planet* to contribute to them. Although sometimes I think there are things that are wrong that I'd like to criticize about our financial operations."

One of the interventionists said that he was still not certain that Q did not consider a discussion of his department taboo. Q said, "Will it help at all, if I say what I thought I started out this morning to say, and maybe didn't, that I did feel the thing wasn't right primarily, and this is the point you won't fully accept, but anyway, primarily because I don't feel that I adequately or properly answered the situation. If I can get the floor later (to answer B) as far as I am concerned, the taboo is off. I don't consider it a taboo. It is quite true that I did not think it appropriate matter in the context of this morning. I'm quite willing to withdraw that and say that I don't think that now, given everything that's gone before, in the last two hours, in the last two days, that I will just simply say that insofar as I am an obstacle in this, I'll say no, I'm not an obstacle." Later: "[Looking back on last night] I was dissatisfied with my just saying no last night. I wanted this morning to give a rationale of my department, as I see it, because I did not want to leave the gentlemen in this room —and maybe this is face-saving, hell, I don't know—but it's my own view of the feature."

One of the interventionists then asked the group members if they would state how they reacted to R's views about Q's area. Nine did not agree and four did agree with R. Thus, Q learned that he had much support within the group, and that his fears about a "false glitter" were not valid for the majority of group members.

Session VII. Session seven was a short one. Most of the time was spent in conceptualizing the progress that some members felt had begun to occur. Also some persons who had been very wary of the process began to say things that indicated they were publicly admitting the importance of feedback, interpersonal relations, and group process. Some typical examples were: "Too often we have not taken responsibility in making decisions. We have felt our task was to scream [and let P make the decision]." "We have a missing link to helping each other. We don't have enough criticism of each other's work." "We have a reluctance to speak and be critical of each other's work." "We're afraid that the other fellow will give us feedback."

Session VIII. I opened the meeting by reminding the group that it had made a commitment to discuss leadership styles, especially P's. P then asked, "Where do we want to begin?" There was a long silence. C broke the silence by starting a discussion of D's leadership style during the discussion of the new feature. Instead of letting this continue, I asked the group to look at the process by which it had focused on D. C admitted that he had started talking about D because he wanted to break the silence.

P then said he would like to start by discussing some of his problems with several of the members of the group. He began with F. He felt that F's way of advising him was not helpful: "F brings me problems but rarely suggests solutions. If I knew the answers to the questions you raise, F, then I would have them solved."

F responded that he had always been taught not to make decisions that were the province of others; as a chief staff officer, he had conceived of this job as raising issues. He now realized that P wanted him to take more initiative in the decision-making process.

The discussion then left leadership styles and focused on some knotty issues about budgets and budget people. This time, a member of the group intervened to say that the discussion had strayed from P. P agreed, and then added that he was tired of much of the minutiae that H, F, and several others were sending him. R asked if people did not send this minutiae because they felt P liked it. Q said that this was his view. The discussion returned to F's relationship with P.

E then asked if F had really gotten everything off his chest. F replied that he did not understand. I intervened to say, "Perhaps your way of dealing with P is not attractive to him, so he goes around your end and deals with your subordinates." P agreed with this, and said that he wished F would bring him information upon which to make decisions. F responded, "I try to."

Several people then returned to an earlier theme, the destructiveness of P's pattern of going directly to their subordinates without telling them. Again, this led someone to remind the group how many activities had been changed for the better during the last five years, primarily through P's initiative. Several others then began saying the same thing, just as the discussion had come to focus on P.

This time I decided to confront the issue. "Why do some members feel the need to remind people in this room of P's accomplishments?" I asked. "Is there an implication that some of you see P as having weaknesses, which requires that he be supported the moment some of his negative impact is being discussed?" No one answered, and instead the discussion moved on to long-range planning issues. I waited for another opportunity to raise the question again. About half an hour later, an opportunity arose. I asked the question again, and again it was not answered or discussed.

I was feeling frustrated and disappointed. The group had run away from this issue several times, and I began to despair of the members ever saying to P what they had said to him during the pre-seminar interviews. Finally I said to P, "I'm beginning to wonder if this is the group that will give you the feedback you need to become more effective. They seem to hesitate the moment they come to areas that may be your weaknesses."

H: [Somewhat irritated] What do you want us to do?
P: I'm not clear.
X: I'm saying that you may feel unsure of yourself about certain decisions:

P: Right.

X: If I hear this group correctly, you may deal with uncertainty by acting precipitously or by delaying decisions.

P: That's legitimate.

R: Well, I'm puzzled about this evening. F started to discuss his relationships with P and others. But the discussion hasn't hit a response. Something's wrong. We're not really digging in.

H: Well, P, as I said before, you have a tendency to do too much one-to-one. . . .

P: I know, but some of you want this.

C: We have criticized P for his style of using one-to-one relations. The real issue is not his style but what decision-making structures to suggest. My question to you is how do we create the structure to serve P?

X: I'm not ready to agree that a structure should be designed around P's defenses.

E: Based upon my knowledge of this group, we have so far, quite deliberately, withheld information.

P: If the theory is that you can learn from your associates, well, I haven't learned very much.

Q: I, too, don't think this has been very productive. My criticism of your style is that you have made decisions too quickly.

P: That's a valid criticism.

Q: Believe me, I'm open to being criticized. But I must say that I find it difficult to invite people to talk about me. It seems to me that this would interest me and no one else. I feel it would be boring and egocentric. Why would ten colleagues want to center on me?

X: They would if they were concerned about your effectiveness, as well as the impact of your behavior on them.

Later: X said [to P]: "Perhaps at the interpersonal level, you are surrounded by a group of 'yes' men.* " This irritated several members, who questioned the accuracy of the observation. C said, "When we finish with this exercise, you go back to your school.

---

* The group could also be conceived of as "yes" men to me, for they had promised me to attend the seminar and experiment with the process. Perhaps I was partially projecting.

These men have to live with each other. Your idea is to force us to tell the truth directly to P. This will somehow be clarifying, and you think that it would be purifying. I think it could be destructive. That explains the silence in this room."

I had two reactions. One was a feeling that I deserved the hostility because my intervention could be experienced as punishing by members of the group. The other was the thought that C's comments illustrated my thesis—that the individuals were silent because they feared what might happen to their relationships if they were to become more open.

I responded that I could not see the destructiveness that C was identifying. P had said he had not heard anything new, and the group was very much in control of what was being said. "I will protect the group's right not to go further, but I also believe that I have a responsibility to identify the consequences. Also, I feel you are correct that I am anxious . . ." [cut off by F]

F said he felt he was being treated unfairly; he had leveled completely with P and yet the group did not find it involving nor did P find it helpful. P responded that he still did not know what F wanted of him.

I decided to make one more intervention. I looked at P and F and said, "My bind is that both of you have told me things about the other that you are not saying."

R: [questioning the propriety of this remark] You have violated F's confidences. After all, he told it to you in a personal meeting. F is a reticent man who has tried his best. You've become very impatient with us. The conversation was not going at your pace, and you reacted.

E: That is not true in all respects. We all know what he expects of us. We agreed to come here. He comes to the meeting and finds almost complete reluctance.

X: I think R is correct that I have felt impatient. I wanted the group to go further and probably faster. I have been on the fence about making an intervention that may have violated the pre-seminar interviews with F. . . .

F: I don't think so.

X: Nevertheless, you are correct, I am feeling impatient. It's
    not that I think the evening is lost; it's that I wished
    we could go further. However, I value your confronta-
    tion of me, and I want others to let me know if I have
    gone too far or too fast.

R's and E's comments seemed appropriate to me. E
focused on the fact that many of the members had agreed to
come to talk about issues that they were not mentioning. In this
sense, they were not meeting their commitment and thus not
giving the experiment a fair chance to succeed.

However, the commitment was more external than internal. Many of the members (but not R, nor more recently, Q)
were ready to let me, the interventionist, be responsible for
progress in these difficult areas. I, in turn, was willing to take
some of this responsibility. My theory was that if people took
some risks they would find them worthwhile and therefore become
less dependent on me for further progress. Q was an example of
a person whose internal commitment had increased after he was
able to explore his feelings about R's comments and vice-versa.

Again P took the lead. He said, "We did come down here
to try something. My friend F seems to be willing to try. It is
true, I have said things to X that I would not have said to F.
Tomorrow let's both take our hair down and try."

Session IX. The meeting began with several members
asking for time at the beginning of the session to say that last
night they had not said everything because they did not realize
this was necessary. Several maintained that they were not familiar
with the rules (even though a lecture had been given on the value
of all participating in giving and receiving feedback). This was
another attempt to hold the interventionists at least partially
responsible for their behavior.

C said that he had now made a conscious decision to
experiment. R, one of the members who had been most open,
noted that his commitment varied with the subject. C responded
that he could now see why the process was taking so much time.
E said, "Last night before I went to bed, I wrote this down. This
process pushes at the heart of the P–F relationship and it touches

on the relationship of P and the vice-presidents. If people are honest, this could be very bad, and if they are not, it could be meaningless."

That statement eloquently expressed the bind that an increasing number of participants were feeling. It also verbalized an increasing awareness in the group that the interventionists had worked hard to help the seminar, that it was now up to the group, and that the interventionists would permit the seminar to fail if the group members were not going to take responsibility for its success.

The group returned to F and P, and the discussion seemed to reach a deeper level of analysis. X helped F to understand that P could be threatened if all he had were vice-presidents who brought problems to him. Perhaps that is one reason he liked people who provided possible solutions.

F said he found this helpful because all his life he had assumed that he was doing his job well if he only explained the consequences of various possible decisions. He never thought of the possibility that this could be threatening, "although 'threatening' may be too strong a word." "No," said C, "It's not too strong a word. P is under many pressures and, if he's not careful, they could become overwhelming."

The talk about being threatened led Q to comment on a concern that threatened him, namely power struggles. "I have a deep hesitation to talk about them. I feel I have never looked for power but I'm afraid that at times I'm interpreted as talking about seizing power. I would like to discuss this, but now let's get back to F."

X: If I were a subordinate of yours, I would have difficulty in being aggressive toward you or saying something that would easily hurt you.
C: I have felt the same way until the meeting. F has shown more guts than I expected him to show.

Several commented "yes, yes."

P: I too felt that we have been more open. But I'm still not sure how I can handle the situation when we return.

X: Perhaps the next time you feel frustrated with F's way of
    dealing with problems, you could discuss it. Perhaps
    you could even tell him when you are reaching the
    point of wanting to go around him.
P: I wouldn't know how to say it.
C: Perhaps you already have.
P: That's a good point.

The group turned to E, who said he had some feedback
that he wanted to give B. As E began, it was clear from the tone
of his voice and from the extensive notes that he had in his hand
that he was going to tell B something which might be negative.
He then proceeded to give fifteen minutes of uninterrupted feedback. Some of the main points that E made were that he and
others saw B as: (1) working hard, and at times somewhat ruth-
lessly, to become the next President or the next Executive Vice-
President; (2) pressuring the organization to become "tough,
ballsy"; (3) deliberately pushing people as far as they could be
in the direction that he wanted them to go; and (4) claiming to be
in favor of participation, yet exercising his leadership through
highly controlling and manipulative behavior. For example:
"You're seeking allies all the time. This sets a pattern—for a takeover." "The appeals for sharing, I think, are phony. If you wanted
to share, you would have asked before you took action." It's easy
to say you feel lonely—but if you wanted to share, you would do
it." E ended by saying, "This is my very open contribution—
though it's slightly foreign to me because I see hypocrisy as an
essential element of decent human behavior." * [silence] A:
"Take my name off the list for receiving feedback." [laughter]
P confirmed several of the points made by E about B but
not others.

C: One thing you can't ignore is the strength of E's feelings.
    Obviously something has happened. Let's not duck the
    question. B has aroused strong personal feelings in E.
H: I'm ready to go ahead and say something further if that's
    in the rules of the game.

* This is *not* an open contribution because it could close off responses from the recipient and others. Openness is a quality of relationship, not something within people (Argyris 1971).

B: I want to hear more, especially about how I can become
   more effective. I want to make my needs more congruent with the success of the organization. I don't
   think it's fair to leave me put down as an ambitious
   fellow.

Here the group stopped for lunch.

Session X. After lunch, B opened the session by com-
menting further on the feedback: "It was very useful. I learned a
lot. Perhaps I can put something into practice. I thought that
attributing motives to me, however, was a bit unfair. What should
I do?" The group was not ready to discuss this issue yet because
several others had feedback for B. H, for example, said that B
never respected E's job. And A said, "You have spoken to me
negatively about a large number of people that you know I like
and am fond of. I'm worried that if you say it to me, you would
say it to others. You've been very mean, if I may say so." B soon
said, "You're making me feel I should shut up," but listened as
more examples of his behavior were given to him.

B: Funny, I don't feel set apart, as this session might indicate.
   I feel very much among you. I don't feel thrown out—
   not yet. I've had things said to me here that I had not
   heard before. My question is what the hell I'm going to
   do when I get back. I still don't have any clear idea
   of how I'm going to behave.
P: I hope you are clear that I feel there are many positive
   things about you. I made the assumption that in these
   sessions we would focus on the negative.
B: But I don't feel rejected by the group. I asked for it.
X: I've been trying to say something for a long time. I
   would like to explore the way we have given feedback
   to B. How effective was it? Are there other ways to give
   feedback?
H: Yes, that would be helpful.
X: I would like to begin the next session with a discussion
   of giving and receiving feedback. One of my goals is
   to return to B's question of what can he do when he
   returns.

Session XI. The session began with a short lecture on giving and receiving feedback. The ineffectiveness of giving evaluative and attributive feedback was stressed. Examples were taken from the session on B to illustrate the points.

As I translated some of the feedback given to B into less attributive and less evaluative terms, P looked bewildered. He said the feedback now sounded very stylized and stiff, and added: "If I stop being me and talk this stylized English, B is going to know that this isn't me. I can't imagine such a discussion."

I responded by agreeing that this language would seem strange, and that if it were accepted mechanically it would never be helpful. The language should not be used unless it mirrors what the speaker really feels. Thus one important step is for people to learn to recognize moods in which they want to make evaluations and attributions, and to ask themselves why they feel that way.

Y added that the difference is more than just changing words. The idea is to change from telling someone something about himself to telling him something about you.

Q: That's egocentric.
X: It depends. Egocentric behavior is when A decides how B should feel. If I can tell B how *I* feel in such a way that he can express himself, then that is helpful.
H: That makes a lot of sense to me, but it's going to be difficult.

The group explored several other examples. At one point I said that from certain behavior data which I had identified, I inferred that D tends to be highly controlling in his leadership style.

C: This is fascinating. You have deduced from that data that D is a steamroller. Well, you are wrong.
I: Have you ever seen him lead a meeting? How can you make that statement?
X: Well, you have the data, plus my inference. It seems to me you have a clearcut basis upon which to reject my view.
E: Yes, he did give us his data and his attributions. This gives us a chance to reject it.

R: The question is whether the technique is valid and not whether X has a perfect box score.

The session closed with a discussion of the effectiveness of the seminar. All members reported that they felt more progress had been made than expected. Several members were much more positive, saying that it was one of the most meaningful experiences that they had had with the group.

The discussion then turned to the possibility of remaining for another extra day. (The group had already remained a day and a half beyond the initial two and a half days.) C said that this was impossible for him because he had a meeting that he could not cancel. Another executive said that he too had to leave. Several said that they had made no commitments but felt exhausted. The group members eventually decided to stop the seminar with this session. Some wanted to set a date for a follow-up session. I suggested that they think about that idea for several days.

6

Evaluations of the Learning Seminar

I left the seminar with the belief that it had helped unfreeze the group members from their fears of being more open with each other. The amount of unfreezing and learning varied with individuals. R and Q probably learned the most, and P perhaps came next, with C close behind. The first three could become the focus of new learning experiences, with C supporting them ambivalently. The seminar also provided one of the first experiences for the group members in examining the dynamics of their decision-making processes and relating their behavior to the effectiveness of the living system.

However, about half of the members left with little new insight into themselves because they did not become involved in the activities. This lack of involvement was primarily their own responsibility. They chose to participate minimally, and not to rock the boat, because of their beliefs and fears about the group (especially about themselves and the President). Some of these participants left the session feeling disappointed in themselves.

Others left blaming the group process and believing that the experience was at best worthwhile but could have been shorter and administered more efficiently by the interventionists.

One of the lessons learned about unfreezing values and behavior is that the process works best when individuals are presented with discrepancies between their own rhetoric and behavior, between what they say and what they do. This means that the learning process does not begin until the individuals expose their beliefs and their actual behavior. The amount of time the process takes varies with the members' willingness to discuss their values, expose their behavior, and experiment. The group, as a whole, was on the low side on all these criteria. This is not surprising, given the fears that they expressed and the brittleness of their relationships.

Another lesson learned is that people are rarely interested in unfreezing themselves until they have confirmed for themselves, that they are not behaving as competently as they desire. The process of confirming must be uncontaminated by the influence of others, so that the individual cannot find a way of assigning the responsibility for his incompetent behavior to anyone else. People will not accept responsibility for their incompetent behavior unless they can see that they are clearly responsible. Moreover, we all tend to give verbal and nonverbal cues to others that indicate that we are uninterested or uncomfortable about becoming fully responsible for our ineffectiveness (Argyris 1968, Argyris and Schon 1974). The espoused theories of adults may be full of rhetoric about self-responsibility, but their theories-in-use are often empty of such behavior.

Perhaps this is one explanation for the fears these men expressed about attending the seminar. Perhaps becoming aware of the incompetent aspects of their own behavior would be too much for them to accept. Perhaps they believed that others would not accept them if they knew of their limitations. Underlying this hypothesis is the fear of rejection. If I cannot be the person that I think I should be, then I cannot accept myself and others will not accept me.

The irony is that the others *are* aware of many of the faults and limitations that we may try to hide. They hide the

fact that they accept us along with these faults, because they sense
that we do not accept them (and indeed may not be aware of
them), and because they believe that to express recognition of
them would be an act of threat and rejection. This sustains relationships in which individuals believe they can minimize the
chances of interpersonal rejection by hiding their incompetences
—or by providing legitimate organizational causes for them if and
when they become public and undeniable. Others may sense this
strategy, and play the game, in order not to threaten or upset
the individuals. This collusion may act to create assurances that
in another context others will not violate the rules of the game
they may have to play with us.

 All this results in hidden agreements. Each individual
may come to believe that he is effective because he has successfully hidden his faults or because others have learned to tolerate
them. The eroding aspect of these agreements for the individual
is that he learns that he is accepted as incompetent in certain
ways and that his relationships are designed to help him remain
so. The eroding aspect for the organization is that such agreements reduce the effectiveness of activities that require discussion of information that may be threatening to individuals.
Thus part of the reason that the new feature had been under
discussion for four years, as we shall see, was because it raised
issues of organizational power and control, issues that all participants refused to acknowledge in front of each other (but discussed in private meetings with the President).

 The fourth lesson learned is that individuals will not try
to generate a new competence until they are relatively certain
that they can learn it. But they will not discover whether they
can learn it unless they feel free to expeirment with it. They
will not feel free to do this unless they are acting within a culture,
or a setting, in which experimentation is sanctioned and the fear
of rejection by others is greatly reduced. But the fear will not
tend to be reduced unless the others also want to learn about
themselves. This is true because in order for A to feel that he is
not rejected when he owns up to and accepts his own incompetent
behavior, others must own up to the fact that they have also
been accepting this behavior, perhaps for years. A, upon learning

this, will probably ask why, and B will find that self-exploration becomes necessary.

A three-day seminar, even with the most open and unconflicted group members, cannot set in motion all the processes just described. Yet all of these processes must be started if new skills are to be learned. Since even the first process—exposing individual beliefs and behaviors—was not adequately achieved, little learning was possible that would lead to new skills. The most we were able to do was to provide a short lecture on giving and receiving feedback. Since about half of the members had not yet unfrozen, we felt that our lecture was effectively understood by less than half of the group members. Of those who understood the lecture, many found that the implications of practicing the new skills ranged from embarrassing to unbelievable.

Thus we would expect to find, upon returning to the offices of *The Daily Planet,* little or no behavioral change among the group members. However, we predicted that some (such as R, Q, P, and C ambivalently) would seek new learning opportunities. Others would wait for the next session to see if they could generate the strength, or courage, as one participant described it, to create conditions to learn. Others would try to reduce their fear of failing, and still others might stiffen their position that learning is dangerous or needless by refusing to cooperate in future meetings. Only one senior executive, however, insisted that he never wanted to participate in another such session. He was never asked nor coerced to attend such sessions, nor did he, to my knowledge, directly or indirectly coerce the officers reporting to him to agree with him.

The evaluation by the participants. About two weeks after the seminar, I interviewed all of the participants. They confirmed our expectation that little behavioral change had occurred. However, as one executive put it, "The group will never be the same. You can't erase such an experience from your mind." For some, the experience would produce varying degrees of internal guilt and anxiety, since they had come to realize that they were not as effective as they wanted to be and as the organization needed them to be.

However, others were trying to put what they had learned into action. Several made efforts to become more open during certain substantive meetings, but said they were uncomfortable about taking the risk; they reported, however, that they were equally uncomfortable, for the first time, about *not* taking a risk. Some began by defusing the potential risk of experimenting by experimenting only with fellow seminar participants and by prefixing their comments with, "In the spirit of Roundtree" (the place at which the conference was held).

R felt very positive about the potential of the seminar and asked if a program like this might be started within his own group. He also asked for advice about the most effective ways to convene a meeting. He wanted to increase the probabilities that the individuals would attend, but he also realized that they had to be able to reject the idea. "What if they say no?" he asked. "Then," I said, "we'll have to respect their views." "But," R retorted, "I don't want this to die. It's too important. On the other hand, I understand and believe what you just said." As we shall see, R came very close to violating his beliefs out of his genuine desire to increase the effectiveness of his group and the quality of life within it.

E felt that no behavioral changes had occurred. Yet he, too, talked about the number of times the members had called upon "the spirit of Roundtree" to say something that they would not have normally said. E also said that he hoped the idea would continue but doubted its long-range viability because "We need hypocrisy to survive and that is why we won't change."

C reported that he had been intellectually against the seminar but now realized its importance. "The more we talked the more I began to have a feeling that there really was something here. We began to break through into honesty, not all the way but part of the way."

P also reported no significant behavioral changes. However, he felt that others were freer in their confrontations and showed some signs (in his opinion all too few) of taking initiative.

The others' views ranged within these evaluations. Thus the entire group reported positive feelings, although, as we shall see, one person had lied. He was the one who asked the President to exclude him from all future learning experiences. It is interesting to note that this man conceived of himself as tough, straightforward, and willing to let the chips fall where they might. Yet he was unable to give me his honest evaluations. One of the advantages of long-term research-action activities is that such discrepancies eventually become clear.

About a month after the first learning session, a meeting was called to assess people's views and, if desired, to plan the next step. The group discussion confirmed the comments made above and provided further in-depth views of the members' reactions.

P: I guess we're gathered here, now that we've had a chance to gather our wits, to discuss where we've been and where we want to go from here.

X: It would be helpful to me if you would bring me up to date a little. If anyone has any further thoughts that would help bring me up to date as to where you are on your own feelings about the seminar, then we can go from there.

G: I can say a little bit. I think that at the end of everybody's little talk about how they felt about it, I tried to sum up the consensus of the meeting. There was a divided opinion in the group but the consensus, the weight of the expression, was to go ahead with a further step.

R: There was not equal enthusiasm, as I understood that meeting; the weight of the expression was to go ahead. Another direct result is that we agreed to go ahead and have a discussion about the new feature, and from there, either tonight or some other night, to a discussion about the general thrust of the organization.

X: There are two questions that I'd like to ask. One is, some of you in the last evaluation felt that some of the experiences may not have been helpful. They may have been destructive to others. Question one is, looking back on this one month, does anyone see signs of destructiveness or harm, or does anyone see any signs in the other way?

G: I see no signs of any harm.

A: Well, B has disappeared. [Laughter. B was the recipient of E's attack during the seminar. He was now on vacation.]

I: I haven't seen enough of B to be able to answer that question for you. I think there's a bitter residue there, it's underneath. I get it in remarks and comments he makes.

H: I'd agree with that, he hasn't forgotten it. But I don't particularly try to psychoanalyze B. I haven't particularly seen any real change.

R: I haven't change in any way at all, I suppose, but I'm conscious of things we're talking about, and sometimes I try, usually futilely, to practice them. So one day we were all sitting around the table and somebody said, "Well, I think such and such." I forget what it was about, and I said, "I don't agree." Then I said, "Well, let me put it this way. It's interesting that you said, but analyzing all the factors and so on, I think it's a lot of shit." * [laughter] Half of the room collapsed, and the other half looked completely bewildered. [laughter]

H: I know one thing, X, when I went through, I read two articles you were kind enough to send. I thought it very useful to read them, and I would suggest that other people read them. It gives you a much greater idea. I read the articles and they were very fine, and I think it makes sense to read them, now that we've gotten our feet wet and this sort of thing.

C: I agree.

R: Yes, I read a couple, I think, I'm not sure what I would have gotten out of them before I had gone to this discussion.

P: Frankly, I think the first test we're going to put to any of this, in a meaningful way, will come this evening, when these learned gentlemen on my left and I are going to gather together to resolve the new feature question.

---

* As pointed out previously, this is not an example of competent behavior. It may be honest, but not competently so because it does not encourage the other to express himself.

D: Aren't you going to be there?

P: Yes I am, but I haven't figured out in what role yet! [laughter]

X: I made some observations about our session that I should like to mention. I saw the group to be a difficult group for at least three reasons. First, there was a substantial number of people who were uncomfortable about the need to talk about interpersonal issues in order to be more effective on substantive issues. Second, I felt that there were many questions in people's minds as to the necessity for a cohesive executive group. This, by the way, was a new experience for me. I've never been in an executive group that didn't feel some sense of commitment to develop themselves into an effective group. There was a high proportion of people who felt that the process could be dangerous. Third, there was a high proportion of participants who felt that the best way to serve P was to be as open as they could and let him make the decisions. This sub-group would tend to back away—as a group, not as individuals—from decisions that require interdependence. This was the first time I have met a President who was as ambivalent as I see you to be. For example, you want an effective executive group and yet you prefer to work with small sub-groups; you want people to be open with you, and yet you don't want to get rid of historical legacies; you were open about your feelings toward others, yet, as I listened to the tape, I don't think you were as open about your own feelings toward yourself.

As I look at the seminars, I believe that one sub-group came in with, or soon developed, the idea, "OK, we're going to experiment with this and see if it works and we're going to try to make it work. We expect X to help us, but we're not going to be dependent on him." I experienced that to be the smallest sub-group. Another sub-group came in with the view, "We will come but it's up to X to get this thing going and to keep it on track." Their participation was genuine, but it wasn't very frequent. Also, they tended not to be particularly open about themselves. So I felt

there was a kind of responsibility placed on me by the
largest number of the members to get the seminar into
orbit.

The executives agreed with my description. I added that
as a result, I felt myself in a double bind. On the one hand, I knew
that the experiences I considered growth-producing, they considered threatening. On the other hand, if I did not press for
genuine experimentation with these activities, they might never be
experienced. Someone, I believe R, remarked that some members
probably felt the same bind. I agreed.

The discussion turned to a re-exploration of some of the
more vivid episodes during the learning seminar. Apparently
they were still providing food for discussion and thought. For
example, several group members recalled the interchange between R and Q. Q felt that R had attacked him, but after listening
to the tape, Q realized that actually he had attacked R. They also
recalled that individuals such as Q tended to insist that they did
not perceive attacks, such as the one R was accused of, as being
personal. However, the onlookers saw it as personal, and that was
how they interpreted Q's view when he said that the dialogue was
destructive. Why did Q deny that he experienced R's attack as
personal?

G: I think it was part of the game, to say that, but he really
felt it was personal.
X: I'm suggesting that Q makes it difficult for someone to be
critical about his new feature without seeming to make
it a personal attack by the way he responds to it.
Q: I think we're playing with words here.
B: No, I think X is correct. You came in swarming with 700
flies. [laughter]
G: I think we're all playing around with something. When R is
critical of Q's department and Q comes back the next
morning and starts in about R's department, of course
these are personal attacks. You'd have to be made of
stone and wood for them not to be personal attacks.
R: I think there's a definition of personal here.
G: You think I'm wrong?
R: No, I think you're right. But when I criticized Q's depart-

ment, I certainly didn't intend to say that Q was a bad man, or that Q was a harsh man.

The members began, for the first time, to explore openly the intimate connection between success on their jobs and feelings of personal self-esteem. This discussion was a sort of milestone, since up to this time people had denied that their personal selves were directly related to their work, or had admitted it only during the interviews with me. Q, as we shall see, still stuck to the notion that he could distinguish attacks on his page from attacks on him as a person. He suggested that it was easier for him to deal with personal attacks than with attacks on his area of competence.

R: I can see that Q is very involved in his work. It is his life, just as the news is part of mine. So when you're saying he is not running his page right, or I'm not my department right, nobody is saying that I'm a stinker, but it's personal in that I have to face up to what's wrong.

C: Q's department is much more personal than the rest of the stuff in the news and there is a much closer relationship.

G: As the editor, he is personally wrapped up in what he's doing, ask R, this is my life—love me, love my dog—it's this idea, it's part of you, so much that it can't help but be personal.

Q: As a matter of fact, one thing I was thinking about after this is, it's much easier for me to take a degree of personal criticism. A guy could fly off the handle or scowl or whatever. It would be easier for me to take personal criticism than to hear someone saying that the basic thrust of the paper under my direction is wrong. That's much harder to take.

X: Q, perhaps that's where our energy to keep working like hell may come from. It places an enormous responsibility on us to create that atmosphere in which people can then feed back to us the very kind of data we need, for example, how they feel about your department.

Q: If I understand correctly, what you're driving at is, given these facts, people like R and me have to learn to roll

with the punches, so to speak, have to learn to absorb
this without reacting too much.

X: I would say not just to absorb it but to invite it, because
unless you do it will take years to make important decisions, because everybody fears hurting someone else
and therefore they hold back.

Before the meeting ended, I read off a list of questions
that had occurred to me during the meeting.

(1) What was the nature of the feedback that was identified as helpful and that which was identified as destructive? How
did they differ?

(2) How can dependence on the interventionist be reduced while still using his skills and knowledge?

(3) What factors influence people to see the same reality
so differently?

(4) What are the sources of the dependence on the P?

(5) Are there some hidden fears about the long-run
effectiveness or capacity of the P?

(6) To what extent is the interventionist seen as a manip-
ulator or pressurer?

(7) How do we deal with conflict?

(8) How aware are we of the emotional and personal
involvement in our intellectual work?

(9) Do we invite feedback from others about emotional
aspects of our work, or those intellectual aspects that others
believe have important emotional roots?

(10) How can we create a climate that will be safe for
members who prefer not to participate? How do we create
processes that enhance or increase freedom of choice?

The meeting ended with all the members committing
themselves to an evening meeting to discuss the next steps, and
with the majority committing themselves to another seminar.

Some notes on the seminar. The seminar illustrated the
group members' reluctance to discuss openly their leadership
styles and the impact they may have, upon each other and upon
the organization. Yet during the interviews, the members had

given vivid examples of the negative consequences of each others' leadership behavior.

One possible reason for this reluctance could be that the individuals feared for their jobs. This fear did not seem relevant, however, because all of the executives had legal job security (contracts) or the security that came from being leaders in their profession. Moreover, the President repeatedly asked for candor in order to help make the organization more effective. In the few cases where this was attempted, he did not resist the feedback.

Another reason was suggested by a member during the seminar. If an executive discussed someone else's leadership style, then he would be open to having his own style discussed. Why should the prospect of learning about one's own leadership behavior be threatening? Part of the explanation may be that in a living system experienced as containing deceit, hypocrisy, and competitive win-lose warfare (both open and covert), individuals may have built up many feelings of anger, frustration, and rejection that they have consciously suppressed. Discussing behavior might eventually make it necessary to discuss pent-up feelings that have been suppressed or even denied. For example, as we have seen before and shall see again, Q has felt misunderstood, attacked, and rejected, but he has denied that he is involved personally. The discussions eventually led to Q's becoming aware that he was personally involved and that he could not separate the attacks on his department from himself as a person. To accept this possibility, however, could lead one to ask why has he maintained this separation between self and job. Moreover, there is the question about the impact upon his subordinates. If they felt that he was highly involved in his work but denied it, then they may have found it necessary to collude with him in this defensive stance. If they collude in accepting the separation between job and self, what impact does that have upon their view of the relationship between job and self?

Moreover, how do those who are editors deal with reporters' and writers' emotional responses to having their work edited? They may, for example, become blind to, or annoyed with, the writers' responses to their editing. This could lead the writers and reporters to feel misunderstood and rejected. However, since their behavior is controlled by the living system, these issues will not be raised directly. The response may be an organizational action—for example, defining the relationships between the editor and the writer more rigidly and formally.

No matter what the reason for the reluctance to examine leadership behavior, the result was to make it difficult, if not impossible, to resolve certain critical organizational issues. For example, most of the seminar members believed that the executive committee meetings were a waste of time. When the President asked why, the quality of the discussion was reduced because at the heart of the problem, in their eyes, was the President's behavior. Since they hesitated to discuss the issue, even after identifying it, the President hesitated to discuss his views that he was being misused and mistreated by the members. Similar problems existed with the news meetings, yet they were not resolved because to do so would require an examination of leadership behavior. One news meeting problem was resolved because the solution was to cancel it (which therefore required no one to examine behavior).

Moreover, the decision-making processes related to the new feature page were indicative of another problem that faced the group. The idea had been discussed for four years and no decision had been reached. As P said, every time they had a meeting on the issue, he felt that they would give him some ideas and then leave with many unanswered questions. The willingness— indeed the insistance—on the part of the top executives to force the President to make the decision could be related to their concept of the proper role of a subordinate, namely being dependent and submissive. Besides leading to ineffective executive group dynamics, this could also easily lead the subordinates of these executives to act in accordance with the dependency concept that they see their superiors using with the President.

We may begin to see how individuals may create a living system such as the one described in Chapter One, and also how they tend to act in ways to make it difficult to change the individual, group, or intergroup behavior as well as to alter organizational forms (executive committee, news meetings) or generate innovative products.

But the fact that some of these issues were faced indicates that there is a degree of intellectual integrity which leads the individuals not to deny the inconsistencies, and in some cases, to do something about them. For example, Q has written several articles on the importance of a society being free to discuss any issue that impinges on its quality of life. In these articles, he argued vehemently that society should never define "taboo areas." Yet he realized, especially after Y's comments (in session VI) that he was responsible for creating taboo subjects during the seminar. Or C, who believed that it was important not to embarrass others, found himself attacking D's conception of the new feature page by calling it a distinguished example of compromise and mediocrity. This example illustrates that when it came close to a decision, men were willing to disagree, did so in ways that could be punishing, and denied that this was their intent. It also suggests that a moment of "brutal honesty" had to be faced when no alternative seemed available and a decision had to be made.

This tactic bewildered and frustrated the President, because it led to many group discussions where little of consequence was said, and even more individual and private discussions where much of consequence might have been said, but wasn't. This, in turn, resulted in long delays before decisions could be made in ways that did not offend the participants.

The members did create several episodes where they behaved in ways that could embarrass others. Yet, even in the most dramatic one, where E seemed to explode with a series of attributions and evaluations of B's behavior, no harm occurred. Indeed, B reported that he felt closer to the group.

However, B also felt that he was not helped to see how he could solve the problems. I would agree with him. All that E and several others succeeded in doing was attacking, and they did so in ways that would not enhance problem-solving and increase the level of trust. The issue of trust was discussed in the context of giving and receiving feedback; but given the shortness of time, little was learned that might lead to changes in behavior.

The former issue—how to solve the problem between B and the group—was not discussed, partly because a complete discussion would require an exploration of others' desires to become executive vice-presidents, and their politicking for what one person called "executive goodies"; most of all, it would require a discussion of certain senior executives' jobs that many people felt were more honorific than real.

7

The New Feature

During the learning seminar, one session was spent on the new feature. The President asked to have it discussed because it was a decision that had been postponed for nearly four years. The manifest reason for the delay was disagreement as to the feature's purpose and format. The unspoken or latent reason was fear of opening up certain political issues, such as who would be in control, and who would gain and lose space in the paper.

The President had told me, before the seminar, that he had spent many hours in one-to-one meetings with the key news and editorial executives. As he listened to them, he came to feel that their differences over matters of substance were quite small. The differences that loomed large were the political reasons. He felt that their feelings on these issues were so strong that they could not be discussed openly. He also felt that he was already pressing hard enough on executives involved in other areas, such as budget cutting and reorganization, and he did not want to overburden them with another set of problems. Finally, he was not confident of his ability to discuss the issue openly with the four key persons because he feared that their political biases would tend to prevent them from hearing each other's views, compromising intelligently, and developing a solution. He did not add at this time, although it became clear later on, that he wanted to select his own candidate to direct the new feature, and was concerned about the degree to which the four would accept his choice.

Because of the first three reasons, the President had asked if the decision could be discussed during the learning seminar. The issue was therefore discussed early in the life of the seminar, but with little success. However, during a discussion of the dynamics of that session, the following new facts were revealed. Executive D, during the lunch break, had taken a walk with the President. The President found occasion to say how strongly he wished that a decision could be made on the new feature. Executive D, who for organizational reasons had the least political investment in the matter, promised to do his best to help the group come to a decision.

When the session began, I asked if someone would like to be chairman. The President suggested D, and D graciously and humbly accepted. D took over the discussion, controlled it tightly, and in fact pushed so strongly that he was dubbed "the steamroller." He objected to this sobriquet, but the group members agreed (for one of the few times during that discussion) that their "award" was well-deserved.

It was during this meeting that one news executive suggested that the editorial page had a "strident" quality. This upset the representative of the editorial group; indeed, as the reader may recall, he later called the meeting destructive. The two interventionists led the discussion that helped Q and R to begin to express their views about each other and helped Q to see that the majority of the members did not agree with R's evaluation. Because the discussion began to face up to important issues, and because these issues were worked through rather effectively, many of the participants learned that such sessions need not be destructive and that important organizational issues that had hitherto been considered taboo could indeed be discussed. These learnings turned out to have important consequences for the meeting we are about to describe.

The meeting began with fewer pleasantries than was

usual. Executive A turned the discussion to the issues by saying that the seminar experience had helped him to think through his ideas completely. The discussions had also helped him, he said, to see that he "had not understood others' views correctly." C added that he had had doubts about the value of the seminar but had come to realize its importance. "The more that we talked, the more I began to have a feeling that there really was something here. We began to break through into honesty—not all the way, but part of the way."

"On the new feature, I got an idea. I want to be tough about this. *I realized* [during the seminar] *that we were not dealing with the problem but with the politics of the problem*" (italics mine). The other members immediately agreed. This created an impetus to attack the problems that had smouldered for years because people had said they could not be confronted. There followed a very productive discussion, in which agreement after agreement seemed to be generated. Then C stated:

C: All right now, let's face up to the tough issues. We've been hung up on three issues: (a) Who runs it? (b) Will the material impinge on D's job? (c) Will the space be taken out of the news hole without diminishing the hard news?

D: [turning to R] Would you be willing to consider your position [he is cut off]

R: I want you to forget everything I've said about the new feature because the most meaningful things I've said, I've said tonight. And [I'll admit that one of my big concerns is] if we are going to lose 10 percent of our space I'm going to be stoned.

X: For being a traitor?

R: Yes, we're going to have to justify this. I'm going to have to prove [to my subordinates] that it's going to be good. C just asked if there was agreement on the three questions. I don't think there is.

Q: No, I don't think so either.

A discussion followed which did not seem to me to raise any important questions, so I said, "Let me ask if the issue is not that you, Q, want to manage it and you, R, believe that you

should manage it." Q answered: "Well, I wouldn't put it as
crudely as that—but that is essentially what I think. . . . Yes,
that *is* what I think." R also agreed with me and then added that
if the new feature would need the services of the reporters and
writers, then his department should be in charge of the enterprise.
C supported R by saying "If the new feature is not under R, it will
shut itself off from the news people, who are a great resource."
The President added that the person managing the feature could
report to him, but he questioned the advisability of such an
option. The others shared his doubts.

     D then told Q that C and R had made several compro-
mises, and that it was now up to Q to do the same. (D had returned to his compromise strategy.) R asked if anyone had really
given up anything; he said his reason for being willing to give up
space was that would be best for the paper and for the new
feature. D then decided to ask Q if he would be more open about
his concerns.

Q: Well, there are several things, not personal but institutional
     —well, maybe to *this* degree it is personal [for the
     first time, owning up to the personal dimension], there's
     a long history of my involvement in this. So it seems
     to me the most natural and normal, almost inherent,
     part of my department. [Note how personal Q can, un-
     realizingly, become.]
R: I understand your feelings perfectly. I'm not bullshitting.
     I know that you were thinking of the new feature long
     before I was. Now let me ask you honestly, in the spirit
     of Roundtree, should your department also be responsi-
     ble for selecting what should appear in the new feature?
Q: Yes, it's a reciprocal function. It's much more appropriate
     than the news. I feel that your department is getting
     into extra-news activity [and that is wrong].

Here C said something that supported R.

P: I've got some honest-to-Christ confusions in my mind.
Q: You've got, for the first time, some honest conversations,
     I'll tell you that.

P: Yes, I have, and if I didn't have to leave to catch a plane,
  I wouldn't ask to turn it off. [Turning to the inter-
  ventionist] Should we stop and regroup our thinking?
Q: I would suggest that we stop.
P: [To the interventionist] What do you think?
X: I'm very clear. It should be a group decision.

Q insisted that there should be another meeting. P asked
if the next step should be a set of one-to-one meetings. No one
supported this view. He then asked if the group wanted him to
make the decision. There was a spontaneous and resounding
"No!" "One more session!"

I then asked Q if he was feeling that he was losing and
wanted to delay the decision. He nodded, but before he could say
anything, C said that the new feature should provide an additional
opportunity for the younger and brighter news people to contribute. Q responded that they had that opportunity already, and
said that he thought too many reporters were already expressing
opinions and that he did not want to support that trend. R and C
said that if that happened, they too would be against it. Q responded that by then it would be too late.

R then turned to P and said, "OK, you can't leave now!"
He told P and the group that he had been terribly concerned that
the paper, in the last few years, had gone toward the left politically. "This [has] bothered me more than anything else in my
professional life. And I would feel equally strong if it went to the
right. The editorial page has gone toward the left; the columnists
are liberal to liberal left; and many of the bright reporters have
come out of an atmosphere of advocacy. All of us—something
has happened. At times, during the Chicago business, I felt that
the paper was in trouble. I felt that my job was to pull it back to
center. This paper should not be politically discernable."

P said that this was a critical issue and one that the paper
must discuss. The meeting ended with a promise to meet again.

No such meeting ever occurred. The President, several
months later, announced his decision to place the new feature
under the control of Q's department.

I was bewildered. Progress was being made toward developing an effective group and reducing the dependence upon the President for decision-making. R's reaction was one of mild anger and disappointment. But he insisted that he was not surprised. "P does whatever he wants to do. That's the trouble with all this stuff. If the man on top doesn't really believe in it, then I wonder." C was out of the country and could not be questioned. When I did interview him about three months later, he said that P must have had good reasons for his choice. They had their day in court, he said, and what more could they expect. He repeated his often-stated position that the President must have the choice in these matters. Q was, as we might have predicted, very happy. He believed that the decision was a correct one. He did not express any disappointment that they had not met again.

I interviewed P. He felt that at the end of the meeting, R, C, and D would have voted together. He felt that he had to support Q because Q was alone. He evaluated R's ideas about the new feature as poor and he reported that C agreed with him (but in private). I asked P why he had not said any of this to R and his response was, "There wasn't enough time." "Besides," he continued, "this decision has been over four years in the making and I knew they weren't going to make it, so I made it."

I said that his behavior was now incongruent with his espoused commitment to being more open and collaborative with his top people. I predicted that he would now be accused of taking the old route in order to get his own way. He acted surprised with this interpretation. Both of us had to leave to go to another meeting. As we walked out the door, I told him, "I'm beginning to question your commitment to the kind of management process we are developing or your understanding of it." He objected to this and asked that he be tested further by how he behaved in the future.

On the basis of the interviews, I would have to agree that the executives were predisposed to having P make the decisions. But I also believed that they were beginning to examine the unintended consequences of such a stance. Moreover, the meeting had been, as they pointed out, a relatively open and candid one, where the issues were dealt with directly and honestly. In my judgment, the President's actions delayed the day when such problems as overdependence upon him would disappear. It was difficult not to question the President's depth of commitment to genuine involvement of the top executives. G's continual assertion that P basically wanted to run the organization by himself began to have new meaning for me. I decided to observe the President more carefully and if necessary to confront him on this issue.

In the meantime, Q said that he was concerned about the hostility emanating from R regarding his (Q's) department. He said that there were deep difference between himself and R as to what the paper should look like. "Mind you," he added, "this is not personal with R!"

X: Have you considered talking to him about it?
Q: No, I have not. That's not my responsibility. Would he not rightly see me as meddling in his affairs? I would be glad to talk about it, but I don't have any authority. . . . Mind you, this is not a personal thing against R. My relationship with him is fine. His view is perfectly reasonable and rational. But I would be very diffident about discussing it with him. This is not my jurisdiction.
X: But if I recall correctly, he believes that your area is responsible for the loss in circulation. So we have the two top people each feeling that the other is responsible for a problem but not talking to each other about it.
Q: I think R would resent it. It would be absolutely futile. I know I would resent it if he came and told me how to run my shop. I guess that I would consider a meeting where we really worked through these issues as the impossible dream.
X: R would find it unhelpful if the purpose of the meeting was to tell him that he was wrong. However, I saw another scenario. It would go something like this. "R, I believe that you see much of the responsibility for the loss of circulation as related to my department. I see it as related to your side. I may be distorting the picture and would like to explore my views to get your reactions. Also, you may find there is something in my views that may be of help."
Q: Do you want me to set up such a meeting?

X: Yes, but it should come at your initiative.

Q: With or without you?

X: I prefer that the meeting be held without me rather than
    not held at all.

Q: Let me think about it.

X: I might add that I believe whether or not I am invited will
    depend on how comfortable R thinks you are with my
    being there.

Q agreed to give it serious thought. He also asked me to join
his group for one of their lunches.

      Several days later, I heard that R felt that he had been
ridiculed and hurt by Q at a luncheon meeting. I met with R and
quickly learned that he was very upset about Q's reported behavior during the lunch. He felt Q was "out to knife" him, that
he was unreachable, that he never seemed to learn. I asked if he
would consider a meeting with Q. His response was "What's the
use?" I said I could think of two reasons. If two top officials
such as themselves had more effective relationships, the whole
organization would gain. Also, if they learned how to handle
these difficult situations effectively, they would have gained as
human beings.

R: But I understand him. I accept his different view.

X: Why then the anger?

R: That's a good question. [later] But do I have the time and
    energy to work out all these issues?

X: If you don't work them out, it will probably cost you even
    more energy.

R: But maybe these are basic differences.

X: Fine; how about a world in which these differences can be
    discussed without individuals mistrusting each other?

R: Yes, yes.

Several weeks passed and I received a telephone call from R,
saying R and Q wanted to meet with me for a discussion of these
issues.

8

Editorial and News Explore Their Problems

"The fundamental question," T began, "is how much mutual agreement should we strive for, mutual agreement in the sense that we treat each other as rational human beings; you know, we don't hack at each other?"

As T talked, several thoughts flashed through my mind. I wondered if T was telling R, as openly as he can, that he would like the norms for this meeting to be focused around rational dialogue? I found it interesting that T, who six months ago was worried about the organizational development program creating conflict and setting individuals against each other, was now apparently concerned about too much cooperation. The reality was that the living system rewarded polarization. I was asking these men to spell out the reasons for the conflict and deal with them openly so that they could design whatever relationship would make the most sense to them and to their repective groups.

T continued by saying that the news and editorial leaderships should not have to be in full agreement about editorial and

161

news activities. What did bother him, he said, were reports that people, especially in the news department, thought that "Our editorials are dreamed up and unfounded. Here I think it would be helpful to discuss this and cooperate with the news department." T cited several memoranda that he had written, including one telling R and his group that he would be very receptive to any thoughts they had on the editorial page. He repeated his invitation to talk with reporters, in meetings large or small, private or public. He ended his introductory comments by saying, "I really think that there is a good deal to be gained by making it clear to the people in the news department that I would welcome criticism. I would rather get it directly than behind my back, and I know that some of it goes on behind my back."

Here is a good example of the difference between espoused theory and theory-in-use. T's espoused theory is that he is open to criticism. His theory-in-use is that if he is criticized—as he had been by R during the seminar, for example—he becomes defensive and calls the attempt destructive while simultaneously going to his files to make an objective case as to why the criticism was incorrect. Note also that T's belief that he can separate himself from his job is not part of the theory-in-use. In these comments, T was pleading that he, as a human being, was open to criticism.

R responded that he remembered the memorandum, that he thought the idea was "theoretically a wonderful idea," and that he had talked about it with his people during a meeting. However, he added, discussing the memorandum had made him somewhat uncomfortable. For one thing, such a discussion could be construed as encroaching on editorial policy and prerogatives; and the separation of news reports and editorials was as important as the separation of church and state. Furthermore, R had been confronting reporters and editors on the problem of subjective and interpretive reporting. He was receiving increasing pressure, especially from the younger reporters, to permit more subjective analysis. R believed that this was a dangerous trend in the news. T said he was pleased to hear this from R because he, too, was concerned about the trend; and he said he was chagrined to realize that the memorandum, which he had written to be helpful, had actually made R's task more difficult.

R: I have a feeling that you think that there's more criticism about your área than there really is. The thought just struck me. When I hear criticism about myself or the department even though it may be low-key, it sounds like it's on a loudspeaker, it sounds profoundly important. For example, you jibe at me by calling the newspaper a "magazine" and I go home and get mean to my wife. We have strong reactions, I mean it. You say one word and I spend a whole weekend brooding about it, trying to get it off my mind. After the weekend is over, I realize that it was childish.

T: And I feel the same way when you use the word "shrill" regarding editorials.

Here we see that R went directly to a very important issue. He asked that T explore with him the extent to which they unintentionally magnified criticism. This invitation, which no one had made before the seminar, is very important because rational discussions will not be very effective if the individuals have built-in magnifiers that distort messages, for these magnifiers lead them to make attributions about the others' motives, which in turn make it very difficult for the others to behave rationally.

Magnification of criticism is not only a personal attribute. It is characteristic of the living system. This means that if the problem of magnification of criticism is to be resolved, interventions will have to occur at the individual and interpersonal level (as is the case here), and later at the group and intergroup levels.

Finally, the predisposition to magnify may be an important reason why the executive group was so concerned about anyone being hurt at the seminar. In fact, at the seminar there were at least two episodes that would rate as explosions compared to the way criticisms were made in the normal work situation; yet there was overwhelming agreement by the participants that they were not destructive. The apparent contradiction is resolved

if the problem is not the criticism a person receives but his inability to explore it (caused by the norms of the system and the
members' lack of interpersonal competence). During the seminar,
when T and R had such an episode the two interventionists
helped the members to talk through the issues instead of sweep-
ing them under the rug. In the case above—and it will be repeated below—T made what he thought was a harmless remark
to R, but R exploded inside and suffered several days of despon-
dency and suppressed anger before "overcoming" the impact.
According to my interviews, this was the typical way of coping
with such an interaction—typical because the living system does
not sanction exploration of the issue. In other words, the group
members were not free to explore rationally the impact they have
upon each other.

How effective is this mode of adaptation? How much can
a human being take if anger is suppressed and managed through
depression? What impact do these psychic states have upon his
leadership behavior? If one of R's subordinates were to sense R's
depression and ask him about it, let us say, R might say "Well,
T let me have it again at a meeting." From remarks like this,
the subordinate could learn to tell when his boss is hurt, and he
would also learn that R prefers not to discuss the problem with
the person involved. Thus the subordinate is introduced to the
taboo: it is not possible, for superior or subordinate, to say something like, "I've wondered whether I ever say things that upset
you, or others; if I do, please let me know." If such questions
could be asked, they might elicit helpful feedback, which would
tell human beings when they are unintentionally upsetting each
other. System processes would then be developed that would result in new norms in the living system, norms which would sanction more constructive openness. This, in turn, would begin to
reduce the magnification by individuals, and a self-reinforcing
process would be created.

Returning to the discussion, T heard what R was saying
but he had difficulty, I thought, in accepting the possibility that
he might magnify and distort when he becomes upset. One reason
for this could be that T conceived of himself as being against

distorting reality, no matter how painful. His editorial policy is based on the assumption that one must call a spade a spade, even if it upsets people. But to be free to call a spade a spade, one must also be certain he is speaking the truth. Since truth about opinions is relative, it becomes important that opinions be arrived at rationally. This requires minimal distortion caused by external pressures. Since the *Planet* is scrupulous about not permitting external pressures to influence editorial opinions, the only pressures that can operate are internal.

There are two types of internal pressures. One is pressure from others within the system. As we have seen, R and T were scrupulous about keeping out of each other's domain, but they were causing pressures for each other. The second kind of pressure may come from within the individual. As R illustrated above, there may be internal processes that act to distort one's perception of reality. R was owning up to this possibility when he talked about magnifying criticisms he received from T. T, on the other hand, was having difficulty owning up to the same process.

I began to wonder if R was correct, and the editorials really were more strident than T felt they were; giving T's genuine commitment to honesty and rationality, he might have been unable to experience the feeling of stridency, after suppressing his feelings over nearly three decades of work in this living system. This hypothesis receives some support below, when T says he has felt that his department was never taken seriously until after he was put in charge, and that he has not had as much influence over the destiny of the newspaper as he wished.

T's response to R's comments of self-exploration was to nod understandingly but to keep repeating, in various ways, "I honestly want to improve our editorial knowledge, and it isn't that I'm not accustomed to criticism, but what I don't like is unfair and unjust criticism." R agreed and again asked Q to consider the possibility that the criticism might not be as loud or strong as he felt it to be.

I then asked R if he had not felt that T had criticized him during a recent luncheon meeting. R tensed and his understanding smile disappeared as he said, "Oh, that's a different matter!"

Then, for the first time that I had observed, R added that perhaps at that moment he was magnifying T's criticism. This made it easier for T to respond to the issue and be more rational in what he said. After T gave his version of what happened, it became clear to R that T had no intention of hurting him. T then added:

T: We mustn't get into a disagreement here because we are in absolute agreement. You see, I feel just as strongly as you do that reporters should not become editorial writers. Indeed, I would fire some of those bastards.

R: I contend with this every day. Not with what gets into the paper but what does not get into the paper. Not only what we cut out but what I know they would like to do if they could do it. That's not an enjoyable life. I know what they are feeling and saying about me: OK, you son-of-a-bitch, this is the way you're going to run this paper. OK, but we don't like it. And that's not very comfortable.

Here is another set of tensions and pressures that become bottled up in a person. If this happens frequently, where do these pressures go, since R cannot discuss them? To be sure, R has written memoranda about the differences between objective and subjective reporting. In them, he has shown keen sensitivity to the needs of the younger men, a commitment to high quality reporting, and a deep concern for maintaining the high integrity of the paper. If this analysis is correct and R feels as I have just described, then what must it do to him when reporters confront him on this issue or attempt to write something that violates the guidelines?

T recommended that R feel free to fire some of the worst offenders. R responded that it was not that easy. Even in the most flagrant cases, there could be repercussions, and he wondered how much backing he would get from the paper. I then commented that both were in strong agreement about the need to separate editorial opinions from news, and I asked T if he felt he saw editorializing in the news more clearly than R did. T said yes, and added that he would be less permissive than R.

R said this problem did not trouble him as much now

that he realized that T and he were in agreement about the proper aims for the newspaper. His problem was:

R: You believe that I'm steering the news the wrong way. I'm just as sensitive to this as you may be sensitive to criticism of editorials. . . . You think we're making the paper too much like a magazine, that we're not giving enough attention to what happened yesterday, etc.

T: Yes, I think that you've put your finger on it—since you've raised it. You're damn right I believe that too much attention is being paid to sociological developments and trends. I feel there is too great a degree of subjective interpretation.

R: You think we're making the paper into a magazine.

T: That word magazine really bothers you.

R: Yes, it does. In fact, you have a whole vocabulary that [laughs]. I'm just teasing.

X: Maybe you're not teasing, but letting T know what words trigger you off.

T then gave several examples to illustrate his charges. R responded with his views. As the discussion continued, both men were making points that the other agreed with but the agreement was not occurring because each felt so misunderstood and disrespected that he spent most of the time rebutting the other person. For example, T would argue that a trend in an African country which was leading the natives to become Christians was not news; R would maintain that it was.

R returned to the issue of feeling misunderstood. He asked T to compare the early and late editions of the paper and see if soft news did not get cut out or greatly reduced. R also recalled the luncheon session where they had discussed a particular news story about a trend in land values.

R: I looked at you and I knew you didn't like it. Somebody else said that he liked it and another story, and I knew that you didn't like that one either.

T: Yes, that was the [cut off].

R: You were sitting there cooking and though you hadn't

come out with it, you should have said that you didn't
like either one of them.

Note how much "analyzing" R does of T. This sort of
activity occurs frequently, between two persons who were worried
about a seminar that might focus too sharply on personality. What
is actually going on in the system is that the executive *are* per-
sonality-centered. They *do* analyze each other and make attributions about each other's motives, but these attributions are never
tested for their validity. Consequently they serve to reinforce the
living-system problems, such as magnification and distortion of
reality.

R then added a new factor to the discussion. He said that
the criticism from T bothered him not only because he respected
T, but also because T was close to the President and had an influence on his ideas. T said he doubted whether he had much
influence over the President's thinking. As he attempted to document this assertion, R asked T to focus on the influence he had
over R.

R: You have a great influence on me. More than you realize.
     You use words like magazine, that's soft, that's driving
     things out, and boy! You write these elegant editorials;
     the one yesterday was great.
T: Parenthetically, the President wasn't too happy.
R: I know, he asked me about it and I told him it was great.
     I think he expected me to detest it, but I didn't. But
     when you talk about the news, I think you're damaging.
     It's as if I sat with you and the President and called one
     of your editorials "shrill." Boy, I used that word once
     but never again, because now I can see it was an ex-
     tremely hard and damaging word.
X: But another strategy is to help develop a milieu in which
     neither of you becomes upset with the other's language;
     or better yet, an atmosphere in which you can explore,
     as you are now, such issues as "shrill" and "magazine."

R then said that his deepest concern was finding a way for
R and T to come together. Some of R's sub-editors have disap-

proved of his trying to develop better communications with T. They argue that it is their business to do the best news job they can and to remain outside editorial influence.

Here again, the issues may be unnecessarily polarized: on the one hand, R's personal feelings about the impact T has on him, and on the other, the fundamental separation in a newspaper between the editorial and news functions. But if the interchange above means anything, it is that both men strive to keep out of each other's territory; both meet or interact through normal business meetings; both focus keenly on each other's comments; and both tend to leave feeling misunderstood and hurt, which leads to increased internal tension and an overcarefulness about what they say during meetings. To the extent that this excessive caution occurs, the meetings will be less productive than they could be because people are not freely presenting all the ideas that they have on substantive issues. It is understandable that under these conditions, group meetings will become unproductive.

T said he agreed that R's question about the separation of news and editorial functions was a basic one. He then reassured R that he did not have any "axes to grind." "I realize that you don't have axes to grind," responded R, "but look at what happens to us after those meetings." T answered that all he wanted was to feel that his comments were being taken seriously by R.

I intervened here to say that I was hearing that both wanted a more open relationship in which each felt that his ideas were valued and his competence was not questioned; but that I could see that when they attempted to discuss issues with each other, legacies from the past and their way of communicating with each other tended to negate their own aspirations.

To raise this intervention from the personal to the organizational level, we have two departments whose product influences each other and the paper. The way to maintain autonomy under these conditions of interdependence is not to ignore each other, or when meeting, to polarize positions by overinterpreting each other. The way is to conduct open discussions, which should aim at producing three things: a clearer idea of whatever has inhibited communication and understanding; a more valid view of the policies and practices of each department; and a clearer view of the limits of each department.

These results, coupled with an increased competence in human communication, can free individuals to say exactly what they believe because they know that others will openly explore issues that are threatening. The strategy is to maintain autonomy through interdependent relationships.

The meeting came to a close and T set a date for me to meet with his group. Both men said that the meeting was very helpful, that they wanted to do much more thinking about the issues, and that the meeting represented the beginning of a dialogue.

Two weeks later, when R and I had a brief meeting, he reported that the session had not solved the problems but had showed that they were solvable. This was as much as I could have hoped for from such sessions. Both men had more feelings to expose and explore with each other, and both had more to learn about how to do this competently. R was ahead of T in being able to own up to his feelings and discuss them in such a way that he could hear the other person's; but both had limits beyond which they would lose their effectiveness.

We must not forget these men were but two persons in a large system. Unless what they were learning could be learned by others in the larger system, they would have difficulty maintaining their hard-won growth.

The chances for increasing the learning and enlarging the scope of the discussions between T and R seemed good. One important area for enlargement involving T and R would be their relationship with P. What were P's views about the long-range purposes of editorial and news activities? How much freedom can editorial activities have, given the fact that a newspaper is a business that must survive economically? The reader familiar with journalism will recognize these issues as fundamental ones. If my informants were correct, these issues were rarely discussed openly and candidly with the President. Let us turn now to some sessions in which this was precisely what was attempted.

9

The President and the Editorial Department

T believed, and the President agreed, that both might have differences in opinion that could profit from an open discussion. T was clear that the President's views were the views that would ultimately be found on the editorial page. T had no interest in challenging the President's right to this influence. He did believe, however, that he had a right and an obligation to influence the President's views on this subject. He also felt that *The Daily Planet's* integrity required it to side with the "public good," and that it should continue to do so even when it might affect the paper's earnings. Although the President agreed with this basic point, it was not clear to T where the President would draw the line, especially when the issues were financial.

The meeting began with T controlling most of the conversation. His ideas tumbled out one after another, almost tripping over each other in a rush to escape long imprisonment. The essence of T's position was as follows: The President had final

171

authority over the editorial page; he had a veto power over any editorial written by the editorial group. The President should consider very seriously any disagreement between himself and any members of the editorial group; he should not publish a view that the board believed was not in keeping with the paper's mission. The mission of the paper is such that the paper never speaks for any given special interest, economic or otherwise; it does not permit itself to become a mouthpiece for any party, any sect, or any corporate interest—including its own. This could mean, for example, that the paper should not hesitate to endorse a particular city tax because that tax would cut into the paper's earnings. T was especially concerned that some publishers have used newspapers to advance their own economic interests. "They have a constitutionally protected position which some have misused."

The President asked, as a hypothetical question, if it would be proper for him to write a letter to the editor if he felt that a city tax on advertising would harm the newspaper. T said yes, he could do that, and he could also go to City Hall to complain against the tax even though his paper had published an editorial supporting the tax for the public good. T added that he believed that the head of the editorial group should not be an officer of the company.

The President did not agree with T on the tax example. He said, "I should do about any goddamn thing to stop it. That's the difference between you and me." "But," pleaded T, "What is more important than any tax or bill is the reputation of the paper. There is no year in which you can afford to sacrifice the reputation of the paper. There are no sabbaticals on integrity." "I understand you," replied the President, "but we have to keep this corporation going, and so we have to perform some very dangerous balancing acts."

The President then said that if he followed which he did not want to do, he could not serve as President and publisher at the same time. I asked how he felt when someone presents a case for that position: "Well, I don't know exactly. It's an interesting question. It is one thing that I've thought a hell of a lot about. Maybe as the company grows, these two jobs should be separated. I just don't know. To date, T and I have had very few disagreements. But I think as the paper grows, it will be tougher to let them ride. I don't think it makes much sense to say that I can't put an idea in the editorial page but I put in the form of a letter to the editor." P continued by stating that he wanted to find a way to have more discussions with the editorial group. T said that would be a good idea, and added that it would make the board members very happy.

T then said that one of the problems of being a paper with a conscience was that such a paper served the community best by being critical: "We're helping our city by being critical of all the things that are wrong with it. I think that the best way to help the city is to be critical. Of course, this is different from the typical booster view." P interrupted to ask T, "Are you anti-big business?" T answered, "No, I'm not." "The editorial page," P retorted, "could give some people the idea that we're anti-big business." "That's because businessmen didn't like some of the criticisms that we made," T replied. "I would say that we're as critical of big labor as we are of big business."

Here again T had fallen into his response pattern of attempting to give objective data to disprove P's statement. I asked if perhaps the issue was not what T wrote but the tone of the editorials; perhaps readers react to the tone. T responded that he could not remember any anti-big business expressions in editorials. "I do admit," he added, "that we try to get editorials that use some vigorous modes of expression [laughs]. You know, I've never really been psychoanalyzed; maybe you're doing it right now."

X: I don't think so.
T: I think you are. I grew up with the paper, and for years I
     thought the editorials were awfully flabby and never
     said anything. I was determined that if I made the
     editorial group, I'd begin writing editorials that said
     something. For years, I felt that our editorials were so
     damn low-key that no one read them.

Then T said something which seemed to me to reveal a new reason why he would want to write the editorials that caused people to take notice.

T: The paper for years had a reputation of being a great paper
      except for its editorial page. I think maybe what I con-
      sider to be vigorous and definitive is what you would
      call angry, and what R considers shrill, which is a word
      I don't appreciate but use because he did so.

X: [to P] Do you believe there is shrillness and stridency in
      the editorials?

P: Yes, sometimes, and that concerns me.

T: I don't think they're shrill at all.

P: I think they are, on occasion, and my associates feel it more
      than I do.

T: [returning to a more closed position] I really reject totally
      the criticism that we run a shrill editorial page. I
      really do not believe this is justified. I would say that
      occasionally a phrase gets by that gives some basis for
      that remark, but it is rare.

T then gave an example of how he checks out these issues.
Recently he received a letter condemning the use of a certain
phrase in an editorial. He was astounded because he felt certain
that he had not used such a phrase. Yet when he checked it, he
found that the writer of the letter was correct. "Somehow it
escaped me and I didn't even recall it." Perhaps wondering
whether this example tended to support my own analysis, he
added: "Sometimes I use or agree to let others use phrases that
are unnecessarily aggressive. Someone else told me about this
a few weeks ago." "This is useful to me, because it makes me more
conscious than ever. I thought I was pretty conscious, but I guess
I have to be more conscious of watching the phraseology."

T, talking to himself, noted that the use of unfortunate
phrases had to be reduced. Then he added, as if to reassure himself and others, that the unfortunate phrases crept in not because
of "a philosophical bias against business," but because a concern
for "the good of the general public as weighed against the special
interests." P responded that he didn't have any disagreement
with T that the paper should focus on the public good. He only
objected to editorial positions taken by his paper that he did not
agree with. T asked for an example, but P could not produce one.
He asked for a couple of days to think about it.

The second meeting. The next meeting was held about two weeks later. In addition to P and T, it was attended by another member of the editorial page staff and a vice-president of the company who had spent most of his life on the news side of the business. The topics of this meeting were mostly the same as before, but the discussion explored the issues further.

The President began by alluding to the tone of the editorial page—too much sense of crisis, words too strong, too much on the attack—which had been covered during the previous session. The President then recalled T's view that the role of the editorial page should be to be critical of all institutions that deserve criticism in the name of the public good; he wondered if the paper did not also have a responsibility to suggest ways of correcting the errors and weaknesses it identifies. T began his answer in his personal style of attempting to correct any misperceptions P might have about his position. He then said that the paper did have an obligation to present positive suggestions along with its criticism. The paper ought not to go into detail, he said. "We cannot write a new budget for the government." The President agreed, and one of the new members of the group turned the discussion back to the tone of the editorials, which he described as sometimes righteous and strident. T immediately denied they were strident in tone, but he quickly abandoned his usual defense of trying to persuade the other person that he was wrong, and asked for some examples. Interestingly, no one was able to think of an example. After some discussion, the President recalled an example that he admitted was not the best one to use. Indeed, the examples led the entire group to discuss the President's memos, which they found to be emphatic, strident, and at times hostile.

T then noted that they had agreed that this meeting would begin with the President presenting his views, but that this had not occurred. He was very much interested in hearing from the President. The President said that he wanted to turn away from the stance of his predecessor, who had rarely consulted others. He believed that problems were now too complex for one man to decide by himself on the proper editorial stand.

All agreed to this suggestion and T (joined by the other editor) said that they would cooperate in trying to develop this

new relationship. The other editor then returned to an issue left
dangling at the close of the last meeting. He wondered about the
stance of the paper if the editorial group believed in a policy that
was bound to hurt the paper financially.

P: This is the most difficult one for me. I don't see how I can
    stand up and say one thing and then have the paper
    come out in another direction. . . . I am in agreement
    with the point of view that the paper should be con-
    cerned with straightening out the world. But when it
    comes into direct conflict with something that is en-
    tirely practical to the business, then I lose the call a hell
    of a lot faster than you do.
T: And that is the point that concerns me.
P: This is what may lead me to write some of those strident
    messages. It's very strange for me to divorce myself—
    separate myself—from the organization. It may not be
    strange for you, but it is for me.

The President then described his feelings when, on a few
occasions, several of his corporation board members, men whom
he respects greatly, read the paper to find their company's actions
condemned. T said that he had never thought of that embarrassment. However, he still believed that the correct action for the
paper was to condemn the companies even if their chief executive
officers were on the corporate board. T continued, "These businessmen are great human beings, but they have no feelings for the
tradition of a great newspaper." P replied, "Let us be clear that
news and editorial matters are not discussed by these businessmen. But it is still not easy to divorce myself when I know [that
we have attacked] someone who sits on our board of director. . . . None of these men would even think of trying to influence our positions. But they might say, "You are certainly entitled to print anything you wish, but how on earth did you arrive
at such-and-such a position?"

The three other men in the room supported the idea that
the paper must be free to be critical of any corporate policy, including its own. The President said that he understood that, but

still was not completely certain. He wanted to think more about it.

I commented that if I were on the editorial group, I would feel several kinds of insecurities. On the one hand, I would know that sometimes I would be creating difficulties for P and his business friends. On the other hand, I could never be certain that P would stand behind me. I would even wonder if P had the vision of the paper that I had and wished he had.

The three executives agreed that this was an important point. One man said, "I've always been proud of this newspaper because I knew it was free to state the difficult editorial positions —if we thought they were correct—and I always felt absolutely secure that the President was going to stand behind me, no matter what the pressures were." The President said he understood that, and hoped the day would never come when the paper's interests would take precedence over the public interest.

The conversation returned to the tone of the editorial page. T said that he was now trying to learn not to take these attacks so personally. But, he added, this would take time. Then he restated his belief that since he had become editor, the page was respected; it could no longer be ignored. "People may disagree with it, but they pay attention to it."

I began to connect this statement with one T had made previously that for years he had felt the editorial page was drab and unimportant. I began to see an outline of a person who isolated himself from the main news activities, in the name of separating editorial matters from news and administrative functions, yet really carved closer relationships with valued colleagues. This quality of wanting interpersonal closeness, but denying it or suppressing it by focusing on intellectual and rational issues, was characteristic of many of the top editors. It was as if the way they had learned to get close to people was to compete with them on an intellectual level. I mention this hypothesis because it would be incorrect to give the impression that T was unique in his need for closeness. The overwhelming majority of the news people showed the same need and the same ambivalence. It is understandable yet ironic that these people who needed the rewards of interpersonal closeness had created a living system in which the only way they could obtain some of those rewards was through intellectual competition and from the fame or notoriety accorded them by unknown readers.

This hypothesis, if confirmed, would be another important reason why the news executives should exhibit such a high degree of ambivalence about examining interpersonal relationships. This was an area in which they were less competent, less likely to win, and, if my program "reached" the inner core they so carefully concealed from themselves and others, they would have to confess to their needs for interpersonal closeness.

The third session. In the third session, T and P explored the same topics but began to expose even more of their feelings. For example, T, who had entered these discussions dead set against intruding in anyone else's area—and particularly concerned about maintaining his autonomy and independence in relations with news, administration, and the President—had now reached the point where he was trying to design a closer, more open relationship, within which key issues of the paper could be discussed and where he would receive much more feedback from news people about his editorials.

T began his discussion by asking if he was cutting anyone off. P and the interventionist said no, he was not. T then said smilingly that he was trying to become more aware of dominating discussions. I saw this as another small sign that T was taking the lessons he was learning seriously, but that he had not, as yet, internalized them. He was at the stage of acting them out and thereby alerting others of his intentions. T said: "I've been doing a lot of thinking as a result of these discussions. One long-standing feeling I've had . . . is related to the President's control over the editorial page [which I believe is proper]. I am more clear now that as editor I ought to be in a more intimate relationship with the President and the news activities of the paper. I should have more participation in the long-range planning of the paper. . . . [later] I can't help but feel that over the years the editorial department has been looked upon as sort of an appendix. . . . [later] I'm not speaking personally; I'm speaking in the institutional sense. I feel that my participation, despite others' attempts, is off on a shelf." Note that T still has trouble facing up to his personal needs and integrating them with the legitimate organizational needs of the job.

The President then spoke of dilemmas and frustrations that he had experienced with the top news and editorial executives. When he became President, he wanted to increase the genuine involvement of the top officers but found that he had difficulty on the news and editorial side. As the diagnosis of the living system had pointed out, decision-making had become centralized and his executives had become adept at passing decisions on to him. "I wanted to open up the big issues of the paper. Where are we going? Are we drifting, resting on our laurels? I wanted to get all the responsible editors together and sit down to have a rational discussion that would lead somewhere. Not just have a discussion where all of you get up and go away. I've never been able to succeed in doing it. And I've tried every format I know. Everyone starts to defend what he is doing and we end up with a one-to-one relationship. However, let me say this. I'm willing to start over again."

At this point I wondered whether I should intervene and confront the President with the way he had handled the new feature discussions, in which the top group had made its first genuine attempt to take on more responsibility. I decided not to do this because to raise the issue privately with P could make me the cause of a discussion that would involve other people who were absent. This tactic would have been ineffective for any professional interventionist, and it would have been dangerous in this particular living system, which was already dominated by secrecy and competitiveness.

T agreed that reaching decisions in the top group had been a problem in the past, but said he now wanted to try to alter the situation. He suggested that the top people meet regularly to talk about the important issues of the paper, its management, its policies, its values, and its future direction.

From the interventionist's point of view, this was an important moment. What flashed through my mind were memories of the interviews I had conducted with each of the top people. Many of them had said that such meetings were necessary but that they would never happen because key executives like T and P would never agree to participate.

The next comment brought home some of the hard realities of life. T said, "I want this, and I'll do my best, but I don't know if a discussion with people of our particular make-up is ever going to be successful." The President said that he believed it was now possible to hold the discussions, but that he was worried about whether they would accomplish anything. Would individuals simply return to their polarized positions?

T responded that it should be given a try but that the President should not expect early results. "There are certain temperamental difficulties with people who get to the top. They have strong opinions and strong wills." He then added: "I would hear a lot of things that I really don't like to hear, and this may make me uncomfortable. But I hope that I'm now open-minded enough to recognize criticism that has real validity and be willing to change or take a different direction." T went on to say that although he had at first resented the comments about his department, "these comments have made me extremely conscious, more conscious than I would have been before." He said that in reading copy he had become more aware than ever that the editorial column could be criticized as being strident. He was not suggesting that the problem was completely resolved, or that he would agree in all cases with the criticisms; but he did believe he was now more open to hearing criticism.

The President, perhaps out of disbelief in what he was hearing, pressed T. He asked him how he envisioned participating in decisions that might affect the news side, for example, without being influenced by the news executives regarding editorials. T answered that he was willing to be influenced but that he wanted to participate in a discussion where he and his group had the final choice, and that the same would be true for the other departments. The President pushed further. Would T want input from others about what political candidates the paper should support? T responded that he wanted to enter such discussion; what he did not want was a situation in which an outsider was given a controlling decision over someone's group. T added that he was not clear on all the issues but hoped that they would be worked out. I suggested that the idea be proposed as an experiment.

The President then tested T in a more indirect way by wondering out loud if T really wanted an open discussion of the editorial group. He said he believed that T frightened quite a few of his colleagues, to the point where they would not really disagree with him on difficult issues. T replied that he didn't think he had such an influence, but that if he did he would want to discuss it. I believe this was the first time that T did not go into a long defense of himself when someone accused him of behavior that he genuinely disliked and would not wish to associate with himself.

The President and T both agreed that this had been a very important meeting. It seemed to both of them that much progress had been made. As they tried to define the progress, they realized that it consisted less in setting up guaranteed new actions and more in breaking down old barriers to action, old myths and attributions, and in creating expressions of willingness to experiment and to learn from experience.

The President said that the next step was to hold a discussion with C and R present, as well as a few more top people. Months passed and no meeting was called. This tended to reinforce the view held by T, R, and C that the President was simply game-playing: he would become involved in opening up the climate to the point where group decision-making might work, and would then revert to exercising authority alone.

I discussed this possibility with the President, and he denied that he did not want to involve people. He kept saying that the problem was "getting these guys together," that a few key executives still had serious reservations and he did not want to alienate them; he said that within a year or so most of the resisters would have retired, and then he could move. I questioned his strategy and asked that we hold a meeting with the executives who had attended the seminar, to test their commitment. The President agreed and scheduled such a meeting.

10

Self-Renewal in the News Department

Soon after the meeting with T and P, I had a meeting with R. He told me that the more he thought about the seminar experience, the more he wanted to explore ways to create more effective human relationships with the editors immediately beneath him (none of whom had attended the learning seminar). He said that he would like to hold a meeting with all of them present to discuss the possibility of such a program. I agreed to participate.

R wondered how we could introduce the subject. I suggested that one way would be to ask them to read the report I had written about the living system. We could open the meeting by asking them to express their agreement or disagreement with it. If there was a substantial degree of agreement, then actions could be jointly designed to correct the problems. As always, the commitment required would have to be an individual, internal one. Also, the rule would be maintained that after each step our concepts and activities would be reviewed, and the group would make a new decision about whether to continue.

R was delighted with the idea of holding a meeting but ambivalent about giving his editors the report. He felt uncomfortable whenever he read it. He believed that he could be identified in it, and that some of his clearly directive behavior, which might be criticized, had been necessary to correct a deteriorating situation. But then R recalled that most of his editors had actually read the report and had a long discussion session with the interventionist. He agreed to schedule the meeting at the earliest convenient time.

Because of my own scheduling problems, I asked the President to consider postponing the other meeting that had been planned until this meeting with R and his group had been completed. The results of this meeting would be important input for a meeting where the degree and quality of the top group's commitment to these activities would be reviewed. P agreed immediately.

The meeting with R and his immediate editorial subordinates. The meeting began with R stating that he had asked for the meeting to explore the issues raised in the report. He turned to me and asked me to make any comments that I wished to make.

I asked if everyone had read or reread the diagnosis made of the organization, and said I would like to know how they had reacted to the findings. I said that if the group agreed with the findings, they might focus on planning action steps and learning activities that could begin to overcome the problems identified in the report. I continued:

> I see this group as unintentionally creating problems for people—for example, problems of conformity and overcontrol. Some of the strongest conformity is created, and overcontrol exercised, when [members] are performing their regular professional activities and when they intend to have the opposite impact.

Subordinates who deal with members of this group tend to feel inhibited in expressing feelings and opinions, especially if they believe them to be threatening to other members of the group. The content that is threatening, and the degree of the threat, varies with the different individuals and their subordinates.

I believe that I can help you to unfreeze the situation to make it easier for your subordinates to do problem-solving with you and to help you to be more effective with them. I'm interested in helping you to increase your effectiveness in dealing with people, and your interpersonal competence—to increase your problem-solving effectiveness as well as to raise the quality of life within the organization.

Immediately after these introductory comments, the questions began.

R: Can you be concrete about the problems you've mentioned?
X: Yes, I can. I can give examples and identify individuals in this group, if you wish.
B: Yes.
C: Go ahead.
R: Sure, by all means. We're all open here.
X: Well, Mr. F, during my observations of your meeting [with subordinates], I found that you were initating most of the ideas and actions, that you seemed to use your subordinates more to help you think through and express your own ideas than for them to express theirs. [Some examples were given here.]

Also, at times after the meeting when I would ask a particular subordinate why he didn't tell you about [a certain idea], his response would be that he didn't feel he could. I would ask him how he had arrived at that conclusion. His response would be, "Well, look at his enthusiasm; see how he cuts people off without even being aware of it; the last thing in the world I'd think of doing is telling him how I feel. He wants to hear good news, and I can understand why— he's so harried!"

I might add that people report a high degree of respect for the professional competence of the members of this group, but less respect for their interpersonal competence. By the way, the people who are most critical of you—your subordinates—tend not to be any more effective with their own subordinates. Many of the younger supervisors believe that they would be more effective. My data would not support that view.

Am I getting at your questions?

The members nodded affirmatively and two said yes. Then one person asked how I would propose to help them overcome these problems. "Would we work individually with you?"

X: No, not at the outset. I recommend that the initial learning steps be taken as a group. There are several reasons for this. One is that each of you can be an important resource for the others during the learning. Another is that you can be of help to each other after we have returned from the initial experiences. This would hasten the day that you no longer need me. Finally, it is much cheaper in time and money expended.

D: Well, what kinds of meetings would these be?

X: Before we talk about the possible content of the meetings, I'd like to emphasize two points. First, I'm not suggesting that we become amateur psychologists and try to change each other's personalities. In the first place, personality changes aren't made that easily. I'm asking you to explore the way you deal with people, your leadership behavior, and see if it's having the desired effects; if it isn't what can you do to make it the more effective?

Second, I don't think learning occurs and change develops unless the individual is genuinely willing to explore his own part in causing the problem. Thus, your subordinates and I may believe that your interpersonal competence is not as high as it should be, but that is not the important point. The point is what each of you believes.

The kind of learning that I'm talking about requires internal commitment. This means that you will be involved in designing and managing the learning, or killing it, any time you wish. Unless you have the freedom to kill it, I can't see how you can be internally committed to it.

OK, I recommend that we plan a meeting that will last for several days. The topics of discussion you bring there could grow out of the issues raised in the report and any other issues that you may wish to identify. We can talk about professional problems, people problems, technical problems—anything that we believe is important if we are to make this organization more effective. Periodically we will stop and examine our behavior. We can do that by listening to a tape recorder or by recollecting it. We could ask about the degree of competitiveness. How much openness and risk-taking was there? How was the discussion led and by whom? How effectively were people heard? How effective was the decision-making process?

The members reveal fears but resist exploring them. In the first phase of this meeting with R and his group, I spent most of the time describing what I conceived to be the objectives of the learning experiences and the likeliest ways to go about achieving these objectives, while noting the possible dangers and misunderstandings.

The next phase seemed to consist mainly of three-stage interactions of this sort: a member would reveal his fears; I would respond; and if my response seemed to indicate recognition of the member's fear, he would respond in a way that blocked further exploration of his fears.

For example, the first fear to be exposed came from C, who felt that the result of the learning experiences would be to "homogenize" leadership styles.

C: Aside from solving problems, we have to make people feel that they are effective. I have the sneaky feeling, not that you are trying to put anything over on us, but that leadership styles will get homogenized. I'm not

convinced that any single leadership style works the
same way for everybody. You learn from your people
as well as they learn from you, and you adjust to them
as they adjust to you.

R: You don't have to accept any views he has.

C: No, but I'm trying to be as open as I can.

As C was speaking, I noted that he seemed to think it
was his job "to make people feel effective," which suggested to me
that he might hold a mechanistic concept of leadership by which
leaders "make" people have certain evaluative feelings about
themselves. I looked for a good opportunity to point out an inconsistency in what C had said. My hypothesis was that one way
to test C's interest in learning was to demonstrate that persons
who are relatively open to, and interested in, learning will value
exploring any proven inconsistencies in their own behavior.

The opportunity I selected was the issue of homogeniza-
tion. The logic was as follows: C says he is against homogenizing
people; the subordinates of C and others have reported that
they were being homogenized; therefore C and others will want
to explore the inconsistency between what they espouse and how
they actually behave. So I said: "That's helpful. Let me make
several responses. One is that the subordinates reported that they
felt homogenized. So the leadership styles may be different, but
their impact seems to be one of homogenizing all of the subordinates."

C replied that it did not make sense to him to be fully
open and fully honest with everyone all the time. This seemed
to be a polarization of my position. No one had suggested that
openness meant to be fully honest all the time.

R: Are there any conditions where complete clarity is
possible?

X: Under conditions of concern, individuality, and high trust.

R: Suppose there is little of these.

X: Unilateral openness can be damaging under conditions of
low trust. If I understand your [group of] subordinates,
this is one reason why they may hesitate to be as open
with some of you as they would like.

The discussion then turned to the possibility of harming another when being fully open.

At this point, I was wondering about three things. (1) Why do the group members continue to polarize the issue of openness, so that complete openness means running the risk of hurting others? (2) Do the members have their own problems of openness, their own fears of what would happen if they were open with each other? (3) While preparing the diagnosis, I learned that private "gossip" sessions about certain individuals tend to occur frequently. People reported that it was difficult to trust others with a secret or attribute a willingness not to gossip.

The group begins to reject the learning experience. It was difficult for me to think of a way to raise any of these issues without strengthening the resisting forces. In any event, before I could say anything, E made the first open rejection of the idea of a group learning experience:

> That raises a point. You're asking a direct question. What do we think about a weekend in which we sit around? So, I'll give you a direct answer. I think it'll be a waste of time. The reason I think it'll be a waste of time is because we've been talking for maybe an hour and nothing relates to me. I have problems and I had one last week, a personnel problem, serious at the moment. But it may fit into D's bag. And I'm not interested in D's problems.
>
> And another thing, it creates an artificial situation. Because if you bring us all together like you're doing now, this is not the way we normally discuss problems. This same group does not meet when I'm having an individual problem. I go to R, I go to B, I go to C upon occasion, and I go to F upon occasion, if it's a joint problem there. Much less to D. On the other hand, if you're talking about problem-solving; if you want to come and sit on my desk and notice the time frame in which I have to solve a particular problem, and the particular pressures that are on me at the moment I have to solve that problem; and then, at the end of the day, you know, you kibbitz me and we talk;

then that's a different thing. I think that might have some relevance. But we don't have councils of war like this. When you were here before and we had those morning meetings, they were under different management, so to speak, and they were bullshit, if I can be blunt; they didn't amount to anything and they didn't take me anywhere.

Before I could ask how others felt about E's comment, F brought up a fear of his, the familiar one of having only negative aspects of one's behavior discussed, of having "weaknesses" exposed. In this case, F openly lamented the fact that he did not get "pleasant" feedback from me:

> One thing that puzzles me. I have a large, complex staff which I like and feel I get along with quite well. You know, a lot of time has passed since you were here last. I think the staff likes me. We work pretty closely together, and we get a lot done. There's a lot of personal satisfaction on both sides. What bothers me is every time I discuss something with you, your approach to me is negative. You've never viewed my role in a positive sense.

Before I could respond, E returned to his attack. He said that the report may have been valid when it was written but that by now it said little that was true about his shop. He repeated that the problems of other department heads did not concern him, and that he would find it a waste of time to discuss their problems with them. He concluded with these remarks:

E: I'm not interested in spending a whole weekend talking about F's, B's and C's problems, which are different from mine. Maybe you can draw up all the principles on how to handle people, but I sort of reject that! [said with emphasis]

X: What kind of data or information would you accept that could disconfirm or change your beliefs?

E: I don't know. You're running up against a long-standing, strong prejudice on my part.

This question of mine did two things. First, it helped make public the fact that E's resistance to the entire idea of exploring behavior had roots in experiences which occurred long before this session, but that his resistance remained strong even in a situation where he could help design and control the learning conditions. Second, it set the stage for a possible examination by E of the inconsistency in his behavior: his willingness, on the one hand, to invite the interventionist to observe his leadership behavior, and his insistence, on the other, that he has a strong prejudice against behavioral science theory and method.

The discussion was so animated at this point that I was unable to explore these issues, but R offered a statement in response to E's objections. He said that he had participated in the first experimental session with a group of company officers who had less varied backgrounds and interests than members of this group, but he felt that he had nevertheless learned a lot. He also observed that E's problems were not that much different from those of F, B, and others. Moreover, some of the personnel problems facing F today might face E tomorrow if these men were transferred to E's department. Also, R felt that E had several men who were similar to the men with whom F was having problems.

After R made these points he turned toward E and told him that he was an excellent leader. He said E had built up his department by "cheating and stealing, yet nobody's mad at you."

I wondered how other department heads could not be angry at someone who stole professionals from their groups. One possibility was that E stole ineffective people. But how could one compliment a leader for that? Moreover, the "stealing" had actually become such an annoying and difficult problem that R had to write a memorandum ordering a halt to "stealing." R statement that no one was angry and E for stealing personnel seemed to be a glossing over of reality.

I wanted to follow up this inconsistency but I felt compelled to reply to F's fears of focusing on negative behavior and the prediction that the younger men would leave. I reminded F that the prediction made was that the better young men would leave if they had better offers, or remain physically but leave psychologically—that they would, in effect, moonlight on company time (a practice which was increasing rapidly).

D and E brought the discussion back to the fact that the report was now nearly a year old, and said that things had changed for the better. I said that from what little information I had, I doubted that changes had occurred, but added, "if you as a group believe that there isn't much to be learned at this point, fine. I'm not here to try and sell you something."

E responded that he was not saying that he could not benefit from the interventionist. "If you came to our native habitat, we might find that you could be quite helpful. But I do question the benefits to be gained from sitting around a table through a whole weekend kicking things back and forth." C said: "I subscribed to what E says and extend the hand of welcome to the monitoring of the animal in its natural habitat. I cordially invite you to sit with me. I have a lot to learn, but I can't learn in terms of general principles. I endorse E. You've got to watch me and tell me what I'm doing wrong."

R then said that he would like to see the group meet more often to talk about the long-term problems of the organization. "Sure, I know there's a high degree of trust in this group. We know each other—we can read each other. F is sore, aren't you?"

F: I'm not being sore.
R: You're not sore? Why you're cooking! You're furious, right?
F: No—not that furious.

R continued that he wanted to have more meetings at which the crucial issues of the organization were discussed.

C suggested a new set of factors that might be operating on some of them—the pressures, frustrations, and feelings of not being fully appreciated:

> You know, there's another aspect of this thing,
> if I may bring it up, because it relates both to what R
> is saying and to the things that you're interested in [X].

Many of us may be developing gripes against the company ourselves. Because when the chips are down, the kind of a group that you have here always makes the difference. It's very easy to draw a blueprint somewhere, and you [X] have so many other resources to deal with the situation. But in the last analysis, we know that the buck stops here, in effect.

People added more examples of the pressures on them. C summarized by saying that "these are not easy times." I agreed and said that it was my hope that if the project worked effectively, they could develop ways to decrease the pressures on themselves. F responded that the interventionist had not been around for a long time. "Things have changed; everybody feels free to raise everything with me now."

I then suggested that I might return and make some new observations to study the differences. If things had changed, then I would agree that I was not needed. "But," I added, "I doubt that things have changed that much." F responded, "I think things have changed dramatically in the last two months." Then F spoke of another fear he had about the presence of the interventionist.

F: I feel that when you come down to our organization, things open up. My people have always complained. I was a professional for many years. Anyone around this table will tell you this—that they've always complained. It's the nature of the men to complain about their bosses. They complain about their fellow professionals. They complain about anything you can think about. When they know that someone is there to listen to complaints, the complaints come—and an antagonism builds up. Almost an artificial antagonism.

X: I have several reactions to your comments. One is that the behavior I observed in the meetings you led is not much different from behavior I've observed in other corporations with other executives. And I've seen things happen there which are similar to the things that happen here. So either things systematically get distorted in all organizations as soon as I arrive, or things are not being distorted systematically. Perhaps I saw some bit of truth, some bit of reality that was important enough to look at. I guess I need to defend the possibility that they may be acting, but I doubt that there is that much of it.

C: But I keep coming back to this point. I invite you [X] again to sit down with us and go through, you know, minute by minute, what we do. And then after you do that and have, you know, some feel for what we're doing, then I'll have the confidence I need—conversational confidence I mean, I'm not speaking about personal confidence, obviously. And I think then we'd be talking about concrete things.

X: I have no problem with that; I've done that with quite a few people in this room. I buy that.

R: I have two advantages over the rest of this group which are not typical, but I'll tell you what they are. The first is that I've been through a three-day session which I found interesting. The second is that I'm your boss. As you know, I saw the interventionist as a threat to me. I told you that I've never reread the report that he wrote; it hurt me so much that I haven't reread it even to this day. I saw myself everywhere in that report. Therefore there was some truth in it. Everything I saw that was bad, or mean, or domineering, I said, "Shit, that's me, that bastard!" and so on. I no longer see him as a threat. I'm not sure whether anybody in this group regards the interventionist as a threat to them. I would rather doubt it, and yet it may be so.

X: I feel that.

C: Do you perceive yourself as a threat?

X: I feel that I am threatening to some people around the table.

C: You perceive that we regard you as a threat?

X: Yes, but it varies in amount with individuals and with different conditions.

At that point F asked a question which surprised me. "Do you regard anything said here tonight as opposition? E has expressed himself in opposition to some of the things you reported. Certainly I've said things that can be construed that way. Do you recognize any validity at all in what we say?" I was about to respond that I recognized that they felt their view was valid but that what troubled me were the inconsistencies, but before I could respond, C added that he didn't believe that behavioral science was a science and "it's only fair to begin with what my prejudices are." X said, "I don't feel bad because people have genuine questions and concerns about my field and my views. I do believe [turning to F] that there is validity in what you are saying, and I also think there is resistance—both."

B then joined E in questioning the advisability of the program, but the reasons he suggested added a new dimension, one that partially contradicted the view that they did not, as individuals, have interpersonal difficulties: "I think we would become more aware of some of our shortcomings, our abrasiveness and so on. I'm not at all sure that it would help us, that just becoming aware of something is going to help you to a solution of that problem. For example, I'm aware of a certain amount of my abrasiveness, to a point where after I've been that way I get angry with myself and say, 'My God, if I had to contend with B, wouldn't it be terrible.' [Sometimes after a discussion with R], for example, I see personal ambitions that I have, and I say, 'Jesus Christ, you're despicable, and if I were in his place, I'd hate you.' I'm aware of it. I'm sure that I have a lot of other shortcomings. But you know, I can't help myself just because I'm aware of these problems. It may be my state of life and I'm hardened into it." Some of the more important messages in B's comments were these: he has feelings of self-disparagement and resignation about change; he expects that a program to increase personal awareness would be more painful and cause even more pressures on individuals; and he thinks that an awareness of problems is sufficient to change behavior. (I could have taken the opportunity to illustrate with B's comments that self-awareness without self-acceptance may lead to self-disparagement.)

B's view that time was a critical factor was supported by A, and I repeated that the group would be in control of the amount of time that they spent (again I missed the more important issues of self-disparagement, self-resignation, and so on).

C then raised a new issue: "If I tried something new, wouldn't they perceive me as putting on one of my phoniest performances ever?" I agreed that phony behavior would be dysfunctional. Indeed, the objective would be to develop changes in one's own behavior, but it is also true that genuine changes do not occur overnight. Thus, there would be a period of time when the behavior would be experimental and not genuine. During the transition period, it would be important for the subordinates to be invited to give C, or anyone else, feedback when they believed their superior was acting phony. C would have to invite his subordinates to give such feedback, and to make this invitation openly would mean that C would have to admit that he was trying to become more effective. With this, we come to one of the most difficult problems for many of these men—making an *open* admission that they were not as effective as they wished they were and that they wanted to alter their behavior. This reluctance is understandable given their predisposition to be competitive and to create systems with win-lose dynamics. Making an admission of ineffectiveness, to subordinates, would probably seem to them a sign of weakness. Moreover, there is the simultaneous fear that their subordinates would also see them as weak and ineffective. Competitive individuals would tend to be threatened by these conditions, because they could be interpreted as laying the basis for loss of control.

R then observed, "There's something funny about this meeting." He pointed out that the people who were usually very vocal were not, and that some of the behavior seemed more defensive than he had expected. B responded by attempting a historical explanation. He reminded everyone, "We've just been through a period of great turbulence. People have gotten scared. While there might be benefits to be gained, this was a time the group could benefit from quietude rather than from further discussion." He continued by saying that, in the name of organizational effectiveness, many people hurt each other. "Now the situation has changed dramatically in two ways. We have come into much quieter waters. The other is that we have a new and more direct but informal leadership style. [Gone are two people who, each in his own way, inhibited this group.] Now we are confronted by a diagnosis that was developed during that period."

Agreeing that some changes must have occurred over time, I added that I had some data which suggested that the basic issues identified in the report still remained valid. E shook his head negatively, and R said, "I feel things have changed dramatically. No question about it in my mind."

I then asked R if he would invite me to conduct some new research to study and document the changes. R said he was not sure, and asked me what I felt might be the impact of a new set of observations and interviews. I responded that I would be concerned about the impact that a new set of interviews might have; if nothing has occurred that is connectable with the first diagnosis, persons might feel annoyed about going through another round of interviews. As for observations, I said I felt that these could have a positive effect, especially if R told his group that he was inviting me to help him be a more effective executive and the group to become more effective.

R's response not only indicated clear resistance to the idea but, it seemed to me, raised serious questions about how healthy and effective the new climate was in R's department: "I've worked very hard these last three to four months to stabilize the climate. I've put a tremendous amount of energy into this, and time, and a great deal of effort. Not only myself, but every other executive. We've tried to use our own amateur psychology. The staff is more or less, as far as I can see it now, at a point where I wouldn't want things upset."

I turned to G and asked him how he would evaluate the validity of the report. G's response supported my conclusion that the report was still valid and supported B's, C's, E's, and F's belief that the impact of the program on the group might be damaging to its effectiveness: "I think my general reaction would be that there is still truth in what you had to say then. At the same time what concerns me, as a result of being here tonight is, I think, what B has touched on. That [loss of effectiveness] may be the price we'd pay to come to grips with this problem; it might be a small one, but it is going to be too hard on us because of the [recent turbulence] within this group and within the organization. I don't know."

Before I could ask the group members if they felt as G

did, R said that he was becoming increasingly perplexed by the discussion. If the two people who had inhibited the group were no longer in the group, if this group now had new and open leadership, then what was the problem?

R: Have we removed the elements of fear among ourselves? We don't fear each other. I don't believe we do. Are people afraid of me? . . . Has something inhibited us tonight?

C: I pretty well know what my problems are, and there are some of them that I don't want solved in a convenient way.

R: What do you mean?

C: There are certain people whom I can mollify, and my aim is to mollify them.

R: You're assuming he's going to tell you how to softsoap everybody.

C: No, I don't know.

R: He won't tell you anything as a matter of fact.

E: I'm going out and when I come back, I'm going to make a major pronouncement. [laughter.]

C: I've pretty well isolated my problems. I now have to think through my problems, how to solve them in the best way. Some will get solved, some I'll let drift and they'll solve themselves.

Defining the decision-making process and making a decision. R then pointed out that the meeting was in its fourth hour and perhaps the time had arrived to think about coming to some conclusion. He asked the group if they would turn their thoughts to the processes by which the decision might be made. Personally, he did not favor a vote, but he was not sure about the most effective way to make the decision.

The response to his question was very illuminating. Almost everyone said that the correct process was for R to make the decision.

B: As far as the decision is concerned, each one of us has to say to what extent this meets our needs, including you, R. I think you have to say, as the director and the guy

who runs this team, whether you think it's going to help
you personally as well as the team as a whole, and then
we arrive at a consensus.

C: I don't think you [R] can duck the responsibility. . . . I
   think ultimately it's got to be your decision since you're
   not going to have—this is not the kind of thing where
   it'll be a yes-no vote.

F: I think this is a very close group. We all know each other
   very well. And I think *you* have to make the decision.

R: So I decide, huh? E?

E: Yeah, I think a case can be made both ways. If it were a
   democratic vote, then I'll get to vote against it.

R: You think it should be done on a vote basis?

E: No, but I really think that despite the vote, if a director
   feels that this [project] would be beneficial in his relationships, then we ought to do it no matter what.

G: I don't think it should be done unless we have the unanimous consent of F, E, and D, because I think we're
   essentially talking about their relationships, relationships with their subordinates. And I think if they are
   not willing to pursue this, or don't think it's worth it
   for whatever reasons, then I think it would be a
   frustrating effort, worthless.

D: I have one postscript to my earlier comments. I don't
   really believe that the decision, the final decision, really
   should be his [R's] in a sense. And the reason I say
   that is because if the final decision is his, in the face
   of an unwillingness of a substantial number of people
   around this table to go forward, it's not going to work.
   We need a consensus in order to make the process
   work.

R: What consensus?

D: Well, a consensus would be that everybody feels that it is
   useful enough to be worth the effort, even though they
   have some doubts about it.

R: [to X] How would one arrive at a decision like this?

X: I think that as a minimum, everybody has to agree that
   for himself, it's worthwhile enough that he won't hold
   R responsible for his attendance. If an individual can
   hold R personally responsible, even in the most subtle
   way, for his being there, then he will hold R reason-

sible, and indirectly me, for the success or failure of the learning activities. Under these conditions, the activities will probably not be very effective. And you could be harming yourselves rather than helping yourselves.

R: I'm not sure I agree.

X: I think there was a high degree of commitment that you [R] make the decision. . . . The feeling I have is that if you ask this group, the preferred way of making a decision about this is for you to make it.

R: You don't approve of that?

X: Oh no, I wouldn't do it under these circumstances. You could be harming yourself.

R: I don't see that at all.

X: Well, OK.

R: I feel that's not the way to do it, but I don't see what harm I'd be doing myself.

X: I would feel that I would be held responsible for [cut off]

R: I'm not talking about you, I'm talking about me.

X: I'm talking first about me. They'll expect me to make the session work, and you [R] know the process—it must be in their hands, and it must be in their control. And if they're waiting for me, you know what will happen. I'm not going to be doing very much on that level. And I think they're going to be saying, "What the hell did we come here for?" I want to make my position clear. I don't think I would want to be part of any session in which the group isn't genuinely committed to experimenting and learning.

R: Why not?

X: Because it seems to me that would be a violation of the very thing that I believe in, namely that every individual has a right to really have personal responsibility for his decision.

R: You get unanimity in all cases?

X: The cases I work with, we strive to the point where there is unanimity to try, to experiment. There need *not* be unanimity that it's going to work.

R: Let me put the question—and if it's not the right question, let's change the question, OK?—The question is, and I'll address it individually, do you think that there is, are you interested in making an initial commitment to our organization to pursue the question of whether or not the techniques that the interventionist has been talking about would help us in any way? That is, with the staff, with each other, whatever. It would be an open-ended thing because obviously we might find ourselves talking about each other. In other words, do you think you're going to get anything out of this? And are you willing, if you're not positive—what a question!—to put time into it? Yes or no is what I'm talking about. Awful question, terrible question.

X: It's an awfully loaded question.

R: Terrible question, I don't, what the hell—you want to go on with this or don't you want to go on with this? Isn't that what the hell the question is?

X: I think that's what you're feeling.

B: The ground rules for going into this thing have been stated by the interventionist. And that's why I said . . . that I think you almost have to have a consensus on the thing to go into it, otherwise from the point of view of personal commitment and involvement the procedure isn't going to work.

R: I might have said I really don't think it's going to work but I'm interested in going into it. What's wrong with that?

X: I have heard this frequently among members in groups that are willing to take risks. I have not heard it tonight. That's why I would want to support B's perception. My perception is that this group is saying that the interventionist can't really guarantee a success, and we need a lot more information than he was able to give us tonight. I'm saying that the information they want they they can get by participating, but they're not interested in doing that. And so I think B is right; we shouldn't do it.

D: I'm not sure. I think we're not willing to take a risk, possibly. But I think there's also the fact, which may be stronger, that the group doesn't believe it will work.

X: Perhaps these aren't separable. Let me try it another way. Let me ask you to face my dilemma. I don't believe these learning experiences are effective if anyone is even mildly coerced. I think the best kind of learning comes when individuals are saying to R and to themselves, "I'm not sure this is going to work, but I think it's important enough that we ought to try it. I'm not holding you responsible; I'll give it a try. But if I see it's not helpful, I want to tell you I'm going to blow the whistle." That's the minimum commitment I get with the groups that I decided to work with.

R: All right, so what's the question? Are we willing to, do you want to go ahead with this thing? Is that the question? Are you willing at this point to invest the time and energy to go ahead with this, knowing what you know and knowing what you don't know? Is that a fair question?

X: Sure, a very fair question. But I also feel—I'm concerned about the dynamics, because I trusted the other answer as being genuine.

R: What's your answer, B?

B: My answer is no and for the very simple reason that the dynamics I sense around this table right now are that it won't work and that it won't be useful.

R: C?

C: I give you a flat no.

R: Well, obviously, this decision has not been taken.

X: Well, it might be reconsidered someday, but I think it's been taken.

R: I would still be willing; obviously my answer is yes. But it's one, two, three, four, five against; one firm yes and one who, I don't know whether it was yes before and no now, or vice versa. All right, take two. I'd be willing because I do have a responsibility and also because I think you would trust me to take a decision to reverse it and ask you to reverse it. Except that X [the interventionist] enters into this. He wouldn't do it.

X: I wouldn't do it. I can give you names of people who might.

It seemed to me that R was very disappointed about the way the decision had gone. Once I refused to participate in a session where R asked his subordinates to attend, he turned to examining the reasons for the vote. His disappointment and frustration became evident in the manner and content of his questions.

R: All right. I don't think this group has shown itself. [pause] You're certainly competent to make the decision the same way as any group—but I'm puzzled; you don't know what the hell's taking place at a meeting like this! That's what puzzles the hell out of me. The answer is no, we're not going to do it. OK? But what do you lose? Now that the decision's been taken, what would we have lost? Is this worth discussing? What the hell would we have lost? A lousy weekend. Maybe we would have won something. What the hell would you have lost, F, by sitting up there. . . .

F: Maybe the problem is that we lack time.

R: We have plenty of time to do it. I think we piss away a lot of time. We confront each other at the wrong times, then when we do get together, we don't use time well. Now what I was saying, what I meant was, I feel that this is a very good group, the best group of people I've ever worked with in my life.

Interviews after the meeting. R was feeling disappointed after the session. He asked me about the next steps. I replied that the group members had made a decision and that should be respected. R wondered if he could have said something that might have swung the meeting the other way. I asked him if he could think of an example, and he said he could not. Then he voiced bewilderment that F could invite me to study his group and yet swear that he had offered no such invitation. (The transcript indicates that he gave at least two such invitations.) R was also surprised by G's anger and vindictiveness. Then R listed some factors he thought might have caused the resistance: pressures from publishing a paper; pressures from cost control; pressures from trying to design a new paper; economic conditions; a history of very ineffective relationships.

    Several days later, I had an opportunity to obtain each person's reactions to the meetings. B expressed surprise about the decision. He felt certain that the members would eventually agree. But then he added that he felt certain that R did *not* want the meetings to occur. I asked him why R would then call the meeting. He said because the President was probably pressuring R. This surprised me because I had no indication from anyone that the President was pressuring R. Also I doubted that the President was pressuring R, and if he were, I doubted that R would succumb to such pressure. B told me that he told this to R, who expressed great surprise and added that this proved that they did not understand each other because he very much wanted the program. But B still did not believe R. Moreover, he added that he questioned the advisability of the program because "there remained old wounds and scars within the group."

B gave several examples related to F's behavior. Apparently, one of F's subordinates came to B to appeal what he considered an injustice against him committed by F. The subordinate did not feel free to talk to F. B said that he would help him if he promised to keep this appeal to him confidential. B did not want to seem as if he were meddling in F's affairs.

The depth of the difficulties began to become clearer to me. Here was B, who was so convinced that F could not deal effectively with a valid problem that he was willing to collude with the employee and secretly arrange to help him. Not only did this raise serious questions about B's assertion (made during the meeting) that the group members were open with each other, but it undercut F's relationship with his subordinate and denied him an opportunity to learn. B was aware of these potential negative consequences, but he was certain that F's competence in these matters would not permit an open discussion. He felt it was necessary to use the "slightly deceptive approach, perhaps deceptive is not the correct word, perhaps tactical."

I asked if he had considered talking directly with F. B replied that he had little confidence in such an approach. He added that F had decided to exercise tight personal control over his department because he wanted to show his superiors that in addition to being a very creative editor (which everyone believed) he was an effective manager (which some doubted). F wanted to show that his department was free from tension, even though there might be heightened feelings of mistrust. B repeated again that he did not like the role of working behind F's back, but that F's people had been so infuriated with F in the past that they wanted peace and would not want to rock the boat by confronting F.

E began his discussion with me by saying, "As you know, I came into that meeting with my mind made up and you were not going to dissuade me. Also, I think my department now has much better morale and I don't want anything upsetting the boat." He continued that the learning sessions I was suggesting could do harm because the group had just been through a lot of political maneuvering and there were scars. He gave examples of how he had had to "steal people" from others in the group and relationships had become strained. "Moreover," he added, "I believe that each editor should remain autonomous and we should not become a team."

E also said that he was very much worried about F's participation in the sessions. "F is a very volatile guy; he gives off sparks, always has, always will; there's no way of changing him. He's a very, very bright editor. We need him, so let's get along with his faults."

E also said that he believed R did not want the meeting held, although he assigned the responsibility for the meeting to me and not to the President. E also felt that I had made a mistake when I "forced F to undress in front of the group. That was painful." I was surprised, because I did not recall doing this to F or anyone else.

X: What did I say that forced F to undress?
E: You didn't say anything. But when he started to talk, you didn't stop him. I found that personally painful. But no, I don't think you forced him. . . . You handled it very well, but I just don't think this sort of thing was a good idea.
X: Do you think that there may ever be a time when we can involve F in these attributions?
E: Nope.

I began to understand that E may have his own fears in this area. Thus, I didn't force F to "undress" but I didn't prevent him from talking and saying things that were painful to E. Perhaps E had similar fears about himself. E indirectly corroborated this guess later, when he said, "Also, if I get into such a meeting, I might say things that I don't want to say. There are things that I don't want to come out. I have a good working relationship with the group and I don't want it upset."

I asked if it would be fair to conclude that there was almost nothing that I could say that would be convincing. E responded affirmatively, and then added more information about his lack of confidence in the group members: "It's nothing that you did or would do. Place these people in this situation and they can harm F." E ended by inviting me to study his group and give feedback to the entire group. "I'm just trying to protect others; I guess that I must sound like God. But I think that I have at heart the best interests of the newsroom."

C said in our interview that he was not surprised with the outcome of the meeting. He repeated his genuine doubts about the value of social science techniques, but quickly added "Let me emphasize that I, and all the others, feel that you're a very likeable guy—indeed, a thoroughly good human being. During the first several meetings I even wondered if you were for real."

C said that none of the editors had been trained to be managers. He believed that there would be more difficulties in the future because financial constraints would reduce departmental autonomy and increase interdependence.

He also invited me to study his group any time I wanted to, and predicted that his people would rate him high as a manager. (Two other members of this group said that C's people rated him low to "lousy" as a leader, and did not believe that he could be told this directly.)

C also believed that the sessions could open up old wounds. "It's like the old unfaithful wife story; she tells you she strayed but has stopped it now. What's the sense of bringing it up again?" I said that in my judgment the problem here was that she says she has stopped but she hasn't. C ended the interview with a statement that I could not relate to the substantive issues discussed during the meeting. However, it was said with a strong sense of emotion: "As I told you before and as I tell my people, the paper will break your goddam heart. The paper does not owe you a goddam thing. I tell my people that they should work like hell because that is what they really want."

G, in my interview with him, also expressed surprise over the hostility and vehemence of E and C. He wondered, too, why I had not made a presentation that would have guaranteed the group some measure of success. (After listening to the interviews, I was pleased that I had resisted the temptation to make such a presentation.) He said that the group members behaved secretly, that there was much they did not tell R or each other. He believed the group members felt that R was pressured into holding the meeting by the President. He guessed that their biggest fear was that a new session might open up old wounds. He believed that they (not "we") were afraid of what they are capable of doing to each other. What they feared most, he thought, was hearing criticism from each other: "Take C, for example. He's a terrible boss. He has many problems with his subordinates. His subordinates have learned to say yes to him and then do it their own way. Would it help C to learn this? I doubt it!"

I repeated that I did not believe criticism or "clobbering" of people is helpful. But what, I asked, would lead them to believe that is what would happen? G answered that he believed that if they were honest with each other, they will necessarily hurt each other. He ended by saying, "The more I think about it, we seem to be swinging from fear of punishment to diplomacy. And I guess diplomacy doesn't work either."

D reported in our interview that the resistance had been greater than he had expected and blamed A and me for not being more convincing and compelling. This theme ran through many of the meetings. Subordinates were ready and willing to have superiors control them and make decisions; they could then continue to withhold personal initiative and commitment to the organization.

D did not believe that anyone had pressured R. Nor did he believe in the sincerity of C's, E's, and F's invitations to study their groups. "It was a way to put you off." D's biggest criticism was that the meeting was not structured by me or by R and me. Then he said,

D: I prefer to be perfectly candid.
X: Candid about what?
D: I like to pursue free trains of thought. I don't want to be constrained!

I then asked him how he had felt when E had said that he was not concerned with his problems.

D: I was surprised. He has similar problems.
X: Why didn't you say so?
D: Well, perhaps I don't want to be candid.

D concluded by assuring me of his interest in the program, especially if it could lead him to get one more column of space!

Finally, I met F. He reported that he was surprised by E's "tremendous resistance and the power of his rejection. He behaved as if he were protecting someone." I asked him why he did not mention these feelings during the session. He replied that he had seen no point to it, *and* "those people have weak egos and you have to be careful." He believed that now was not the right time for a session to explore communication because of "past emotional upheavals" and "scars."

F then turned to his own department. He repeated that "things *are very much* better" and said "it is easy to voice discontent in my shop without it becoming a problem." (F spent a good deal of time, however, telling me that he was concerned about a researcher interviewing his subordinates.) He then said that he felt that he had learned a lot since I had come to the organization; he is now more open, encourages communication, and listens more. He added that many of his reporters are in need of help. He believed that 10 percent of his staff were getting some sort of psychiatric help. Then: "But to return to the topic, I really think things are much better. I'm more frank with people." (Note that he does not say whether people are more candid with him.) A few minutes later, F admitted that he feared my coming into his group could cause his sub-editors to wonder if there was something wrong.

I asked F if he would describe what it was about the sessions that he feared. The ensuing dialogue was instructive for its openness and honesty, and showed a strength to express fears that others were not able to muster.

F: Well, what if you changed my behavior and made me a less
       effective editor?
X: I can now better understand some of your fears about me.
F: Yes, I've given this a lot of thought. You know, this is one
       of the most demanding jobs on the paper. I can't take
       a pee without someone stopping me.
X: How could I make you change your behavior if you didn't
       want to change it?
F: I don't know. I feel this way. You're telling me to be
       honest with you.
X: Yes, I value your responses highly.
F: Let's say you make me work at a slower pace. I don't think
       this job is manageable without a fast pace.

I tried to explain again that I had no interest in trying to coerce people to change or to move at a slower or faster pace. I wanted to help them to be in a world where they could obtain the valid information they needed to make free and informed decisions. F noded understandingly and said that he had heard me say this before, and from what little he understood about the seminar, I tried not to coerce people into anything. Then, "You know, the more I think about this, the more I realize that maybe I don't want you to study me. It'll make me self-conscious."

F next described how he had disliked being evaluated from a very early age. I then asked him to return to the case of the reporter who didn't do well. I asked him if he would role-play a bit about how he dealt with the man. He agreed. His face took on a very scornful look and he said, in effect, "You haven't been doing well; you've got to tighten up your work; I expected you to do much better than you have, you've let me down." I told F that during the role-playing I felt punished and guilty. He looked surprised, laughed softly, and said, "So I may do to others what I dislike others doing to me." He then tried to role-play a new approach, but before I could respond, he stopped and said that again he was being evaluative and punishing. The interview with F ended shortly after this.

Conclusions drawn from the meetings and interviews. There are several major threads that run through these data. The first is the knot of inconsistencies between what was said in the group meetings and what was said in the interviews. What follows is a list of all the inconsistencies uncovered from the transcripts. In the left column are statements made in the *meetings* by at least two of the six group members; in the right column are statements made by at least two members in personal *interviews* with us.

We are a group that understands each other. We understand each other even without talking. We know each other well.	We don't want to say things that might hurt our relationships with others. We behave in ways that range from fear of punishment to diplomacy. I'm not really sure how the others would have responded.
We trust each other.	People do things secretly around here. There is a lot that we don't tell each other. I think we may be afraid of what we can do to each other if we really leveled.
Things are much better in our department. Morale is much higher.	Yes, there is a decrease in tension but there is an increase in mistrust. I predict a blow-up in two years.
We face issues squarely.	There are some big professional egos in our group. We're always externalizing causes; the problems are always out there.

People are our most important resources.	The truth is that most of us cannot put this learning project on a high priority.
We prefer to make our own decisions.	The subordinates, when asked how how they preferred to vote for the program, asked that R make the decision. Also, those who came to the meeting feeling receptive to the idea of attending an off-site learning experience expected that X or R would say something that was convincing and compelling.

The second major theme evolves around F. All of F's peers considered him bright but extremely sensitive. All but one believed that he was a poor administrator, that the causes lay deep in his personality and were unchangeable, and that F's job is the most demanding one on the news side of the organization. Most of F's peers did not believe that they should be candid with him in a group setting because it would embarrass him terribly. During my interview with F, he resisted the idea of exploring his leadership style with his peer group, even though he liked what he was learning from me. Perhaps this validates their fears.

Let us assume that F would be harmed by an exploration of his leadership behavior in front of his peer group. If this assumption were proved correct, it would tend to invalidate the group members' view that they were open and cohesive. This raises a question. Why couldn't the group members find a way to make an invitation of this sort: "We need this help, but we respect your discomfort with such learning; so you could join us and take only an observer's role, or you could choose not attend, and let us try to learn in our meetings anyway."

C, D, E, and F all said frankly that they did not have confidence in the idea that people should be more honest in their relationships. All of them spoke of scars from past wounds. When asked to give examples, all of them described cases in which someone had been highly evaluative and attributive, and had imposed his own meaning on reality. Thus one could understand why wounds could be opened.

When I agreed with them that this type of behavior is destructive but can be changed, the editors expressed grave doubts. They believed that the causes of such behavior lay in early personality development and hence the behavior was unchangeable except perhaps by prolonged psychotherapy. Thus they had little motivation for exploring new behavior.

One also gets the impression that the most common way each member dealt with his and others' competitive win-lose behavior was to suppress his own behavior, to strive to ignore the impact that others have upon him, or to excuse others' behavior ("we're all under pressure"). Acting in these ways could produce, on the surface, a climate of tolerance and patience. Below the surface, however, the individuals could be seething with frustration and anger. As these feelings build up, the individuals will have to generate more and stronger defensive behaviors in order to avoid blowing up. As E pointed out, another of his fears about the program was that a session might cause him to say things to others that would not be very helpful and would not encourage others to be helpful.

Why didn't group members strive to create a climate in which they could work on their individual leadership skills without threatening F or rejecting him? Perhaps one reason was that the members were not much more interpersonally competent than F. If they explored their group dynamics, they would have to face doing, saying, or *not* saying to each other things that were not particularly helpful. For example, two members questioned C's leadership skills. Three members reported that D enjoyed bringing up his personal problems because he liked to attract attention to himself. Two members questioned whether E was as effective as R believed, and so on.

The third theme is the consonance between the behavior in the group's meetings with the interventionists and the superior-subordinate relationships as seen by the subordinates. The members "fought" R and the interventionist with the same dynamics that the subordinates felt their superiors used on them. For example, the subordinates stated in the interviews that when they were invited by a senior person to be candid, and when they did so and their views were in disagreement with his, he did not tend to listen to their views or explore them, but instead attempted to rebut them, especially by using information that was beyond the immediate reach of the subordinate.

The members reacted with the interventionist in the same way. They began by acting interested, by asking questions, and by listening. But when their questions were answered, or when an inconsistency in their behavior or views was pointed out, they ignored it or brought up a point whose content they could not independently validate. Thus the superior depended on "winning" by expecting the subordinate not to question his view of the world.

To give another example, the subordinates had difficulty with the apparent defensiveness of their superiors about exploring new issues, especially given their superior's professional and organizational position. Thus the frustration and bewilderment that R felt with his editors—"What do they have to lose? Nothing!—was exactly what the subordinates felt when their superiors became defensive for no apparent reason. The subordinates reported that when they arrived at an apparent impasse, the superiors tended to react with, "Be patient; things are getting better. It used to be worse. Trust me and give me a chance. Let's not rock the boat."

Finally, there were the gaps between what people said and how they behaved. For example, if it was true, as many of the members stated, that this was a group with high openness, trust, and cohesiveness, then (1) the views individuals held about each other would be accurate and stated openly, or (2) if an individual got information that disconfirmed his views about others, he would tend to discuss it in order to get clarification.

In re-examining the typescripts, I was able to identify the following situations that could have provided data to confirm or disconfirm the group members' diagnosis.

(1) Three members believed that R did not want the program. Although they admitted that R had said that he wanted it, several times over several hours, they did not believe him

nor did they discuss the issue with him at the meetings. Two of them did discuss the issue with R after the meeting, and he assured them that he wanted the meeting. A week later these two reported to me that they did not believe him.

(2) When I asked them what forces they saw acting on R to make him go ahead with the program if he did not want it, they responded that the President was probably pushing him. Yet they did not feel they could discuss this diagnosis with R.

(3) Several members *did* believe R and did not see him as being coerced by the President. Although they were aware of the others' diagnosis, they did not want to challenge it and work through it because, as one stated, "It might upset people and would probably do no good."

(4) Four members reported that they were very surprised by the strength of E's anger toward the program, yet none of them felt free to discuss this with E during the meetings.

(5) Four members reported four different surprises about others' views or reactions during the meeting, yet none of them discussed these openly.

(6) All but two men believed strongly that the program could hurt F; that F had greatly improved but was still very sensitive; and that it would not be worthwhile to slowly and carefully test this view of F's brittleness in discussing his leadership style.

(7) B had an opportunity to discuss "the Mr. W case" with F. However, he not only refused to discuss it with F, but colluded with W, and joined R and W, in colluding to keep the solution they developed away from F (who, the reader may recall, was W's immediate superior).

(8) E insisted, during the meeting, that the editors were a highly cohesive group. Yet he said that he didn't want to discuss D's problems, and didn't feel he could learn anything from such discussions; and he told me that it would be an incorrect strategy to weld the editors into a cohesive group—the best way to manage the entire division was to leave each editor alone, and if any editor needed to make contacts with others, he could do so on a one-to-one basis.

(9) During the interview, F reported several examples

of "significantly more open" relationships with his subordinates. But I experienced them as open in only one direction—F may have been more open, but not in a way that encouraged his subordinates to be more open. F agreed with my points.

(10) During an interview with me, R said that he had asked for suggestions from all the editors about improvements. He received extensive notes from one editor, but said he found them "trivial" and was going to file them away. He said he had no interest in discussing this opinion with the author of the notes, but he agreed with me that such a silence might well be interpreted by the author as indicating a low opinion of the notes.

About two months after the long meeting, I had several discussions with F, at his request, to explore questions of leadership style and indexes of effectiveness within his department. During these sessions, F explored openly and effectively important leadership issues, including his own commitment to perfection. During these few sessions he showed a high capacity to understand himself. It was ironic that this man, whom all the group members (except R) were certain was oversensitive, unreachable, volatile, and brittle, was the only one who took some initiative to develop himself.

During one of our sessions, F asked me if it was true that the group members saw him as brittle and oversensitive, and did not want to hold the diagnostic session for his sake. I said yes, that was true, but explained that I couldn't tell him which group members had said so, or what they had said. He said he understood that, but wondered how he could learn more about why they felt the way they did. I suggested that one step would be to meet with the group and ask them that question.

F: Wow, I'm not sure that I can do that.
X: It won't be an easy meeting, but it could be a very profitable one for you and for them. If the other group members realize your personal strengths, perhaps they will have to ask why they had diagnosed you as uninfluenceable and unchangeable.

F agreed that the idea made sense, but said he remained uncomfortable about asking for such a meeting. I responded that I understood and would certainly not press this idea beyond our relationship. Later F asked if it would be a good idea for him to talk with R first, to sound him out. I supported the idea and the meeting was held. F described the idea directly to R, who responded very positively to it. F explained that he didn't want to do anything to harm his relationship with his peers, especially since they were becoming easier to deal with during the last three months (an observation confirmed by four of his peers during my second interviews). R said that he understood that wish, and would explore the matter more in terms of his own inquiry. I added that I would be glad to be of help, and that I was glad relationships between F and the others were becoming easier, but that if they were to become more effective, issues like these would have to be openly discussable. I reiterated that the others stood as good a chance to learn more about themselves and their relationships with each other as F did about himself and his relationships with them.

I suggested that I should also interview each of the individuals to obtain a sense of where they stood about possible next steps. This would be expected by them, since I had suggested during our last interviews that I would take another reading in several months. The second series of interviews confirmed, as I mentioned above, that most of them felt that F was "less uptight." Also the anger and resistance toward individual and group developments were reduced. However, there was no positive commitment, no sense of seeing these activities as worth experimenting with, and only a slightly higher sense of curiosity. Interestingly, during the period that I was conducting the second round of interviews, I learned that two of the members were having serious difficulties with their subordinates, and that these subordinates were uncomfortable about confronting their respective superiors any further.

R's soundings were somewhat more positive, but not so much more so as to suggest that a meeting should be held. I met with F and told him that I believed the only way a meeting to discuss the issues could be held was for him to ask for it. He seemed reluctant to discuss the issues, especially in the group. He said that if he explored them, he would do so in one-to-one relationships.

I concluded from these experiences that the members

had created a group whose dynamics and norms were defensive (because they emphasized such behavior as not being open, lying to others, and mistrusting others). Moreover, the members made many attributions about each other which they rarely tested openly. The probability that they would obtain valid feedback was therefore low. Inconsistencies were frequent, were frequently denied, and were rarely discussed. The predisposition toward self-sealing processes was very high.

I also concluded that these individuals could use help in becoming more effective, but that the help would have little chance of succeeding because they were not internally committed to learning. Moreover, it would be difficult to help a group whose members simultaneously rejected the help because the process could harm F, who lied that they were trying to protect F, who refused to test their hypothesis about F, and who preferred to remain a group in which covert manipulation and artful stealing was a norm and when successfully carried out, brought praise from others.

These group dynamics illustrate the dilemma created for the interventionist who values free choice and internal commitment. Given these values, defensive groups, like this one, may choose to ignore self-examination and self-renewal. Yet such learning would be important for their effective functioning.

Some have suggested that the interventionist should push harder and pressure the individuals to attend learning seminars. I doubt the advisability of this strategy. Indeed, the material in this chapter represents, I believe, evidence that group members cannot be forced to learn. The members killed the possibilities of learning during the session and united to place the blame primarily on the interventionist. People who are genuinely closed to being open cannot be made to be more open. Nor should one make such attempts because, out of self-protection, the members may, at best, go along with the education, only to reject it at a later date. At worst, some members could strive to learn the rhetoric of openness and trust in order to manipulate people even more subtly. Another reason, therefore, *not* to push for the group members to attend the learning sessions is to protect the more helpless and less powerful subordinates from new strategies of manipulation.

I believed that the relationships within the group and between these members and their subordinates would get worse: at some point, another cabal might develop, new pressures might be created through professional unions, and more professionals might become more difficult to deal with or might withdraw from participation in order to use the paper as a base for larger operations.

Finally, there was the issue of the choices to be made by the top management people. Would they choose to alter the quality of their relationships? If they would not, would not this group have good reason to fear that learning new behavior would only compound their problems?

Let us turn to the top and see.

11

The Top Group

My involvement with R and his group postponed the meeting with the top group for several months. This was partially my responsibility, since I had asked that the meeting not be held until I had developed a more accurate assessment of the interest in R's group. If it remained adamant against undertaking further developmental activities, then the advisability of expanding the program to other parts of the news department seemed questionable.

Several weeks later, I had an interview with the President. I told him that I was ready to meet with the top group. I suggested that if development were to have a respectable chance of occurring at the lower levels of the organization, the top news and editorial officers should first be helped to alter their behavior. If they did so, the impact of their new behavior might help to unfreeze the editors at the next levels and make trying some next steps more worthwhile. He agreed and promised to call such a meeting.

Three more months passed before I heard from the President. He apologized for the delay, saying that several top people had been unavailable because they had been traveling, and asked if I would come in to talk with him. I agreed.

As I walked into his office, P said that he had invited R to the meeting. I was delighted, partly because I knew that R was a strong supporter of the program. P began the meeting with the question that I had promised myself (X) to bring up if P did not do so.

P: I think you know how much we value your relationship with us. We have learned much and I realize that we have a long way to go. It's in the interest of moving forward that I raise the question. I wonder—and I think R would agree with me—how you're going to help us if your visits are now scheduled once every three months. It seems to me that your commitment, and ours, has to be stronger.

X: I'm glad you raised the issue. I agree that the issue of the quality of commitment is an important one. I'm more than willing to increase my visits, but I haven't been invited to continue any of the programs or explore new ideas.

R: I want to support what both of you are saying. I think we need what X represents very badly in the organization. I don't think you're going to help us unless you're here more often, and unless we develop a plan we're committed to. And [turning to P] if the top does not really commit itself to movement, then I doubt if I should take much initiative at my level.

P agreed and said that he was ready to call a meeting. The meeting was scheduled with the top officers of the news and editorial side. I left the meeting very pleased; two of the key people now seemed to be taking more initiative to develop their internal commitment to the program. I also felt that the strategy of placing the responsibility for the success or failure of the program squarely on them was an effective one. The top was confronting the issues, and whatever decision was made would theirs.

The final meeting. The objective of the meeting was for the President and the three top people in the news and editorial departments to explore their commitment to further organizational development activities. The meeting began with a warmup

phase, in which individuals described problems that they felt
were important.

　　Some of these problems were: (1) how to explore further
the President's leadership style; (2) how to regard the fact that
the President seemed more concerned with profits than with the
Planet's stature as an institution; (3) how to understand the
meaning of loyalty; (4) how to deal with an attempt by R to
undo certain prejudices that might have been held by the others
present about one subordinate who was being considered along
with others for an important top position; and (5) how to deal
with the genuine worries some members had about exploring interpersonal issues. Concerning this last problem, one person
present at this meeting admitted to a lifelong disgust with and
mistrust of psychology. Apparently he believed that psychology
can be used as a crutch by persons to explain away or not take
personal responsibility for their actions. I said I wondered why
he saw "psychology" as being responsible, and not the persons
who choose to use psychological knowledge in these ways. I also
said that I thought his interpersonal style of dealing with conflict, which he had described publicly as using diplomacy to
smooth over interpersonal differences, was relevant and should
be discussed at this meeting or a later one.

　　The President then said that several key positions would
have to be filled during the next few years, and he hoped that
the dynamics of choice could be more effective than before. "Let's
not have some of the unfortunate rumors and misconceptions
we've had in the past after announcing a particular promotion.
In order to avoid these, I believe we need to become more effective in our relationships. I asked X to join us to discuss what he
believes are the necessary next steps."

B: As I remember, both of us said, "Well, why don't we see
　　　whether, first, there is a role for X, and second,
　　　whether he can help us avoid this kind of assumption
　　　about what people are. This guy wants this guy, and
　　　this guy's just angling for that—I don't think any of us
　　　can go through that business anymore. I really don't
　　　think we can. It's all too neurotic.
P: We've got to get more specific, it seems to me, if we're

going to have this kind of a discussion. We just can't talk in a vacuum, about who would be an M editor, because unless you go to the outside and select somebody, anyone you select will have an impact on others. Other jobs are going to be coming along. How do we test for other jobs? How do we make up our minds about who should fill in for Mr. G when we come to that? And all the other things that go on here. I think it's an interesting thing to do, and I'm fascinated.

B: I doubt whether that kind of thing, good as it may sound theoretically, can be done by a committee or group. That business of selection of personnel is very much a matter of individual choice. . . .

P: You're going to have to live with anyone that's picked as much as I will. I'd like to hear what you've got to say about it; I may disagree with you, but [cut off].

X: I don't think anything R said suggested that a group had to make the decision. I though R was saying, "How do we get more information to P so that. . . ."

P: I'd rather not make the decision in a little dark room by myself, and then have arguments with you for the next three or four years—"How on earth could you have taken this guy when he does this, this, this, and that, and where the hell are we going with this organization?"

B: Oh, I don't see why you assume you'd have those arguments with me.

P: Because I have. [laughter]

B: I don't know what you're talking about.

B wondered if open discussion of these issues might not undermine loyalty to P. If subordinates were to be loyal to P, then he should select those that *he* wanted, and not those that his group recommended. I suggested that open discussion and loyalty to P need not be separate, or if they had to be, at least P should know why. Moreover, the group could act in the role of a resource person to help P think through what he wanted and what the organization needed.

This led B to express again his concern about "too much" emphasis on interpersonal relationships. R and I said that it was important to face these issues. P agreed. I agreed but added that it was the commitment, and not my program, that had to become internal.

C: Are you saying, if I understand you correctly, that we aren't making much of a commitment?

X: Yes, although the internal commitment varies.

R: So what we need are more, what shall I call them, therapeutic sessions with you.

X: What I'm asking is for some genuine exploration of your uneasiness, in the context of discussing key organizational problems.

R: Well, I'd like to go with that.

B: But if I hear X correctly, he's saying that we are the problem, the first problem. Isn't that right?

P: We'll deal with us as we solve the problem.

R: Would you prefer that we do it the other way [go into a training group]?

X: It's difficult for me to answer that question. But my inference, after experiencing the degree of genuine resistance here, is that this group would be more comfortable working on key organizational problems first and then examining interpersonal relationships. I'm willing to go along if I can be free to bring up the interpersonal issues when they seem important to me. You can, of course, stop discussions of this kind at any time. But if you stop too many of them, then I'll have to say that I can't be of much help.

B: I have a little trouble with this. First of all, I've felt from the beginning, when you came here, you were arguing for openness.

X: Yes.

B: Arguing for men to say honestly what they felt.

X: Yes, but in such a way that others could also be honest about how they felt.

B: Now, having run through this process, I've learned certain things—like what we just talked about right here, what is the honest, open thing to do with your own men when you dicker with your boss. That's useful. But where I get into trouble is that I would tend to say to a person, "Now look, for Christ's sake, don't come barging in here and interrupt the process," but you would say to him, "Now you have to be careful because P feels as if you're being disruptive of the decision-making process." I'm beginning to think for the first time, "I better be careful with P." I thought I was being open all the way through what you were telling me, but then I began thinking, "Gee, then maybe openness is not what this process produces, but maybe just the opposite. It forces you to begin to calculate your actions."

X: Openness can become destructive if only one side is encouraged to be open. And you were open but he wasn't. Openness is an interpersonal issue, not simply a personal one. If you began to have feelings that you have to be careful with P, then these feelings are discussable. As P said, he would have appreciated knowing these feelings partly because he was having doubts about you.

P: But I think there's a piece missing here, which is, how can you both be as open as possible and allow as many people as possible to say what they have to say, and also be effective?

This led C to discuss the behavior of editor Z, who was being critical of *The Daily Planet* in public, and presenting himself as one who could offer expert opinions because he was a high-ranking member of the organization.

C: I felt very strongly that Z should have complete freedom to say anything he wants in his articles that we publish. My objection was that, as a highly ranked member, I felt he was creating a great deal of confusion.

B: I think this is a very old-fashioned idea.

C: You think my idea is old-fashioned?

B: Very old-fashioned.

C: I don't quite understand.

B then responded that he could understand why C might feel this way, given the way they grew up in the communication business. "That day is gone. The new generation will simply not accept it. You can talk to them all you like; it won't do a damn bit of good." R supported C. He felt that Z had publicly stated that no communication media can or should strive to be objective. Yet objectivity was a cornerstone of *Planet* policy. R repeated that Z had the right to hold that opinion, but he wondered if going and making statements in print did not confuse the situation.

R: If Z believes that our role should be one of advocacy, let's discuss it. But what he is doing is, I believe, detrimental to the institution. I think P has a right to ask him to explore his impact on our people and the organization.

B: Well, I agree somewhat. After he made his statement, I told him that he provoked and incited the audience. I thought this was wrong and told him so. And his answer was, "You know how I am. I got carried away."

C: [standing up] I'm really sorry that I have to leave now because we're getting to a critical issue. But before I go, I have to express extreme dissent from your point that is of view. . . . I think [what Z did] goes to the heart of this institution.

B: What would you have done?

C: I would have warned him and if he continued, I would, at the very least, have reduced his rank in the organization.

R: [addressing B] But what Z was doing that was destructive was asking for advocacy reporting, which we ought to be standing against.

I pointed out to them that when Z apologized for being carried away, nothing further was done. If high-ranking employees, especially those with power, are not willing to explore how much personal responsibility they are willing to accept for their own behavior, then why shouldn't subordinates feel free to decline responsibility?

B: Well, all I'm saying to you now is that I do agree with what you say.

Perhaps, I said, the problem is how to help Z become better able to recognize and control the behavior that he himself admits is ineffective. R cut me off to repeat that Z had a right to defend his advocacy position, but should do it within the organization and attempt to influence the people in this room. The discussion became quite heated. Afterwards, much time was spent identifying the issues. I noted that these were the kinds of issues that required thorough discussion and that was the reason why a cohesive and effective top group was necessary. P agreed and asked the group to get on with listing any other issues. This was done. Soon we again came up against the question of their willingness to explore their problem-solving processes while they discussed these issues.

I asked B how he felt about attending a meeting where both substantive and group-process issues were discussed. B said he would feel fine until such a meeting began to examine interpersonal processes related to problem solving. "That's where you and I always break," he said laughingly. B then elaborated on his feelings in a way that led me to point out a dilemma between his position and his behavior.

B: Now if we sit together and talk about the future, that's one thing. But if you want to get me involved in analyzing P or saying whether I'm getting what I need from this fellow or that, I don't know how you put it in psychological terms, then I have doubts because I think it leads to the opposite of openness. One is open and one is calculating, and I hate the calculation.

X: I couldn't agree with you more. I'm not suggesting that you analyze P or anyone else. Indeed, on the basis of my diagnosis I would say that this very kind of covert analyzing of others is going on right now in the system. This organization has one of the most calculating living systems that I've ever been in.

B: Well, I don't agree with your premise.

X: That it isn't?

B: I don't agree at all. What do you mean, calculating?

X: Everything that was in that report that I wrote three years ago.

B: Oh, I see. Well, I did agree with your report.

X: Also, B, I agree with you that there's no spontaneity when you have to calculate and have to worry about what the other guy is wondering. I am not suggesting that we say something in certain ways in order to please others. Indeed, I believe that you [B] have given many examples of times when you have been calculating as a person. Several times during the past years, you have said that when you see conflict, you calculate. You begin to calculate in your own interpersonal relationships how to deal with conflict so that in your view you can get the most out of the people in the room. Second, sometimes what you do has an impact that you may not intend. For example, when you said to C, "That's old-fashioned," I think C heard it as "He's old-fashioned." Now, are you going to say to me, "X, what the hell do I have to do?" "Do I have to worry about the way C hears it?"

B: Except that I think I *do* have to worry about that.

X: All right, you do unless you want C to sit there and think about all the reasons why you called him old-fashioned. Where then do we differ? I'm not talking about psychoanalyzing everybody.

R: I agree with what X says, when you said to C, "That's old-fashioned," I said to myself, "Uh-oh, I'm forty-five years old and I'm old-fashioned, too."

B: Well, I understand that, and this is one of the great values of this sort of thing.

R: May I ask you one thing, B? I can understand your reluctance to do this, but [cut off].

B: I didn't say that. I want to think about it.

A short silence followed and then P asked if the next step was not to set up the meeting. All those present agreed that this was the next step. There was a pause. R turned to me and said:

R: I really admire you. I must tell you that. The desire to stay with us through all these three years—that's great.

X: Thank you. It feels good to give it a try. But I have my ambivalent feelings.

R: If I were him, I would have walked out two years ago, or a year ago.

P: Don't say that. We don't want him to leave.

After three years, then, the top had begun to unfreeze a bit; people who had never talked to each other about certain crucial issues had began to talk; openness about issues of power and the control of scarce resources (as in the case of the new feature) had begun to occur; self-awareness and self-acceptance had begun to increase; sensitivity toward and understanding of others had also increased. However, in some persons the anxiety about discussing feelings and interpersonal issues remained high. After three years the same persons were still expressing doubts about the ultimate usefulness of becoming more open about these types of issues, even though they readily admitted that what little progress had been made could not have occurred without focusing on feelings and interpersonal issues.

12

Looking Back
at the Experiment

After that last meeting held with the top, I received letters and telephone calls assuring me of "everyone's great interest" in continuing the program, but no further discussions were scheduled. According to the President, there were two reasons for this: vacations and extended travel schedules were one; the other and more important one was the process of appointing a new top management team to run the *Planet*. The President wanted me to continue working with this top team. I said I would do so if the top team itself expressed interest in it, and if it seemed highly probable that I could continue my intervention in news and editorial activities. The President agreed to these conditions.

I doubted that the news and editorial departments would invite me to work with them, however. Although the heads of these two departments had a genuine interest in the intervention, they were also ambivalent. On the news side, there was clear and unambiguous evidence that the members of the top group were not interested in participating (see Chapter Eleven). This led R to become discouraged. His discouragement was compounded by the behavior of the President, who appeared to support more participative management until the final decision was made, or until a decision to be made might upset one or more of the people who would naturally have participated in the decision. Also, R was tired. He had worked very hard to overhaul, redesign, and make the news activities significantly more effective. As pointed out in Chapter One, the living system at *The Daily Planet* tended to deal with such behavior by identifying it as ruthless or insensitive, without also acknowledging the necessity for change within the system. If one has a deep concern for people, and if the others in the system do not seem to appreciate the pain that one is going through while demoting, firing, promoting, and shifting people, then one may soon feel that he is not valued and is misunderstood.

Q, as we have seen, had arrived at a similar view of his organizational life and activities, but by a different route. He felt that he had worked hard to improve the quality of all activities and to make his department something that could not be ignored by the thoughtful reader. The result, in his mind, had not been genuinely appreciated by his peers and superiors. Since he did not consider it proper to discuss these issues with his colleagues, he too withdrew. Having chosen to withdraw psychologically from these issues, but to remain immersed in his work, the idea of participating in an intervention that would naturally lead to exploring his withdrawal was not a very attractive possibility. The same applied to R.

To compound the problem for Q and R, and indeed for the entire top management group, there was P's behavior. Although he remained a loyal supporter of the idea of continuing the entire intervention, he did not hesitate to violate the values that he was espousing, and he was reluctant to explore the reasons for these violations. P withdrew when he wanted to withdraw. Since many of his subordinates, who were confused to see that his behavior violated his espoused theory of management, did not feel free to confront him without the interventionist in attendance, P never experienced much genuine questioning of his behavior. Those who felt P was violating his own proclamations, but did not say so, saw themselves as being "administratively cowardly." One way to deal with these feelings would be to withdraw even further.

There were other factors in the setting that inhibited persons from taking further steps. One crucial factor was that the values explicit in the intervention process, although espoused by many of the participants, were extremely difficult to make part of the living system. The more the participants tried to behave in accordance with these values, and the more they realized the obstacles that would have to be overcome and the barriers that would have to be removed, the more they had living evidence, through personal experience, that they were not, as individuals or as a group, as effective as they thought. The longer the intervention continued, the greater the probability that the participants' sense of effectiveness would be challenged and questioned. Such a challenge and such questioning understandably produced anxiety in the members, and the last thing they needed was more anxiety; the present living system produced enough of that. They were executives with an organization to manage, and they had to make certain that they could get on with their tasks in spite of the effects of the living system.

Another factor was the system's defenses, which were peculiarly hostile to genuine individual and organizational openness, risk-taking, and learning. One example was the defense of projection, which enabled a person to see others as "brittle" and "weak" while at the same time denying these qualities in himself. Another example was the sense of hopelessness and helplessness that the living system produced in people, and legitimized. As one executive put it, "You know you've become a full member of this organization when you genuinely believe that few changes are possible *and* that it is necessary to hold such a belief in order to remain sane."

Finally, many executives openly stated that they felt embarrassed about learning a new language and a new set of skills.*

* Personal psychological factors also operate to inhibit learning. These factors have not been mentiontd because of the lack of systematic data to support the inferences that would have to be made. It is my per-

Part of the reason was that they would have to learn to give up habitual use of their present language and skills. In order to unfreeze the old and eventually incorporate the new, they realized that they would have to explore the meaning and usefulness of a whole set of values and assumptions that they presently held regarding power, dependence, conformity, risk-taking, the expression of feelings, and so on. These explorations would not be easy and they would require much time.

This assessment was somewhat pessimistic. These executives, in only a short three-day session, had begun to pry loose issues that had been stuck in organizational cement for decades. It would take time to explore them, of course—but only a fraction of the time they already spent catching up on what others had done, blowing up at things they considered unfair, or trying to line up support for a pet idea. As R put it, they "pissed away" plenty of time.

The men and women who were involved in this intervention caught a glimpse of the living system that would be necessary for effective self-scrutiny and self-renewal. Some were attracted by it; a few were repelled. All were ambivalent, and all, for varied reasons, withdrew from it.

The executives would, I believe, agree with this analysis, but many would say that it is incomplete. Many believed that through tighter budgeting processes, long-range planning, and management information systems, efficiency could be increased and maintained. I agree.

But I would add that if efficiency increases without reducing the human problems we have identified, it will also increase the factors that restrain, inhibit, and undercut organizational self-renewal and self-scrutiny, and will further depress the quality of life within the organization.

How did the executives feel about the intervention? As part of the contract defined at the outset, when the program was

---

sonal assessment that the individual defenses dovetailed with the system defenses, and that none of them were so complicated that the top group could not, as a first step, reduce the systemic factors that were inhibiting growth and learning.

concluded I was to interview the key officials to obtain their final reactions. The group cooperated fully and I was able to interview eight of the ten top executives involved in the intervention from the beginning. Their reactions, I believe, are congruent with the predictions that could be made from the analysis above.

> The most valuable outcome was that we became aware of our lack of communications. We had to face the fact that we were more or less dishonest with each other, that honesty was rare.

> We've lost our internal commitment to the idea. [One thing I learned was that] it's a healthier way to live— if you can possibly achieve it, it's a better way to live.

> I was probably more affected by this experience than any other experience in my life. It hasn't continued, except that I remember it as something fine that almost came about.

> Yes, I believe that we learned something about the quality of our relationships. I find myself influenced still, thinking about it. But our problem was that we never learned the concepts or the skills.

> We were unable to learn the language of genuine openness. Now, being aware of this has made us somewhat more aware and effective.

The next two comments come from the two executives who expressed doubts about the program from the outset. They believed that it was at best, unfortunate and at worst dangerous to focus on interpersonal relationships.

> Unquestionably we learned. You can't go through such an experience and forget it.

> I would say that there is probably not very much behavioral change. We did become more alert to some of our weaknesses in communication. But people didn't change their spots—and, of course, you weren't saying that they would.

Finally, a comment by a participant who was skeptical at first, involved himself strongly, showed important changes in behavior (while the program was in progress), but now questions the advisability of his participation:

> To be very frank—as usual with you—I don't see much movement resulting from our program. I'm not sure there aren't some negative results. The learning seminar sessions may have been destructive. I'm not sure [these sessions] didn't harm my relationship with S. He has done things and taken actions with respect to the paper that I think are bad. [Later] My relationships with the President have improved in the sense of being franker. That is a plus.

The President and the other executive with whom this respondent reported difficulties described him as having shown some genuine progress but said he was not willing to continue to explore the next (and more difficult) issues with them in a problem-solving manner. They wondered if he would ever change his behavior. I asked if they had tested their assessment of his capacity to continue learning. Each replied that he had not because the respondent had given them cues that he was uncomfortable with the process; indeed, one of them speculated that the respondent probably saw the process as dangerous. The respondent hid these evaluations from the others and therefore he could not test their validity with others. The others sensed that this was how he felt, and therefore hesitated to be more open with him lest they hurt him.

It is interesting to see that in these comments not one of the respondents used the mechanism of denying his own responsibility in a relationship and projecting all the "bad" behavior and motives on the other. Thus the omnipresent defense mechanism of this living system could be unfrozen. All respondents expressed a willingness to meet with each other; all believed that it would be helpful to have a facilitator in the process; yet all were concerned about the depth of their differences on substantive issues.

These differences concerned questions that are fundamental to the newspaper business: for example, what are the qualities of a first-rate newspaper, how can reporting be made more meaningful yet less distorted, and what are the most effective relationships between departments (editorial, news, publisher's office, etc.). We have just seen three experts on these issues (P, Q, and R) who, because of the quality of their human relationships, are not meeting to discuss their problems productively. If this is also the case at other newspapers (and from what I can learn the barriers in some newspapers may be so high that they would not even consider permitting a study like this one), then we should not be surprised to learn that the management process of newspapers tends to be ineffective.

Several *Planet* executives mentioned the possibility that the timing of the program was unfortunate. When I entered the organization, it was pointed out, they did not even have a common language, a commonly accepted plan for managing the newspaper. As a result of several sessions on planning and managing their newspaper, they claim, there is now a plan; there is language; there is an explicit thrust or direction; and there is an explicit way to measure the effectiveness of managerial processes.

Two further points were made by all the respondents on this subject. They believed that the learning sessions had helped to raise the level of openness and candor, thereby making the nuts-and-bolts sessions more effective. All also agreed that the problems of competitiveness, lack of openness, and low trust still existed. All but two believed that these problems would get worse and that something should be done about them. For example, a comment by one of the executives who had been concerned about the advisability of holding this program: "Yes (the planning sessions helped us significantly). At the same time, the behavioral patterns have not improved. In fact, the results may be contrary. We have more difficulties, such as competitiveness and secrecy. I see growing signs of empire-building, efforts at personal publicity, secrecy, unwillingness to tell other people what is going on —and I think it is going to get worse."

These results are not surprising. Studies of the living systems of organizations that pioneered in planning processes have shown that these processes do not reduce the human difficulties, they simply define the rules of the game within which they will be acted out (Argyris 1962, 1965, 1971). There is no reason to believe that this organization will not face the same problems. This is not to say that planning processes are not important. Indeed, I am saying that these managerial processes are very important and that they will inevitably decline in effectiveness if they are placed in living systems such as the one I found in this organization.

I asked executive K, who always believed that the best way to solve interpersonal issues was to have effective decision-making processes and structures, how he felt now about his views. He agreed that the re-emergence of "human frailties" troubled him. But he had not changed his mind.

X: If I understand you correctly, you believe that the development and articulation of a top management planning process was very helpful. However, the "ugly problems," to quote you, of interpersonal relations are now reoccuring with renewed vigor.

K: Yes.

X: How would you deal with them?

K: Well, if we had a President who could confront these people directly, but individually, I think they would change. I have faith in what might be called fatherly advice from the senior man. [The competitive secrecy-oriented people] could be totally changed if we had a President who was capable of calling the individuals to his office and telling them clearly what they are doing—telling them to give up their ambitions. Our President simply cannot do it—and I can't either.

X: May I ask one final question? What if it became policy in this organization for people to deal with business-relevant interpersonal issues openly and as a group (something that you do not like) and imagine the President had a friendly talk with you about your reticence, what impact do you believe it would have on you?

K: In the direction of being more open? Not much, I would have to say.

X: Then why do you believe that these people would alter their behavior if the President told them to do so?

K: That's a point. I'm not sure why.

To summarize: All the respondents reported that the intervention program helped them develop new maps of effective human relationships; most of them reported that their hopes about the quality of life that is possible on the *Planet* have been raised; all agreed that the milieu and the behavior of some individuals did change, but that both changes were temporary and that the group did not show the internal commitment to learn the skills necessary for effective management of human resources nor the commitment to unfreeze old values and generate new ones.

All but one admitted that certain events occurred that were rare—such as the discussions between Q and R, and Q and P, and T and P—and that these events were encouraging. Moreover, one change that did occur has remained:

> There is a change in the editorial page. The editorial this morning is a good example. A year ago they would have had all sorts of words in there that would have upset people.

> Yes, the strident tone has diminished significantly. There are other issues to be resolved, but as to tone, the page is much better.

And to conclude with the comments: "You launched us on an important trip. We just began. We got a faint understanding. I wonder if it was enough to make us want to move forward, or are we frightened by the vision of an open society?"

I would agree that these men are frightened. But I believe that what they fear is not so much their vision of an open society but the ways in which they would be required to live and work if the vision were to become a reality. It seems to me that these people manage to maintain their sense of integrity by living with visions. When they make requirements for actual behavior, they make them for everyone except themselves, and for institutions other than their own.

Individuals of high intellectual ability can live with this paradox by doing to society at large what they have learned to do within their own living system—project their difficulties and problems onto others. Thus they attack local and state governments, national political institutions, business, labor, education, and so on, with impressive vigor, thus fulfilling their role as watch dogs of society. The irony is that newspapers may be performing these valuable services by systemic processes that could eventually distort the validity of their reporting, interpreting, and editorializing.

If this is the case, one could predict that newspapers will vigorously resist the behavior they would require of others. For example, newspapers may demand that institutions of government be open to the press, but they will nevertheless argue that they themselves should be closed to examination. They may insist upon being the artillery of the press, but they will see no reason why outsiders should take aim at their methods of operation. And newspaper officials will be quick to condemn their critics not only because they represent a threat to the freedom of the press, but because an investigation of the internal workings of the press might reveal that newspapers are managed by a system whose characteristics are the very ones they so often denounce.

13

Requirements for Effective Self-Examination

In recent years the press has come under attack from all quarters. According to a study undertaken by the Twentieth Century Fund, the press has lost some of its credibility because it has become increasingly remote and unresponsive to its constituencies, so that the public feels a sense of alienation and helplessness. The causes for this public alienation, the study suggested, included the following: overemphasis on the dramatic; lack of nationwide standards for the profession; lower salaries; decreased competition (Balk 1971); and control of newspapers by persons who are forced to be profit-conscious (Brucker 1972).

These reasons may be valid for many newspapers, but they are not the only reasons and may not be the most important ones. The newspaper studied here, which we have called

The Daily Planet, is highly respected for striving to be objective, and for avoiding a provocative tone in reporting deviant behavior. It is acknowledged by the journalistic profession to be a leader in maintaining the highest standards of professional competence. The salaries it pays are among the highest in the newspaper business. Its owners and managers can proudly say that it has been a matter of public record for more than a century that the paper's views cannot be bought and will not be sold.

The Twentieth Century Fund diagnosis implies that this newspaper is a model that other newspapers may aspire to emulate. Yet within this same newspaper we have seen possible causes for a lack of credibility, a clear inability to examine itself critically, and a predisposition to create conditions that tend to isolate it from the public it serves. Indeed, the top people in this newspaper found it necessary to back away and protect themselves from diagnostic and corrective processes they had agreed to undertake; and they did so, in my opinion, because these processes were beginning to expose the root causes of their problems and therefore became too threatening.

Can externally initiated change processes succeed where those initiated internally have failed? It seems unlikely. I doubt whether individuals can successfully be ordered to reduce such factors as mistrust, fear of openly testing their beliefs about others' motives, management by conspiracy, the magnification of events, and dependence on superiors. Yet these are the factors that are critical in creating the living system of the newspaper. Given such a living system, it may act as a magnet for reporters who will be predisposed to create credibility problems by reporting subjectively, distorting inferences, and selecting news to fit their unresolved, and in many cases only partially recognized, needs.

Admittedly, this study has not shown an unambiguous and clear-cut causal relationship between the distortion of the news or the tone of editorials on the one hand, and the living system and type of reporters on the other. But it has presented enough data, I believe, to make these possible connections worthy of detailed study. Unfortunately, the top news and editorial management prohibited further studies of this sort after they realized these possibilities. The question arises, and it must be answered by people more knowledgeable than I about newspapers: Should organizational resistance to exploring these processes be protected by the Constitution? If such studies were to show clearly that there are no connections, then the newspapers would have nothing to fear or hide. If connections were discovered, then ways might be found to eliminate the problems.

The reader may wonder if I am not making an excellent case for scrutiny of the press by newspaper councils. I do not think so, for several reasons. First, newspaper councils will become organizations themselves. To date, no one has found an organization that is immune to the problems described in this study. Indeed, regulatory commissions have not had a history of exemplary alertness.

Second, newspaper councils have not been designed to analyze and diagnose the living systems of newspapers, the types of reporters who write for them, and the *process* by which news is published. Newspaper councils, if I understand their functions correctly, focus on the *products* of newspapers, and conclude whether they have misrepresented events. The theory behind their operation is that once evidence of distortion is found, presentation of the evidence alone will be adequate to change the situation. But why should the introduction of evidence increase the probability of genuine change? In this study, the relevant people actually created their own evidence of possible causes of distortion; they discussed these causes for days but were unable to correct them, even though they understood the change processes and valued them.

The change processes did not fulfill their potential because the top people did not want to change the living system. As we have seen, the top group actually confirmed the original diagnosis by their rhetoric, by their continued behavior, and by their choice to begin the change processes and then resist them even though they acknowledged that they were getting at important issues.

It is true that some executives at the top felt that many of the problems that were identified in this diagnosis could have been eradicated, or at least reduced to a level at which they would become insignificant, by "better" management techniques such as more clearly defined policies and more effective planning. These tactics were tried and they did help. This should not be too surprising, since the organization had very few explicitly defined policies and no systematic long-range planning before the President took charge.

But, as even the most ardent supporters of these tactics now admit, the problems that were identified by this study still remain, and indeed some have surfaced in new modes that are difficult for them to handle. It is difficult, for example, to deal with destructive competitiveness, expire-building, and mistrust when they are woven into the new financial control and planning processes, and when executives can show by "objective" measures that they are meeting the performance criteria established.

The conclusion is not that sound financial analysis, budgeting, and long-range planning are not useful. The conclusion, I would suggest, is that these managerial activities are necessary but not sufficient to overcome the diseases of the living system. These diseases are relatively immune to the administrative DDT spread by the top management. Like mosquitoes, people learn to immunize and protect their defensive processes, so that future sprays have little negative effect—and indeed may actually strengthen their defenses.

I believe that one of the core problems of *The Daily Planet* is that its living system has now been made unchangeable by the very people who operate within it, even though they say they want to change it. The people within the living system have developed some capacity to identify and diagnose the problems they create, but they are unable to resolve them. Under these conditions, defensive behavior will tend to become compulsive: given a stimulus, it will be triggered off and nothing will stop it, including the individuals who are its creators and recipients. The living system is now disliked and condemned, yet this same hostile behavior triggers responses which seem to prove that people cannot change the system, and a heavy sense of helplessness grows and spreads.

If this prognosis is correct, the low trust, the win-lose dynamics, the dependence upon the top, the deprecation of the

administrative processes, the fear of taking risks, the ineffectiveness of group meetings, the managerial secrecy, the apparent
illusiveness of internal commitment to decisions made, will all
tend to become stronger and more deeply imbedded within the
living system. The effectiveness of decision-making will tend to
decrease. Problems that were assuredly solved predictably re-
appear, and the sense of confidence and pride in the capacity of
individuals to manage the system will deteriorate further, while
the sense of helplessness will tend to increase.

Moreover, the newspaper will have difficulty in managing
critical aspects of its own products. It will continue to be difficult,
and probably become more difficult, to resolve such problems as
objective-subjective reporting; the "use" of their positions by reporters (especially Reporter-Activists) to fulfill recognized and
dimly recognized personal needs; the politicization of the newspaper; the development of a fixed or predictable position by a
columnist; the development of such qualities as shrillness and
stridency in editorials; and the unrecognized mixing of description
and interpretive comment in the news. All of these problems were
recognized by the *Planet*'s editors. All of the problems were discussed by the appropriate editors. These discussions produced
formal memos and informal attempts to influence the "guilty"
parties. Yet I interviewed no editor, at any level, who felt that
these problems were being solved.

I would predict that given the present state of the living
system, these problems are not solvable—not in a way in which
the reporters, columnists, editors, and others are internally committed to make the new solutions a part of the living system.

Internal commitment to change requires full participation of the people involved. Yet during my period of observation
this was the last thing the editors would consider. Although
memoranda were sent out decrying subjective reporting and
upholding the tradition of objective reporting, a systematic
program for examining the problem, especially with the reporters
and columnists, was never developed. A few meetings with small
groups were held. The only larger and more public meetings I
learned of were meetings at which editors lectured at the participants, invoking the deep commitment to the tradition of ex-

cellence on the *Planet,* and exhorting them to remain objective.

Moreover, the topic was considered so dangerous and so "touchy" that I was denied permission to make a systematic study of objective-subjective reporting. The news officials saw no incongruity in assuring me that they now had the problem under control and denying me permission to have discussions with the reporters. Similarly, the editorial officials assured me that the editorial meetings were open and free-wheeling meetings. Yet it took nearly two years for me to secure an invitation to attend such meetings, even though the officials kept telling me, "you must attend one of our meetings." I soon realized how defensive the invitation was, but I never realized the significance of the word "one." I was never invited back, in spite of the fact, as the President noted, that there were internal difficulties.

Similar examples could be supplied for the entire list of critical problems that were related to the *Planet*'s credibility and its openness to hearing and responding to its constituency. I hope I have made clear my hypothesis about why these problems will not be resolved. The reason is *not* a lack of motivation to solve them on the part of the top management. The problems will not be solved because the individuals and groups behave in ways that create a living system which teaches them (they become acculturated) to be hard of hearing, to be unable and unwilling to take action on threatening issues.

The nature of the living system is that it will respond positively to two types of management. The first is laissez-faire. The second is controlling and directive. The first does not seem viable to the top management, given the financial and survival problems of newspapers. And even if it were chosen, we would predict that if the system were left alone it would deteriorate and become self-destructive.

The President has selected the second alternative, but is open, I believe, to a third alternative in which increasing power would be placed in the hands of people at the points where they have the most relevant information and where the decision should be (or is being) made. His openness to the third alternative, however, is sharply limited to, and dependent upon, the willingness of his top people to work toward a managerial system of greater and more genuine participation. Up to this point, he has been given precious little evidence that the executives are capable of operating such a managerial system. One reason is that most of these executives have grown up in a system where they learned to look toward the top for others to change. As we have pointed out, during the learning seminar the top group's ambience tended to create a group of members who were "yes-men" *on the issues of changing the nature of the living system;* and this is a quality that is self-defeating to the policy of genuine participation.

It can be predicted that the President will increasingly look for "strong" people to joint "his" top management team. The President will select those who make him feel confident that they can take affirmative action. These executives will not only be supported by the best staffs, and armed with the President's support, but they will have as their constant ally the present reality—namely, that in order for this newspaper, indeed all newspapers, to survive and remain free, they must become financially viable.

It can also be predicted that the participants in the system will respond to the controlling, prodding, directing, manipulating behavior that will be used to promote accomplishment of these ends. Who can argue against survival? However, the system-characteristics of over-magnification, tension production, over-reaction, and so forth will also tend to increase. Thus, as the newspaper increases its capacity to survive financially, it will also increase the forces of ineffectiveness imbedded in its living system.

The top managers will react by becoming even "stronger"; by designing even tighter control systems; and by creating long-range plans which, if examined, are not to manage the future or to learn about it, but to co-op it. Long-range planning will become a force to make the system more predictable in the future; that is, to make it ultra-stable.

From the viewpoint of the lower-level reporters, editors, and other participants, this ultra-stability will be experienced as system rigidity. Depending on how they decide to react, the top management may find itself again and again faced with repeated attempts to have crucial aspects of the news and editorial activities influenced by reporters and writers. Whatever skill, commitment, energy, persuasion, influence, and credibility, it took to overcome the most recent cabal—and it must have taken great amounts—future responses will require even more.

Two further predictions can be made. First, there are limits to the amount of energy and commitment that human beings can generate; someday the amount needed to maintain stability will not be enough to fulfill the requirements of the moment. Second, "stronger" officials, armed with tighter controls and supported by the necessity to use fear of survival as their motivating carrot, will tend to generate less credibility within lower-level employees, and therefore will be less able to draw on personal charisma to reduce forces of upheaval.

It might be argued that the push from below to make newspapers more active initiators of societal change, and to make them take the sort of positions that Reporter-Activists demand, is now on the wane and may be disappearing. My contacts with some of our brightest youth lead me to doubt the validity of that prediction. The strength of awareness that our society needs change is in fact stronger than ever. What has waned is the idea that effective change comes quickly, or that it can be produced through hostile confrontation or violence. Young people are now seeking to become more competent, more rationally effective, and better able to work within the system. But if these more competent and more reasoning individuals are eventually frustrated, there may follow a new era of upheaval that would be even more violent, because youth will have found, in their opinion, that reasoning and competence are not valued. I would predict that very course of development in this newspaper so long as the living system remains in its present state.

Even if youth has indeed changed to fit the image prayed for by every tired, fearful adult with power and responsibility, there would be a host of new questions to be raised. Might not this new attitude simply produce a new set of personal and systemic distortions that distort the news in different directions? Our newspapers, I believe, should not have the freedom to accept and approve of a more conservative stance by our nation's youth simply because that stance is not threatening to their equilibruim.

Newspapers are protected by the Constitution, and so may have a responsibility to seek objectivity, because they provide the citizenry with feedback about the nation's effectiveness and the information needed to take corrective action. I doubt if newspapers can provide valid feedback to the nation about its behavior if they cannot generate valid feedback within their own system about their own behavior. Participants acculturated to the living system of this newspaper will create newspapers that—even though they become better, according to the Twentieth Century Fund's set of criteria—will still generate problems of credibility and alienation from their constituencies.

Another related prediction is that the inability of *The Daily Planet* to manage its own living system (which is why newspapers have traditionally refused to be studied) will eventually break into the open and become public knowledge. The organizational scenarios that have been so carefully confined to executive offices will then be catapulted onto the national stage, to be played out again with a new cast of critics leveling an old set of charges. Because the newspaper executives have kept their problems secret, the outside critics will not realize that newspaper people have been aware of the problems. Indeed, many of these critics may interpret the newspapers' errors as conscious and planned attacks on them. Perhaps they will sometimes be right, given some of the work done by Reporter-Activists. What these aggrieved outsiders will not know is that editors have made hard and continual efforts to correct the potential sources of distortion and lack of credibility.

I believe that the news and editorial officials of the *Planet* would find criticism of the sort made by former Vice President Agnew objectionable not so much for its substance as for its tone, its explicit anger, and most painful of all, its implicit assumption that newspaper executives are deliberately emphasizing negative news about the Nixon administration because they personally dislike it. This message must cut deep into the feelings of the *Planet*'s news and editorial executives, who have worked hard to maintain a newspaper that the nation can point to with pride. Countless meetings, spot decisions, and carefully written policy memos all carry the same message: this newspaper is to be as objective, truthful, and honest as is technically and humanly possible.

The problem lies in the factors behind the phrase "as humanly possible." The difficulties, for this paper, are not lack of technical competence, high standards, or vigorous competition. The problem is that the living system sanctions and rewards the forces that cause these problems, and simultaneously makes it difficult for the editors to overcome them. The underlying difficulty the news and editorial officers would have with their critics is that they misread their motives; they do not realize that although their titles may suggest that they have power, the realities of the living system make it difficult for them to use it effectively. They feel a genuine sense of helplessness. They wish they could be more effective, and say they could be—if only the others would cooperate.

Helplessness: denial and projection. That wish brings us back to the effects of a sense of helplessness coupled with projection upon others and denial of one's own problems.

We found a feeling of helplessness at all levels of the organization. The reporters, copy editors, and editors work in a living system that makes their work difficult to achieve and results in a relatively low quality of life. They doubt if anything could be done about it. Many of the senior editors, officers, and, at times, the President agree with their employees' views. They, too, feel a sense of helplessness about the living system. Working as the interventionist, I have never felt as helpless as I have in this organization. Many agree that change is necessary, and the people in power are in favor of it; the less powerful are also in favor of it; the employees do not resist it; and there are no known laws or internal policies to prevent it. Yet even the smallest step toward genuine change seems to exact an enormous amount of energy from everyone concerned.

The feeling of helplessness has many causes. In social science jargon, it is overdetermined. This is not unusual; indeed it is characteristic of complex social systems. For example, the group dynamics are not supportive of change; the intergroup dynamics between the news and editorial departments, and more importantly between groups within the news department, are still not as effective as they could be. The norms of the living system discourage openness, risk-taking, and other behavior that is indispensable if change is to occur. Finally, most of the individuals are deeply pessimistic about the capacity of human beings to change their behavior.

This mechanism of denial and projection has infected all levels of the organization. The executives, we may recall, diplomatically but strongly resisted the initial learning seminars by insisting they were concerned lest others be hurt, because they might be interpersonally weak and brittle. They continuously denied having any such feelings about themselves. It was not uncommon to hear near-unanimous or unanimous votes in favor of the seminars in group sessions, and near-unanimous anxiety and foreboding about them in private interviews. Often I felt that I was the only one in the building who had faith in the executives' capacities to learn. Not often enough did I realize that this was precisely the situation that the executives were accustomed to create—a situation in which someone else is made responsible for change.

Q, for example, felt a sense of helplessness about ever getting R to realize that the news was subject to criticism. Why the sense of helplessness? Because R would deny that he was closed to discussions about these issues. Yet Q would become emotionally tense and upset when such discussions began. He would feel this way because R insisted on separating his personal needs from his job, while everyone else participating in the discussion was convinced that R could not possibly do this.

The reverse was also true. R felt a sense of helplessness about ever getting Q to realize that his department's work was also subject to citicism. He in turn felt helplessness because Q insisting that he wanted to focus only on the job, yet whenever anyone started to question the tone of the editorials, it was Q, as a human being, that became defensive, and it was the questioner, as a human being, who became tense.

Both men insisted on separating themselves from their jobs, while all others respected their insistence and made it into a cause for a *self-sealing process*. If Q or R insisted that they were not personally involved, when they were clearly seen to be personally involved to a high degree, then Q or R were diagnosed as being very defensive and brittle. The others would decide not to push too hard on Q or R for fear of upsetting them. The helplessness, in these cases, was caused by others hearing the individuals in question deny key aspects of themselves, as when they would insist that the group should focus on organizational or structural issues; and yet seeing, when discussions of these organizational issues began, that the personal defensiveness was not reduced. Indeed, solutions would become more difficult to achieve because Q and R could resist by saying, "Let's keep personalities out of this—we're talking about organizational policies and structures."

The combination of denying personal feelings while projecting those feelings into descriptions of problems in the environment is a difficult one to break into, especially when groups band together to support the denial and projection. R's group did precisely this when they projected onto R their reason for rejecting a learning experience and denied that their rejection had anything to do with personal feelings and anxieties. The Reporter-Activists also did this when they denied their needs yet became impatient, angry, and punishing of those around them who manifested similar needs. The President also manifested this mechanism frequently. He scheduled, for example, the second meeting on the new feature and then denied that it was canceled by him; it was the others' responsibility. *He* was sure that they would never come to a decision. He agreed to a group decision about certain appointments, yet he made them himself. He promised me several times to make certain that I would be told when several key meetings were held, yet I was never notified and he blamed others for the "slip-up."

Why is this phenomenon so dramatically represented by persons in the newspaper business? Is there something about newspaper work that encourages such defensive strategies or attracts people who habitually use them? Probably both factors are operating and interacting with each other. Unfortunately, I was not permitted to obtain direct information that might shed light on these questions. What follows is therefore speculation.

First, we must keep in mind that we are talking about selected groups of people, primarily the editors (at all supervisory levels) and the Reporter-Activists. Second, the phenomenon of denial and projection was observed under specific conditions: it tended to occur when individuals were requested to take action that might lead to self-awareness and exploration of their personal effectiveness. For example, the strength of the denial-projection increased in the top group when they were asked to become involved in a learning seminar. The Reporter-Activists' denial-projection came to light as a result of interviews and discussions about the meaning of their work.

The denial-projection mechanism was also aroused by organizational requirements. It appeared at times when individuals were required to take managerial actions that might upset others (to transfer reporters, evaluate their work, fire incompetent people). These pressures, as we have shown, had increased dramatically during the past several years because of financial constraints, the internal confrontation of sacred cows (objective-subjective reporting), and the credibility gap with the population at large. In short, denial-projection tended to occur when it was necessary to carry out difficult managerial decisions and when self-exploration was being requested.

Next, the reactions varied with individuals. Q and R, for example, denied and projected, but their personal emotional processes were not so tightly bound that they could not change as a result of receiving valid feedback about their behavior. Both showed genuine signs of change, although the process was long and the learning only a small part of what was necessary. The Reporter-Activists, however, had internalized more formidable barriers to learning. One hypothesis would be that societal problems were frightening to them, and that in addition to disappointment and disillusionment they felt a strong need for action and personal commitment. But they, too, were uncomfortable with direct action. So, hoping that the pen may indeed be mightier than the sword, they sharpened a pen as cutting as any sword, only they sliced up the world at a distance. Direct personal confrontation had to be minimized because they had not neither the skills nor the stomach for it. Indeed, many reported that whenever they did become personally and emotionally involved, they blew up or overreacted. Because losing their cool was upsetting to these people, they tried to cut themselves off from personal feelings that might up set them.

Why a credibility gap when the newspapers are performing better than ever? In the words of a member of the Twentieth Century Fund task force, "because the public was feeling a sense of powerlessness and helplessness in its relationship with the press." (Pool 1972). We have now come full circle. We began with the feelings of helplessness that the newspapermen expressed about influencing their living system. We then described some of the mechanisms that make it difficult to change the living system, and showed that the internal system does have some of the problems mentioned by the critics. We ended by discovering that the public's sense of powerlessness and helplessness about influencing the press is confirmed by the executives of the *Planet,* who feel powerless to influence their own newspaper.

Suggested mechanisms for enhancing self-scrutiny. The Twentieth Century Fund study names five things that could help reduce the credibility problem: journalism reviews; underground newspapers; citizens' organizations to improve the press; fair trial and free press activities; reporter power; and ombudsmen and in-house critics. These might ease the problem for the typical to below-average newspaper, but the study also suggests that even if the typical newspaper were to reach the standards and quality of *The Daily Planet,* credibility problems would still exist.

For example, the first four things just mentioned are external, and do not reach the internal machinery of the living system. Reporter power—increasing the influence of reporters and writers in the management of newspapers—flowered briefly at the *Planet* but then collapsed (partly because of effective leadership of top news officials). However, the movement has gained momentum in other newspapers, especially in Europe (Brucker 1972). Although some analysts suggest that this may be a valid response to a thorny problem, I would predict, if my results are valid, that reporter power would make the credibility problem even thornier. I was able to analyze the behavior of the younger star reporters and columnists, who presumably might be involved in the management of the *Planet,* by observing them in meetings and during interviews. I found them very competitive, controlling, and authoritarian. Like their elders, they projected their "bad" behavior onto the world and attacked it wherever it was "reasonable" to do so. They did not deny their inconsistencies as often as the elders did, but when they did acknowledge their inconsistencies they said, like V, that they did not intend to do anything about reducing them. The rhetoric about management used by Reporter-Activists may stress egalitarianism and co-operation; but the way they behaved was authoritarian, individualistic, and competitive.

Ombudsmen might ameliorate conditions somewhat if they were permitted great freedom and if they did not manifest the same interpersonal behavior that their breathren do. To date, the results that have been reported have shown ombudsmen correcting lower-level infractions that rarely, if ever, occur inside the *Planet.* But the real trouble with ombudsmen and press councils is that they are outside of, and cannot influence, the living system, the defensive interpersonal relationships, and the competitive win-lose group dynamics. At best, they can do for the organization what aspirin can do for a migraine headache.

The danger with these strategies is that they will unintentionally reinforce the living system and strengthen its problems. For example, a news supervisor could now point to a statement by a press council as a reason for killing or altering a story. Yet if the story should be altered, one should not need external support to make the decision. If there is doubt, then there should be plenty of psychological space for free discussion and constructive confrontation. Also, the official who has been struggling to alter the internal system but has been frustrated may now give up and turn over the vigilant monitoring of his paper's activities to the council or an ombudsman.

The publisher of *The New York Times,* in a thoughtful published memorandum (Sulzberger 1973), has stated that the real dangers to the press are coming from people who can serve their own ends by attacking it (seeking rights to arrest and imprison reporters, to subpoena tape recordings, and so on). His analysis seems correct but incomplete. The other side of the problem is that there are reporters and columnists *inside* the newspapers who are working in ways that serve their own needs; it is difficult for the public to influence these reporters, before or after they have written their stories; and it is difficult even for their own superiors to influence them as effectively as they have wished.

The intervention I undertook at the *Planet*—a program that held real promise for exposing and solving key editorial and news problems—was resisted so strongly by executives, editors, and columnists because they felt that the processes of self-exploration and renewal were too dangerous. The resistance that eventually stopped our progress was an example of individuals working the system to fulfill their own needs.

I am not suggesting that the fears the participants felt (in the learning seminars) about hurting others, and being hurt, were unreal or even unfounded. Although the learning seminar and other experiences showed that the fears may have been magnified, who is to say that with certainty? Perhaps some people really would be psychologically hurt by an exploration of personal relationships and feelings. I do not have the skills, nor do I believe the techniques exist, to guarantee that no personal harm would come to people from the type of activities that I have recommended (although none has come so far). Indeed, I hope that no technology can ever be developed that will guarantee how people will behave. But the facts are, I believe, that feelings, coping mechanisms, interpersonal relationships, and group dynamics may be critical factors in causing the credibility problems of newspapers.

Herbert Brucker has written, "Newspapers are manned by human beings and so are no more perfect than any other human institution" (1972, p. 47). However, he also cites the (Milton) Eisenhower commission's statement, "Few American institutions are as free of some responsible and systematic analysis as the American press" (1969, p. 151). He then calls that the understatement of the year (1972, p. 197).

Here, I believe, is the nub of the problem. Newspapers are crucial for a healthy democracy; they are protected by the Constitution of the United States *and* they are manned by human beings whose behavior is rarely examined from within or from without. This implies that newspaper people are human, and are expected to be superhuman.

Perhaps it is saddling newspaper people with the requirement that they be both human and superhuman that helps to make them so defensive. Imagine the personal burden of knowing that you are given great freedoms as part of a fourth estate protected by the Constitution, but that it is largely up to you to define your responsibilities and the limits on your freedom, because you are not subject to most of the constraints placed on other institutions that help to guarantee our freedom. For example, the courts gain their right to influence our life partly at the price of having to make their internal operations open to the public and subject to continual redesign to correct difficulties that are discovered.

The need to externalize one's weaknesses and deny their existence may be partly a defense against the feeling of enormous responsibility placed on the reporter. The disillusionment that the young reporters may feel when they discover that their emperors have no clothes on may be partly caused by the fact that as reporters for a great newspaper *they* are emperors— and they know better than anyone else how naked they are. This suggests one possible explanation for Walter Lippman's comment that the press "is very much more frail than the democratic theory has yet admitted. It is too frail to carry the whole burden of popular sovereignty, to supply spontaneously the truth which democrats hoped was inborn." (Quoted in Hohenberg 1971, p. 468.)

Perhaps this is also one of the causes for the emotionality and polarization around the issue of objective versus subjective reporting. The defenders of subjective reporting note that all news reporting is based on subjective observations, and is complicated by the need to condense reality into a small space without distorting its meaning. With all due deference to the difficulties involved, this task is faced by all human beings. We all see the world through a subjective framework; the environment is infinitely more complex than our information-processing capacity; and most of us are necessarily simplifying to meet real time pressures, constraints, and objectives (Simon 1969). Few of us, however, have these built-in characteristics of human fallibility protected by the Constitution of the United States. The anxiety about being objective, under these conditions, would understandably be high, especially among brighter and better educated people.

The institutional response to this Constitutionally given anxiety is to strive to separate and to polarize. Examples of the former are efforts to separate news from editorial, hard stories from soft stories, financial issues from both news and editorial. Examples of the latter are cautionary policies, such as "those with a personal stake in the news should never be permitted to judge whether or not it shall be published," and "to suppress, to pull punches, for a moral end is just as immoral as to do so for an ignoble end" (Brucker, pp. 27, 53); and statements to the effect that because all reporting and editing are subjective, aspirations toward objective reporting should be discarded.

The objective-subjective controversy. The difficulty with the separation strategy is that it is based upon false assumptions about objectivity and subjectivity, as well as on the assumption that younger reporters will acquiesce to pressures to conform the way their elders have done for years. Let us examine the discussions about objectivity versus subjectivity more carefully. To date, they seem to generate more heat than light. If I understand the meaning of these terms, the heat is unnecessary and the little light being shed may be illuminating the wrong issues.

The dictionary defines objective as being free from or independent of personal feelings and values, as being unbiased by any factors. There is a large and complicated body of literature on the question of human perception and human descriptions of reality. It concludes that there is very little objectivity possible in perceptions and descriptions of human events. Professional reporters are not excluded from these findings (Pool 1959).

We have also seen that the needs, values, and abilities of reporters may influence what they want to see and are able to see, what they want to report and are able to report. Moreover, the living system may also be an important influence on reporters, and that the influence is more covert than overt.

Finally, it is possible that subjectivity may enable one to make a more valid description of reality than detached observation. An observer who is able to empathize (feel or think what the other is feeling and thinking) may produce a more accurate account of certain realities. It is also possible that strict adherence to objective reporting can miss the truth. For example, in writing up an observation many years ago, I reported that Johnny Smith "sat down by the magazine rack (in the local drugstore) and read comic books." When Johnny was interviewed by another researcher, he reported that he had sensed I was following him so he decided to observe me while hiding behind a comic book!

Notice that the crucial issue in both of these cases is accuracy. I should like to suggest that accuracy is the fundamental issue in reporting. Focusing on objectivity versus subjectivity polarizes the problem, and labels objectivity good and subjectivity bad. The concerned reporter who realizes the personal and situational factors that operate to reduce objectivity may understandably give up and conclude that objectivity is not possible. Tom Wicker (1972), for example, advises the reporter to substitute fairness for objectivity, but he never defines fairness.

When we conceptualize the problem as one of accuracy, however, it is possible to ask, for example, under what conditions does objective or subjective reporting provide the most accurate information? If subjective reporting can be shown at times to be more accurate, how can it be made "fair" to the subject?

If a report can be accurate and yet still may not be fair, then what is the added meaning to "fair"? I believe the essence of being fair includes making public the directly observable data upon which inferences are made, making public the logic of inference used, and showing awareness of where others might disagree with the data or the inferences.

A great deal has been written about accuracy and fairness because social scientists, especially those working in real-life settings, have been plagued with the problems of determining them. One of the findings is that accuracy and fairness are a matter of degree. Another is that it is possible to determine the degree of accuracy and fairness by using three kinds of tests. These tests are listed here in increasing order of powerfulness.

(1) The degree to which others can confirm the descriptions of what happened or the inferences made from the description. A consensual validation by disinterested but professionally competent observers increases the probability that the reports or inferences are valid. This is the least powerful of the three tests.

(2) Consensual validation could be, in some cases, inadequate because all the observers could be blind, could have common distortions, or could have been deceived. A more powerful criterion, therefore, is the degree to which one can predict future events, under specified conditions, on the basis of the consensually validated observations or inferences. Such predictions (listed in increasing order of potency) could be of three types: (a) predictions about future events under similar conditions; (b) predictions about future events under different conditions; and (c) predictions that events will not tend to occur when the participants say they will, or predictions that events will tend to occur when the participants say they will not. An example of the first type (c) prediction: the top management predicted that their executive committee would increase its degree of trust, but the interventionist predicted (during the next week) that this would not occur (Argyris 1970, 1971). Examples of the second type (c) prediction were when the top management of the *Planet* predicted that they would not repeat their "great fiasco," and that cabals to discuss increasing the influence of reporters on the management of the newspaper would not occur. Both events, as I predicted, did occur.

(3) The third, and most powerful, test of the accuracy of reports is whether one can *make* events occur, especially events that people state would not occur. For example, people at the *Planet* predicted that the suggested discussions between Q and R and Q and the President would never occur, yet such meetings eventually did occur. The third test, in other words, is to make things happen on the basis of the analysis.

Consensual validation. The main business of reporting has been to describe events that have already occurred, are occurring now, or have been announced to occur. Under these conditions consensual validation is the most promising test. The art of validating the report could be accomplished by presenting two different stories on the same incident, either in the same newspaper or in competing newspapers. But as a practical matter, it is doubtful whether either attempt could be arranged. Given the increasing economic constraints and reporter competition, it is doubtful that two competing articles could be requested, completed, and published in the same newspaper. The test of comparing the report in newspaper A with the report in newspaper B would not be possible, in most cases, because there is only one paper.

The consensual validation may therefore have to occur in the relationship between the reporter and the reader. One test could focus on the reporter's capacity to observe accurately. This could be made by comparing the reporter's description with an actual transcription. This requirement may be more easily met by newspapers like *The New York Times,* which have a policy of publishing extensive transcriptions of interviews, court proceedings, congressional debates, and the like. However, there is no reason why smaller newspapers could not periodically make this sort of check on their reporters. If newspapers will not develop such checks, perhaps this responsibility could be assumed by a national press council. What I am suggesting is periodic reliability checks on reporters, much like the periodic examinations and training sessions that pilots are required to receive.

Sometimes reporters obtain their data by examining documents. Again, relevant parts of documents could be published, or they could be footnoted for the reader to obtain. For example, Tom Wicker (1972) recently stated that he examined the available records and found that there was no historical evidence to suggest there would be a bloodbath if the communists took over South Vietnam. This inference is clearly at odds with the inferences made by government officials. In this case, Wicker could footnote the documents that he and his staff examined. He might also make explicit the process of inference that led him from the data to his conclusions, so that the reader could judge the logic of the process for himself.

It is only fair to say that the reporter is only part of the problem. Rosenthal (1973) has shown that it would be difficult for any reporter, no matter how conscientious, to obtain accurate information from the government and many other institutions, given the secrecy they impose on their problem-solving processes. Compounding the felony, Rosenthal suggests, is the public belief that government should cover up facts, or has a right to do so. Under these conditions, it is difficult for a reporter to obtain valid information. I might add that these conditions also imply an underlying mistrust between the press and some of its subjects, a conclusion documented by Moynihan (1971) and Reston (1966). Under conditions of mutual mistrust, it is possible that the reporter may unknowingly slant the news to counterattack being mistrusted. This response is counterproductive because it can be used by the others as evidence that their mistrust was based on valid fears. We now have circular, self-sealing processes acting to make the situation worse.

Whenever the problem is to break into self-sealing processes, it is important that someone take the initiative to begin to correct the situation. The press may find it advantageous to take the lead because it will reduce the need for outside regulation and control. However, once someone takes the lead, the other parties to the self-sealing processes must respond appropriately.

Predicting future events. Newspapers have rarely predicted events that the participants sincerely denied would occur, or predicted that events would not occur even though the participants were genuinely striving to make them occur. Such predictions require the development of some kind of model or conceptual picture of reality that accurately captures the relevant factors and permits accurate prediction.

An example would be the concept of the living system, and the predictions made from it that were eventually confirmed. Developing the model required observation and interviewing skills plus a knowledge of systems theory. But both the knowledge and the skills are easily taught, especially to the younger, more educated reporters. One can imagine that a reporter on the city hall beat might, over time, develop a very accurate and fruitful model of behavior in city hall, or in any other organization in which he could interview and preferably observe.

Such analyses would develop the basis for making causal explanations of events, for making predictions about future events, and for providing the basis for constructive change within the system being studied. For example, it may be interesting to compare the findings in our newspaper with those presented by Gay Talese in *The Kingdom and the Power* (Talese's findings are in the left column, ours in the right):

(1) Competitiveness and tension on the news floor.

(1) Agreed, but our analysis provides insights into the individual, group, inter-group, and organizational factors that help to cause and reinforce competitiveness.

(2) Tensions between copy editors and reporters.

(2) Agreed, but our analysis explains why present policies of "isolating" parties will lead to more problems, and why bringing parties together without helping them gain interpersonal skills in dealing with inter-group conflicts may be equally disastrous.

(3) Overemphasis on symbolic phenomena (e.g., where one sits) and magnification of the violation of these.

(3) Agreed, but again we were able to suggest hypotheses about why this was the case.

(4) Difficulties between the Washington and New York offices.

(4) We found similar problems (only in different locations) and were able to predict that they would reoccur even though all the participants vowed that this would not happen.

| (5) Difficulties between news and editorial departments. | (5) We found similar problems but were able to suggest concrete actions to begin to surmount the problem. |
| (6) Centralized decision-making is inevitable. | (6) We found centralized decision-making and provided ways to alter it, if the members should wish to do so. |

The last three findings point up an important difference between journalistic analysis—of the type produced by Talese—and our own. Talese describes reality, but because he has no theory of systems to which to relate his findings, and because he has no theory about how organizations may be made more effective, his story is a study of what *is;* it does not say what might be. Talese, like traditional scientists who lack conceptions of effective organizations, becomes a maintainer of the status quo (by saying or implying, for example, that centralized decision-making, competitiveness, and individual value-systems are inevitable and unchangeable).

Making events occur. The third and most powerful test is presumably not available to newspapers. They are not in business to make things happen, in the sense of directly managing events. (Although they may, of course, "make" things happen by reporting or refusing to report certain events.)

Accuracy, therefore, is not a simple binary state—either you have it or you don't. There are many shades of accuracy. The thrust of the effort, however, should be to improve accuracy.

Wicker (1972) has shown how a reporter can have the accuracy of his stories manipulated or controlled by his subjects. If a reporter has only a few minutes to file a story, he may depend too heavily on the mimeographed statement given out by the individual or institution whose activities are being reported. Also, continues Wicker, institutions are inevitably self-serving; their leaders are often out of touch with reality; and they are closed systems, unreachable and uninfluenceable.

Wicker is probably correct in his assessments of organizations (Argyris 1964, 1970, 1971). Now, if these conditions have an impact upon what people see, say, and do in most organizations, why couldn't this be true for newspapers? For example, an angry tone in a description of a powerful public figure could be related to the frustrations the reporter is experiencing in his own living system. A reporter's desire to embarrass powerful people could be influenced by his anger toward the powerful people in his own living system. Anger toward competitiveness might be related to unresolved feelings about one's own competitiveness and the competitiveness in one's own living system. A sense of doubt and mistrust of others could be influenced by mistrust within the living system. And of course the opposite might also be true in all these examples, because these processes are not one-way, but reciprocal or circular.

I do not know if these hypotheses are valid. I am simply suggesting that if the conditions which inhibit and facilitate accuracy are to be identified, these kinds of studies are necessary. Unfortuantely, the top management of *The Daily Planet* refused to permit such studies. The reason they gave was as important as the rejection: they stated that such studies might upset the reporters. If that were the case, then one *should* be worried. Behavioral scientists, for example, must open themselves to the study of the reliability and validity of their observations. They are not free to reject this requirement. They are only free not to be considered professionally competent.

Wicker writes that he became aware of the "misbegotten mess" in Vietnam when he became a columnist and had time to think. The difference was it was no longer required of him "to write down what others—largely official sources—[tell me] they think, or did, or plan, or believe; my job is to think for myself and to say what I think and believe about events, and policies, and men" (1972, p. 16). But with this new degree of freedom, Wicker becomes more of a reporter of his own view of reality. Under these conditions, the requirements for documentation increase sharply. The impact of the living system upon reporters, columnists, and editorial writers can no longer be assumed to be benign; it must be shown to be the case. The impact of a reporter's psychological set may no longer be considered beyond study, because it may have important influences on accuracy. In other words, the harder reporters wish to become columnists interpreting the news, giving their opinions, and making attributions about others' motives and strategies, the more important will be the factors that are at the core of this study. Yet these are the very factors that news and editorial officials refuse to open up to careful study. Rosenthal (1973), in his thoughtful articles on freedom of the press, correctly identifies imposed secrecy by the government (and other institutions) and the uncritical acceptance of that secrecy by the public as the two important threats to the First Amendment. I am suggesting that the same diagnosis holds for *The Daily Planet*. The news and editorial executives are imposing secrecy upon themselves and upon their living system. Moreover, the reporters and presumably some part of the public accept the imposition without careful examination.

Developing the internal capacity for self-examination and self-renewal. The newspaper people, I suggest, have no choice but to take the lead in showing that their behavior and their organizations can be managed from within, by the people who produce the problems, and right at the time the problem is produced. This is not an easy task, but it is not an insurmountable one. After all, progress began to occur within the *Planet* with the help of one part-time consultant and one two-and-a-half-day session.

In making this recommendation, I do not wish to argue against the contributions that could be made by ombudsmen, national press councils, and competing papers. All these can play a useful role. I am arguing that they are not enough. The internal relationships and workings of institutions, especially newspapers, may have been greatly underestimated as causes of the credibility gap, while familiar commercial motives may have been overestimated (Ways 1969).

I am also suggesting that once it is decided to examine internal relationships, the spotlight should be focused on the living system, with an eye toward diagnosing it and helping to change it. This means making public, at least to the members of the organization being examined, many of the organization's internal decision-making activities. If there is a function for outside councils, it may be to monitor the living systems of newspapers periodically to make certain that they do not become committed to compulsive patterns of activity.

But such councils would require living systems of their own that are more effective than the ones they monitor. The knowledge and technology for designing and managing effective living systems is still primitive and incomplete. The techniques needed to begin exploring these areas, however, are available. Any organization with the motivation and one or two highly competent specialists can begin the process of self-examination and self-renewal. Not only will it find, if it proceeds, that it can deal with the problem of credibility more effectively; it will also find that the same processes will help it to attack effectively other kinds of organizational dry rot, which if not overcome and eliminated, may lead, as John Gardner has predicted (1968), to the demise of our society.

The requirements of self-corrective activities. The difficulty with the requirement for self-examination is not in its conception but in its execution. This is especially true when the "errors" in a newspaper are a matter of interpretation, of the organization of the news, of a choice of emphasis, of the information excluded. Moynihan (1971) cites several cases in which *The New York Times* apparently made errors. Yet even after the apparent discrepancies were pointed out to the *Times,* no corrections were made; indeed, the paper continued its theme in other articles which Moynihan suggests were unfairly weighted against the present administration. If the *Times* has problems similar to those found inside the *Planet,* then agreeing that an error was made or a balanced picture was not portrayed reaches to the core of the problem—the individuals involved.

We may recall, for example, that Q and V were perceived by peers, subordinates, and superiors as showing clear bias in their writings. V never took any initiative to correct the situation; indeed he denied it even existed. Q, on the other hand, was more open to self-inquiry *after* he became more conscious of the living system and its potential negative effects on the quality of journalism in the paper. Moreover, Q made genuine progress in altering his views of reality as (1) he received valid feedback (2) from others (such as A and the President) that he now began to trust, (3) as the newly developing living system rewarded him for trying, (4) as other valued peers also tried to alter their potential or actual misperceptions, and (5) as he saw that progress toward this new awareness did not lead to his losing important powers that resided in his role but led to increased influence over activities that he wanted to influence (news, for example).

Q was able to progress when he was able to acknowledge that he might need to change certain behavior and attitudes, but then only as others were asked for help, only as they worked together, and only as others also took the plunge toward greater self-awareness and self-acceptance. The behavioral changes necessary to make the self-corrective processes work occurred as Q opened up the process of his self-development to influence by his peers and superiors. Why is it necessary to open the process of self-development to influence from valued co-workers? Let us take Q as an example. Our analysis suggests that:

(1) Q had to become aware of suppressed feelings that influenced how he perceived the world (such as his feelings of aloneness, rejection, within the newspaper).

(2) The processes by which he kept these feelings away from his awareness included: (a) Conceiving of himself as effectively keeping his personality needs separate from the requirements of the job. (b) Informing everyone, whenever necessary, that he as a person didn't count; the job was the important thing and that is what people should focus upon. (c) Insisting on maintaining a clear-cut separation and distance from other departments. (d) Reacting defensively (without realizing it) whenever challenged and giving the impression that he hated to be wrong (not that it hurt him). (e) Controlling the behavior of others when others did not agree with him.

(3) Given behaviors (a), (b), (c), and (d), the subordinates, peers, and superiors tended to remain at a distance and never discussed these issues.

(4) One result was that Q's feelings of being alone and minimally influential were confirmed and reinforced.

(5) His feelings of not being heard within the newspaper

coexisted with his determination that his department would be effective.

(6) Since people had given up attempting to influence Q they acted in ways that became self-sealing—they no longer tested to see whether Q was influenceable but simply assumed that he was not.

(7) The results were that Q's feeling of rejection and aloneness were confirmed; and his projection that the problem of the newspaper lay elsewhere was strengthened.

R, believing that Q saw the news department as the problem, felt misunderstood and disrespected. Whenever R and Q had to meet for discussions of day-to-day issues, each came to the session feeling oversensitive to the other's defensiveness and undersensitive to his own. The resulting difficulties upset them both, and in an attempt to protect themselves, they were especially careful not to cross the line into each other's areas of responsibility.

These self-sealing processes between Q and R will continue until Q and R become aware of them, decide to reduce them, and ask for help in doing so. The public act of asking for help will tend to be seen by others as a sign of strength on Q's or R's part. This, in turn, will tend to unfreeze Q and R and make them less tense. The lower the tension, the higher the probability that they will seek to make contact with each other, and will do so with minimal defensiveness, or an open acknowledgement of that defensiveness.

The resulting sense of being accepted and heard, of being influential where one wants to be, could help Q reduce his need to be heard through his writing, or R through his. Also, the more Q and R become aware of and accepting of the feelings they have disassociated from themselves, the easier it will be for them to be aware of the unintended negative impact of their behavior. This will make it possible for both of them to talk and hear each other more accurately.

Substantive disagreements can then be expressed more openly because they will not come from a position of mistrust or a climate of defensiveness. The boundary between creative activities will no longer need to be maintained by rigid rules, because it will be defined through open, continual dialogue; the differentiation will be maintained through active, effective interdependence, not isolation.

This scenario was acted out only in part and only temporarily. Much of the progress was due to the openness the interventionist helped to induce, and to the capacity of R and Q to learn and experiment. But the program never reached the stage where Q and R, or others, acquired the knowledge or the skills needed to make the scenario self-reinforcing and self-sustaining.

It has been argued that the attitudes and skills necessary for interpersonal competence and trust are developed in early childhood, and that no amount of work in the type of program I have described would be of help in changing behavior. This hypothesis is a legitimate one and deserves careful consideration. But we should keep in mind that although defensive behaviors are learned early, it does not follow necessarily that one must go back to early life to identify them and change them. Defensive behaviors are manifested in the here-and-now, and one's co-workers have much experience with the impact of them. If a person wants to change some of his defensive behavior, his motivation may be the immediate, here-and-now need to work effectively with others. The method of learning can be for him to use his co-workers as resource people to let him know when his behavior is having a negative impact.

To conclude, newspapers, like most other organizations, desperately need processes for self-examination and self-renewal, and these activities should ultimately be the responsibility of the members of the organizations (Argyris 1970). However, at the moment, our organizations are staffed, at all levels, by persons who are "programmed" by our culture to cancel each other out, especially when they are dealing with important and difficult issues (Argyris 1969, 1971). Moreover, organizations are designed to use structures, control systems, and management information systems that compound this felony (Argyris 1964, 1971). Thus the capacities to produce dry rot and an apparently irreversible trend toward organizational entropy are presently endemic to most organizations, including *The Daily Planet.*

The most effective way to fight the spread of such dry rot

and entropy, for *The Daily Planet* and many other organizations, will be to hire a small but highly skilled staff of specialists in organizational behavior. Such a staff would conduct ongoing diagnoses of the sort described in this book; they would design learning environments to help the participants overcome the problems; and for a newspaper, they would conduct serious and systematic diagnoses in such crucial areas as the relationship between reporters' needs and the living system, on the one hand, and the quality of reporting and editorial activities on the other.

If the processes of organizational entropy we found in the *Planet* are found in other newspapers (and I believe they will be), then newspapers everywhere should want to create and institutionalize procedures for self-examination and processes for self-renewal. Without such processes, and given the protection of the Constitution, newspapers may find their freedom increasingly curtailed or managed by outside institutions.

14

On Effective Intervention

At the outset, I stated that this book would have three interdependent purposes: to consider the requirement for effective self-examination by newspapers, to describe what knowledge we have acquired about the living systems of newspapers, and to demonstrate an intervention process that may have advantages over the methods typically used by management consultants.

The third purpose has not been fully pursued so far. It did not seem possible to describe in detail the design and the execution of the intervention processes without seeming to deemphasize the other two themes. I chose to emphasize understanding the requirements for effective self-examination because of the timeliness of that topic in our society, and because the theory that underlies the intervention strategy is available elsewhere (Argyris 1970, 1971).

The advantages of the intervention strategy and the meaning of progress. To the reader whose attention has been focused on the substantive issues, the events that occurred at *The Daily*

Planet may have appeared to flow naturally. But I would emphasize that the flow was in fact *highly unnatural*. The living system, through its participating agents, resisted the intervention activities strongly every step of the way. The intervention strategy succeeded in producing a few rare events because it did so in ways that were relatively undisturbing to the daily life of the participants. The diagnostic processes did not get in people's way, and the information was gathered while participants were carrying out their everyday job assignments.

Moreover, the intervention activities produced data that were difficult for the clients to distort. This was due partly to the heavy use of observational techniques. We observed many meetings and dialogues that were central to the newspaper's method of operating. It was also a result of our diagnostic techniques. We also strove continuously to obtain data that were central to the clients' interests, and to check and recheck our findings as they were being developed. The objective was to collect data that could not be ignored by the clients and to show continuously that the data were valid. For example, the feedback sessions were tape-recorded and a content analysis was made by a person who had no connection with the project. The results of this analysis were compared with the original diagnosis and with the clients' evaluation of the diagnosis. Moreover, the feedback session was designed so that confrontation of and disagreement with the data were encouraged.

When the top management group agreed to a learning experience, we rechecked the quality of the agreement by holding individual interviews. The discrepancy between the data obtained from these two activities was then fed back to the group. They had to wrestle with the incongruity between what they had said in their group and what they had said in private. This dilemma provided important learning experiences for them because the discrepancy was typical of the living system. The intervention activities therefore had built-in diagnostic processes whose validity was continually tested, and the results of the confrontations became material for the clients' to learn from.

We could have planned a learning experience without the repeated validity checks and tests for the depth of commitment made by the clients to the learning experience. Instead of working within the actual living system, we could have planned and set up an artificial learning environment, and suppressed our doubts about that procedure as counterproductive for the clients. And we could have structured the learning experience so that it would proceed more smoothly and appear more productive. But we deliberately rejected such "effective" preplanning because it would have succeeded in suppressing some of the key problems within the living system (such as the dependence on authority, the sense of helplessness and projection, and the fear of interpersonal conflict).

A third advantage of the intervention techniques used was that a valid diagnosis could be made even though many clients were wary of the entire program, a good proportion of them resisted it, and a few were openly hostile toward it. The validity of our techniques is therefore not dependent upon the enthusiasm and support of all the clients.

Another characteristic of the intervention activities is that all of them, regardless of the level of intervention, were informed by a theory. Thus the governing variables of the intervention strategy were valid information, free and informed choice, and internal commitment (Argyris 1970, 1971). Valid information can most probably be generated when the clients have free and informed choices about the program they are going to experience, and about the degree of internal commitment they wish to make to the program. The three factors that continually governed my own behavior were therefore valid information, free choice, and internal commitment. Whether I was thinking of the long-range design of the program, planning the learning seminar, participating in sessions with the top group, interviewing individuals, responding to questions, or reacting to pressures, I always tried to ask myself how my response would meet the requirements of the three governing factors.

I did not always succeed in behaving consistently with my values. Whenever I was under stress, I found myself seeking more control over the situation, and if the stress became strong enough, I became competitive and I began to seek to win in such a way that the clients would lose. An example of minor stress was my anxiety just before the learning seminar. I wanted the session to succeed, but I was worried that not enough of the participants were genuinely committed to its success. The sessions started slowly and my anxiety rose. When people refused to talk about the issues that they had defined as critical in the individual pre-seminar interviews (the President's behavior, for example), I found myself trying to introduce information that would expose the inconsistencies. As R pointed out, several times I came close to violating individual confidences gained during the one-to-one interviews. I did not violate these confidences partly because R helped monitor my behavior, and partly because I had admitted that I could unintentionally violate confidences because I was eager for the group sessions to be given a genuine test. If they were to fail, I thought it should be because people actually tried to follow the rules and found them wanting, not because no one tried to behave more openly and be more honest. Making that admission, the reader may recall, led R, Q, and P to encourage me not to worry ("the sessions have just begun"), and it may have given them a bit more encouragement to help in giving the sessions a real test.

An example of my competitive behavior occurred during the discussion with R's group. After several hours of very difficult discussion, I began to feel that some members were out to kill the idea of a learning session. I didn't know at the time how valid that feeling was. However, I do remember attempting to test it, and experiencing the familiar denial-projection mechanism ("Who, us? We're not trying to kill it; it's you who are the problem," and so forth).

Except for these moments, I believe that the record will show that I remained relatively consistent in my observance of the three governing variables. However, the reader may respond, the record will also show that little progress was made.

What is the meaning of progress? The problems we dis-cussed in the learning sessions had existed in the organization for many years. People were willing to make bets with anyone that it would not be possible to get the top management into a room to discuss honestly the issues in question. Yet these discussions did occur. We were able to create several "rare events" of this type, and that is one sign of progress.

However, another goal was to help make these rare events become natural events. Although the clients will say that there is a greater degree of openness and trust among some people, I have little evidence that they can create and maintain such a state of affairs without outside help. They never participated in the learning processes thoroughly enough to learn the new skills, or more important, to develop a new set of human values.

Successful intervention, according to the theory that guided this study, requires that the clients learn to design organizations where valid information, free choice, and internal commitment are possible without the continued help of outside consultants. Self-maintaining, self-guiding, self-renewing, self-learning—call these activities what you will, what is important is that they promote control over one's own destiny.

The assumption is therefore that if the intervention processes and governing variables that I used work for individuals, they are also valid for the organization. The temporary system that I created in becoming a consultant, and the behavior that I manifested while I was there, were designed to be genuine models for the clients to observe, so that they could decide if they wished to design their world to conform to these values.

The answer from the top group, to date, is a mixed one. A few people (probably R and Q, with P if he had support, and C if he weren't so frightened by the processes) see the value of these new designs for their organization. Others may see some value in the designs but also describe them as "romantic," or "unreal," and then behave in ways which guarantee their failure.

The client system is therefore conflicted and ambivalent. And that would be the next thing to explore. Some readers might wonder why I didn't push harder or "sell" more. I remember that after a meeting C told me how disappointed he was that I did not sell my values more forcefully to the editors. My answer is that such selling would violate my values, because when it succeeds it does so only by extracting a promised or external commitment from people. External commitment characterizes too many programs. New programs become a fad. A fad is an activity that many people are committed to because some people in power are requiring them to be committed to it. The irony is that if the people in power accept such an external commitment as valid, then they do not value internal commitment, thereby confirming that the program is a fad.

Fads are sad, if not tragic, episodes in organizational life. They are sad because they symbolize the shallow façade behind which people work. They are tragic because they are continual, living reminders that individual growth, learning, and risk-taking —and the whole quality of human life that they require—are not possible within the system.

To put this another way, management consultants tend to act out a theory-in-use that is shared by their clients. They strive to win, and not to lose; to avoid expressing negative feelings; to define the client-consultant relationship in such a way that they control its development; to create maximum client dependence; and to avoid threatening the top management, who pays the bills. If they do this well, they tend to be admired by their clients because they have been playing the game by the client's rules, and playing it well.

However, such a process tends to prevent important information from being discovered—or if it is discovered, from being discussed with the clients. For example, if we had followed the more typical consulting procedures, I doubt whether we could have discovered the degree of ambivalence toward change that existed in the top group. They were committed to getting valid information, but they were not committed to getting free choice and internal commitment. It is as if they knew that they valued truth but feared it. They valued truth as part of the great heritage of the newspaper; they feared its effect on their own relationships because of the defensiveness of their living system. Truth, to quote a phrase often used by some of them, could "blow this group apart."

Nor could we have plumbed the depths of the helplessness people felt, or seen the lengths to which they projected their fears on others. We could not have diagnosed accurately the extent of the brittleness that prevented or inhibited the confrontation of issues that were critical to effective self-examination (issues such as subjective reporting). The same may be said for the scope of self-deception and deception of others. The reader may recall the sessions with R and his group. These men insisted that they understood each other well and trusted each other highly. Yet, as the transcripts showed, they frequently misunderstood each other. They behaved inconsistently, and rarely helped each other. They withheld information from each other, lied to each other, and attributed false motives to each other which they never felt free to check. It was in this climate of "high trust" that one editor did not feel free to discuss with the group whether they ever felt the need to protect him (in the area of interpersonal relationships), and if so, why.

Progress, therefore, requires that the clients begin to become aware of the processes within the living system (including their own behavior) that prevent the system from being able to solve the problems that its participants have identified as important. The intervention succeeded in this respect. The intervention activities also succeeded in providing key participants with real experiences which proved that certain events they believed "impossible" could actually occur. It also succeeded in proving that the fear of "things blowing up" was based on projections, and maintained through publicly untested attributions about individuals and the living system; and it showed how these fears and projections were the basis for self-sealing processes.

The fact that the clients did not choose to continue beyond these learning experiences is a sign of their own failure, not the failure of the intervention processes. We tried continuously to encourage, but not to force, the clients to re-examine their choice not to continue the program. What we are left with is strong evidence that when forty top members of *The Daily Planet* had an opportunity to make their organization one that learns and examines itself, they retreated from the challenge.

It is my personal opinion that those members do have the capacity to succeed. However, at the moment, the human costs of further learning seem to them unnecessary given the costs of their present existence. There is little doubt in my mind that the human costs extracted by their living system will continue to rise.

There is also little doubt in my mind that the credibility problems of the newspaper will continue to exist. Someday the credibility problems will become so great, and the sense of helplessness so deep and continuously reconfirmed, that the participants will either choose or have chosen for them some means of external control.

The newspaper is heading for an unavoidable choice. Will it manage its own destiny or will it choose to be managed by other systems? The second option would simply compound the subordinates' dependence on the President by including another system. The first one, I believe, would lead them inevitably back to their responsibility for changing their own system.

Recapitulating the intervention sequences. The first step in the study was to conduct a diagnosis of the client system. This produced in a map of the living system which identified some major internal factors causing organizational ineffectiveness. The factors were fed back to the top management. All but one agreed with the validity of the diagnosis and the plausibility of the predictions about the future of the system. The one executive who disagreed objected chiefly to the idea of conducting such research, and more important, to its implications for action. He believed that "if people are civilized, all human problems are manageable." The fact that he and others agreed with the diagnosis, and accepted the fact that the problems it identified had existed for years, did not seem to shake this belief in the effectiveness of "being civilized."

After obtaining valid information about the client system, the next step was for the executives to decide if they wanted to take action to begin to correct the problems identified. There was unanimous overt agreement to begin a program of learning and organizational change. Some of the most pressing problems identified by the diagnosis were:

(1) The barriers and misunderstandings between the news and editorial departments.

(2) The barriers and misunderstandings between the news and editorial departments on the one hand, and the President's office on the other.

(3) The coercion of the President to make the difficult decisions and then the freedom, on the part of his immediate subordinates, to criticize him for those aspects of the decisions they did not like.

(4) The competitive, win-lose dynamics in relationships between individuals.

(5) The magnification of events, so that events are experienced in a distorted manner.

(6) The lack of a cohesive top management team in the news area that could serve as more of a resource for the individual members.

(7) The omnipresent mechanism of denial and projection.

(8) The problems raised by the Reporter-Activists, including the issue of subjective versus objective reporting.

(9) The apparent unilateral and arbitrary ways of dealing with demotions and promotions.

(10) The administrative activities that had become compulsively repetitive, such as: the ineffective activities of the executive committee; the labeling of persons who propose change as deviants; the increasing demands by professionals for salary increases and other material benefits; and the increasing use of jobs at the newspaper as stepping stones to other careers, or as platforms from which to launch other career activities (writing books, giving lectures).

After the top executives chose to attempt to correct some of the problems, they faced the task of becoming internally committed to the actions implicit in the decision. The first step was to agree to attend a learning seminar, recommended to last one week but eventually designed for three working days. The reader will recall that generating the internal commitment to the first step was not easy; it took several discussions over a period of months while individuals explored their fears about the learning process. We took every precaution we could to guarantee free choice and internal commitment to attend the seminar. We never fully succeeded, partly because the members kept denying publicly that there were any problems and partly because they were afraid to talk about their fears. Roosevelt's statement to the nation that it had nothing to fear but fear itself accurately described one of the basic problems in the client system.

A second reason that we never fully succeeded was that when individuals took steps toward being more open (in the preliminary meetings as well as in the actual sessions), they behaved in ways they did not expect. For example, one person who was very much in favor of the program was surprised at how quiet he remained during the actual sessions. He expressed embarrassment during the post-session interview that he did not support the processes as fully as he had indicated he would in the preliminary interviews. On the other hand, one person who had serious doubts about the program returned with a deeper respect for the learning processes, a greater degree of self-awareness, and became more effective in his relationships with certain key people.

In other words, free choice and internal commitment cannot be selected and put on like a suit of clothes. They are not even stable qualities which one has or does not have. They are capacities for action which are always in the process of being tested. The learning objective is therefore to design a milieu in which these capacities can be continually exercised and examined.

Even though the first learning session was much too short (the group chose to disregard my advice about the time that was necessary), and even though more members found themselves being more cautious than they had expected, some important learning did take place. First, the members found that others were not as brittle as they had assumed. Second, they learned that "taboo subjects" could be discussed and that issues which many people swore would never be raised were brought up, with emotional release and organizational gain. Third, people began to trust the learning process, which in practice meant that they began to trust each other, and themselves, and the interventionist much more.

Although there was little time to reinforce these small organizational gains during the first seminar, some members took the initiative and tried to pursue learning activities when they returned to their offices. For example, R, Q, and P were involved in some very important discussions that helped to unfreeze relationships, correct distortions, and create new visions of organizational relationships. Also, decisions that had been considered for many years were completed in two sessions. (No new information was added in those sessions. The participants simply discussed openly *with each other* what they had previously shared, in whole or in part, with the President.)

But we should not discount the fact that the members resisted further learning sessions. For example, no one learned the skills they needed to create a more trusting milieu by themselves. A few individuals like R and Q tried to alter their behavior, but they simply had not been helped to learn the skills that were required. The President, the reader may recall, said that he would feel uncomfortable and embarrassed about learning the language and the skills that the interventionists were exhibiting during the learning sessions. The truth is that he (and the others) would probably have experienced more bewilderment than they had anticipated if they had gone ahead, because the language of trust requires basic changes in values, new conceptions of authentic relationships, and new concepts of organizational management.

In one sense I felt, and still feel, a genuine sense of sorrow that the clients chose not to continue. I believe that they had much to gain as individuals, and that their newspaper would have benefited just as much. Ultimately, the credibility of their concept of a great newspaper depends on nothing less than it be managed according to equally noble human values. They may espouse those values; they may believe in them; but at the moment they do not behave according to them.

Could I have done more to encourage the group to continue? It is difficult to answer that question without more research. If I may be permitted to speculate, I believe that the answer is yes, if I had been available more often to the group. The men in the top group were individuals with a high sense of intellectual integrity. They did not like being partially responsible for the creation of "taboo subjects;" nor were they comfortable with the inconsistencies in their behavior, or the discrepancies between their rhetoric and their behavior. Whenever I observed them and pointed out an inconsistency, I was rarely condemned and more rarely was the inconsistency denied. The more frequent response was to defend the inconsistency as necessary. But this defense became the energy source for progress, because the assumption that inconsistency was necessary was invariably connected with assumptions that individuals were making about each other. Once these assumptions were exposed, progress could be made, because invariably the assumptions had never been tested and usually they were only partly correct. And so perhaps more progress could have been made if I had worked at the organization full-time, attended more meetings, and continually exposed inconsistencies and organizational dilemmas.

On the other hand, I believe that this organization (and all others) will return to these issues. Most organizations are slowly decaying from their dry rot and giving out ineffective or incomplete services at ever-increasing costs. As sophisticated management information systems (broadly defined) are designed to attempt to deal with this complexity, the issues we have focused on become central to progress. The fundamental assumption of information science technology is that truth is a good idea. What we have seen here (and this finding has been borne out in all my studies to date), is that people in organizations believe that truth is a good idea *as long as it is not threatening*. In a living system characterized by low trust and little genuine learning, information becomes threatening quickly and easily. I predict that even compulsive censorship within the Pentagon is mild compared to the censoring that human beings perform every day of their lives. Newspapermen, as we have seen, believe that one of their roles is to keep the country honest. They, and others, will find that their quest will be greatly advanced if they begin with their own relationships within their own living system.

The fact that society is beginning to request the power to monitor the effectiveness of newspapers is indicative, I believe, of a trend that will accelerate and spread to other organizations. Organizations are designed and managed in ways that are bound to produce organizational entropy—slow but deadly internal deterioration. This deterioration leads inevitably to a decreasing service or product, and so far with increasing costs. As the quality of a service becomes intolerably low and the costs unbelievably high, society will begin to insist on managing the organizations more carefully. Newspapers are among the first to be attacked partly because their product (news and editorials) is exposed in detail to public scrutiny and partly because that product may have an immediate impact on the individuals and institutions in our society.

There is an irony imbedded in this trend toward monitoring the quality of products and services: if it is done seriously, it will probably require some form of organization, which will soon develop its own organizational entropy. This is why I believe that a more viable long-range solution is to understand and reduce the cause of organizational entropy.

Organizational change through structural changes. There are those who believe that organizational changes should precede interpersonal changes. For example, changes in the nature of organizational structure, changes in decision-making processes, changes in providing more accurate information would tend, so the argument goes, to lead to effective changes in behavior. Interpersonal behavior should be the last factor to be examined, and indeed, some would suggest that it never be examined at all.

Let us consider this argument in light of our findings. The participants focused on two types of changes: administrative and substantive. Let us explore each type.

During the learning seminar several people warned the group members against talking about interpersonal relationships. Interpersonal issues, they said should be discussed only as a last resort. They recommended administrative issues, such as the idea of setting up rules defining effective decision-making processes. They did not believe that it was healthy for organizational decision-making to have certain people excluded from meetings, especially if the decisions to be made were relevant to their areas of responsibility.

Their organizational diagnosis was correct. Excluding officials from discussions that were central to their areas of responsibility would, and did, lead to difficulties. But why were they excluded? They were excluded because the highest officials considered them outdated and not very effective, or difficult to communicate with effectively. During the learning seminar, for example, the reader may recall that the President said he excluded from the meetings two people, who were organizationally entitled to attend, because he did not find them helpful.

What good would it do to define the decision-making process in such a way that the excluded persons would now attend meetings when they were not wanted? As the President said, "if [Mr. U] were to attend, I would simply hold another meeting." The point is that if the living structure does not agree with the formal structure, then it is hardly sensible to make rules that say, in effect, that the living structure should be ignored. In order to get at the causes of the discrepancy between the formal and the actual decision-making processes, some very important personal and interpersonal issues had to be discussed, because personal issues have become a central cause in the blocking of certain organizational changes.

Consider the decision on the new feature. The major causes for the delay in the decision were not entirely substantive. The barriers to progress were related, as we saw, to such issues as power and control. These issues, in turn, related to the quality of the interpersonal relationships with the President and among each other. A decision that had not been reached for nearly three years rapidly reached completion once the subjects that were taboo (power and control) became discussable. When power and control lose their taboo status, their attractiveness as "nasty desires" is greatly reduced and books like Talese's become less interesting.

The same was true for the news meeting that no one wanted but everyone attended because they knew of no way to tell the key official their true feelings. The difficulties with the executive committee were not considered solvable by the members of the group unless the President's behavior were to be altered. Yet when the President asked for discussions of the subject, many of the members, including some who were most vociferous about it in private interviews, either denied or skirted the issue. The irony was that the President sensed that this was occurring, and it served to reinforce in his own mind certain negative evaluations of specific individuals. Like them, however, he never expressed these feelings publicly. When he did take action, it appeared to those affected as arbitrary and manipulative. These inferences confirmed the fears these men held, and the processes became circular and self-sealing.

Also, there was much important information that was not shared about key substantive issues. For example, the relationship of the news and editorial areas was not discussable with all the key individuals present because of fears of a blow-up. The subject was "touchy" or "taboo." This resulted in the subject being buried, being discussed with the President in a one-to-one relationship, or written about in formal and carefully worded memos. The result was that a barrier existed between the key individuals that was so strong that I was offered bets by the people involved that the barriers would never come down.

Yet they did begin to lower the barriers. The reductions came after the key protagonists genuinely understood how their behavior created defensiveness in others. As they pointed out, there was not much sense in thinking that rational discussions on substantive issues would make progress when each person was not hearing the others' words as they were intended.

These results are not new. They have been replicated in every one of our organizational studies. Any kind of change in an organization requires people to execute it. As Mary Parker Follet pointed out decades ago, a decision is not made until it is carried out. Only people and groups carry out decisions. Unless they are internally committed to behaving in accordance with new rules or structures, the aforesaid changes in rules and structures are not part of the living system.

This does not mean that it is not important to generate new rules, to create new structures, to design new processes. The point being made is that such structural and procedural changes have the highest probability of success when the people act them out. I have read hundreds of reports by outside consultants suggesting structural and procedural changes. I have never read of a case, including my own, in which the outsider's plans could not have been made by insiders—indeed the outsider usually develops them after careful interviewing with insiders. For example, I have written a document that analyzed parts of the living system of the Department of State (Argyris 1967). Many insiders were critical of the publication of the analysis and some stated that it was not true. Yet several years later, an internally designed and executed analysis of the State Department by top young career officers generated a diagnosis which, as Levinson (1973) points out, not only agreed with the diagnosis but was actually more critical of the Department of State.

The reason outsiders are hired is usually because someone in power believes that: the insiders will not design, or are not capable of designing, new systems; the insiders are capable, but to ask them to make the changes that are necessary is political dynamite; the top executives want the outsiders to take the responsibility; and the inside organization is not capable of executing changes even if they were able to design them. All these beliefs are interpersonal and relate to such sensitive subjects as trust, respect, and competence. I am suggesting that these subjects are fit for public discussion (they are already overwhelming the private discussions).

However, as we have seen in this case, it is not an easy matter to unfreeze organizations to discuss taboo subjects. This is not only because of the threat surrounding such taboo subjects. An equally powerful inhibition of such discussion lies in the enormous layers of defensive behavior, regulation, and mythology created to hide the fact that there *are* taboo subjects. To expose these can be as embarrassing as to expose the actual taboo subjects.

Once people begin to unfreeze, to respect each other's strengths, to begin to trust each other, then there is a mushrooming effect. The trust developed and the skills learned are usable to explore other areas, to prevent the invention of new taboo subjects, and to design systems hitherto believed impossible from within. As each step succeeds, it leads to further steps and soon the participants can become masters of their living system and not its slaves. Effective structural changes will be designed and executed when there are no taboo subjects related to these changes.

Structural changes may work if the new behavior required is already known. In our project we were asking people to learn behavior that they did not know or perform effectively, or worse yet, behavior they thought they performed but did not (for example, acts of trust, openness, and minimally evaluative and attributive feedback).

Some people suggest that there is a danger in placing too much emphasis on interpersonal relationships; everything and everyone does not have to be perfect, they say. To begin with, those who make these assertions tend to act as if everything must be perfect or look perfect. Otherwise, why are they afraid to discuss taboo subjects? If people and organizations are genuinely free to be fallible, then why can't their foibles be discussed?

Moreover, the usual reaction by these people to ineffective behavior is to discount it. For example, vice-presidents have learned to discount the controlling, authoritarian behavior of their entrepreneurial presidents. They commonly give two kinds of reasons for their behavior: "once you get to know the president, you know he's really warm and soft underneath that tough exterior"; or "we need him to survive, he knows his stuff" (Argyris 1972). Notice, in the first reason, that discounting becomes possible because *after frequent interaction,* one learns that the president can be flexible and accommodating. But how about the subordinates who meet the President infrequently and have no way of realizing there is anything behind the tough authoritarianism except more of the same? Or what happens to the few subordinates who are genuinely threatened by such controlling behavior? Usually they withdraw or become (or remain) relatively ineffective. The president reacts by getting rid of them. Soon the president tends to have around him people who fit his defenses perfectly.

The second reason implies a clear and open dependence on the superior. The difficulty with this relationship is that the longer the relationship lasts and the organization is effective, the greater the subordinate's respect for the president and the deeper his anxiety about his own lack of self-confidence. Soon, the subordinates may learn to adapt to their anxieties by accepting the dependence as necessary. The so-called strong leader then comes to be managed by the anxieties of dependence-oriented subordinates.

Privacy and progress. Some persons fear that exploration of interpersonal issues may violate the individual's right to privacy. They would go so far as to maintain that if the only way the issues can be dealt with is to focus on the interpersonal problems in working relationships, then it may be better to fire the less powerful persons in the relationships or transfer them to other jobs, preferably in such a way as to save face. But as we have seen, this strategy rarely succeeds. Indeed, it usually creates great hostility and animosity that cannot be expressed because the initial act was done in secrecy.

One other difficulty with this strategy is that people who decide that others are not behaving effectively rarely put their hypothesis to a rigorous public test. In my experience, when superiors evaluate subordinates openly, the open encounters are a last resort; both sides know this and tend to be uncomfortable and defensive. But the superior has the formal power on his side, and the subordinate has to be very careful lest he upset the superior. The subordinate is therefore placed in a doubly difficult situation: he has the least power and also the least support. Subordinates feel this imbalance and unfairness, but they are not able to do much about it. They feel helpless and angry; they know they are adults, yet they may be required to behave as dependent children. They also know that in doing so, they will dislike themselves afterwards. They may vicariously reduce some of their self-hate by saying that knuckling under was necessary.

Those who speak of the right to privacy should examine the two sides of the coin. One way to violate privacy is to coerce someone to reveal something that he or she does not want to reveal. Another way to violate privacy is to induce self-hate by preventing a person from expressing his or her genuine feelings.

Moreover, if the superior does not behave *effectively* in acting to test his hypothesis about a subordinate, and the test becomes a self-fulfilling prophecy (Argyris 1962, 1970, 1971), then he is also losing as a human being. Instead of learning about things he does that are having a negative impact (things he is usually unaware of) he leaves the encounter simply feeling in his evaluation of the other. To make matters worse, the others, who are watching carefully (but at a distance) and who may be aware of the limitations of both individuals, see one getting punished and the other rewarding himself; from this they learn a very important lesson—it is dangerous to upset the superior. To the extent that they must put up a façade to avoid upsetting him, they know they are deceiving others. Deceiving others, we have seen, usually leads to self-deception and both types of deception require defense mechanisms to hide the deception from self and others. Defense mechanisms may hide the problem but they do not eliminate the anxiety and tensions; these are simply driven from awareness. Simultaneously, tolerance to tension-producing relationships is reduced; subordinates become even more careful to avoid tension-producing situations in dealing with the superior. As subordinates increase their interpersonal vigilance, their defensive and deceptive behaviors become repetetive and compulsive.

Privacy is a concept which assumes that human uniqueness and individuality are personal qualities that can be controlled and influenced by individuals. This is not the case with interpersonal relationships. Human beings develop and maintain their uniqueness and wholeness through interaction with others. Asking that certain kinds of information be kept secret from others makes sense when one can present evidence that the others would be harmed by it, or that the others would use it to harm the person presenting it. Censorship also makes sense when the censor is not interested in establishing new interdependent relationships. But the luxury of picking your friends is reduced in organizations: co-workers are usually assigned, interdependence is high, and the impact of co-worker relationships on others may be high.

Another way to illustrate both sides of the issue of privacy is to ask if the subordinate who is being covertly excluded and manipulated by a superior would not wish the opportunity to discuss this situation. But how can he ask if his superior states that such a discussion would violate his right to privacy?

Does this mean that individuals should be required to discuss issues they consider private? Obviously not. What I am suggesting is that because individuality is a phenomenon of interdependence, and special kinds of interdependence are made necessary by the nature of organizations, the decision to invoke a right of privacy becomes complicated and very important: it should be taken only as a last resort; it should be seen as a possible defensive reaction; and it should be taken openly.

The decision to keep something private, as a basic right, should be coupled with an equally basic obligation to make the decision public. In this program, I struggled hard to protect the right of individuals to withhold information. I especially supported those who had less power. No one, to my knowledge, was coerced to say anything that he did not wish to. When I came close to violating this rule during one of the sessions of the learning seminar, group member R was quick to point out the danger of my behavior. R was supported by others, and we had a situation in which the group members became responsible for maintaining privacy. I found it helpful, and they found it reassuring that they could influence my behavior.

This argument is similar to the one made in designing effective relationships between the news and editorial departments (or between reporters and copy editors). I argue against dealing with these issues by invoking departmental privacy and building up barriers. I suggest that autonomy can be maintained more effectively when both groups trust each other's motives, including their stated desire *not* to control the other. Autonomy is then maintained not by independent actions but by highly interdependent relationships.

Notes on the Validity of the Diagnosis

~~~~~~

How certain are we that the diagnosis of the *Planet*'s living system is correct? Certainty is an age-old problem in systematic inquiry; no one is ever certain in research. Regretably, any uncertainty about this diagnosis is *not* a result of the fact that the individuals we worked with exhibited uniqueness, unpredictability, and self-determination. Indeed, as we have tried to show, the living system of the *Planet* tends to suppress individualism, enhance conformity, and discourage rare events. Thus, behavior in the settings that we observed became highly predictable. Indeed, in all other cases to date, the diagnostician has been a more accurate predictor of human behavior in the living system than the members. This has proved true even when clients have agreed with the diagnosis and decided that they were going to change their behavior. We were able to predict openly that they would fail. In all but one case the clients reacted in disbelief, and in that one with anger, yet our predictions were confirmed (Argyris 1970). Living systems, then, promote predictable behavior.

A second reason for the predictability of human behavior is that we need to make it predictable in order to make it manageable. As human beings we may be unique, but we are also limited in our capacities to process information. Consequently, in order to behave effectively we have to develop work settings and points of view that artificially limit the diversity of information we shall have to deal with.

In this case, we concluded that behavior in the living system was competitive and win-lose, that innovative and risk-taking ideas were seldom discussed openly, and that openness toward peers and subordinates was low while openness toward superiors was much higher. The information collected in the interview supported these conclusions. However, since I did both the interviewing and the observing, we must consider the possibility that the observations were influenced by the interviews. One way to test for such influence is to compare the observer's scores with scores taken by several other observers, preferably observers who have had no connection with the research project in question. This has been done in several cases with the author, and inter-observer reliability was found to be high (Argyris 1965).

However, since in this study interobserver reliability studies of the analysis of the tapes was not done. There is still the possibility that I was unduly influenced by what I heard, or that what I said I heard was not what the respondents actually said. One way to test this hypothesis would be to have others listen to the tapes of the meetings and the interviews and conduct reliability studies. This could not be done, however, because a commitment had been made to the clients that no one else would listen to the tapes of the interviews, encounters, and meetings. Fortunately, there is another more powerful test available: to ask the respondents if they agree with the diagnosis. Some researchers are wary of this approach because they believe that persons can be manipulated (covertly or overtly) into agreeing with the results. This is most likely to happen when the respondents do not have much of a stake in the findings. Researchers sometimes assure a low level of involvement by giving the clients information about their living system in the form of generalized statistical results (such as results that have been factor-analyzed), which means that the results have been combined into a few general categories. This can become less involving because there is no clear path leading back from the general results to a specific case—no way, for example, to prove that denial and projection are things that Q and R, not just "some people," actually do. In this study, we could go from group results to the playback of any group tape, so that any individual could confront the diagnostician about what happened, or vice versa. So far in my studies, groups in four different organizations have let me thread a tape for playback to them; in none of these cases was I permitted to go ahead and play the tape.

In this study, the feedback of results had a purpose beyond informing the client of what we have learned. The objective, agreed upon by all parties, was to set the stage for changes that would make the organization more effective. Hard-nosed newspaper executives may not become excited by statistical analyses, but they tend to respond and to respond strongly, when a behavioral scientist (who has never written a news article and never met a payroll) tells them that they are not effective. These particular executives were also subject to another important pressure to take feedback of the results seriously. Organizational diagnoses involving the top management and sampling of key sub-editors, reporters, and writers could become well-known to everyone. Employees at the lower levels, especially, could look to see what, if anything, was happening as a result of the study. If nothing happened, it could become more living evidence, in their eyes, that their management will never change. Finally, the overwhelming majority of top executives I have met have a deep sense of constructive intent and a great need for a sense of personal competence. Results that question their competence are seldom taken lightly or agreed to perfunctorily.

In the same way that subordinates validate their diagnoses about their superiors by watching the superiors' behavior, so the diagnostician helps validate his results by analyzing new executive behavior during and after the feedback sessions.

There are at least three levels of analysis that can be conducted during a feedback session. First (and here a disinterested researcher other than the writer should be used), one can analyze the issues that the clients chose to discuss and their reactions to these issues. Second, the session can be scored to note whether the group dynamics are different from or similar to the dynamics described in Table 1. Third, one can infer the degree of validity of the diagnosis from the degree to which the clients, in their discussion of the diagnosis, express belief that it is a valid basis upon which to design new programs and change old ones. In this case, one of the conditions I stated for my continued partcipation was that the design of any change program would have to begin with the executives; this made the decision about whether to proceed with a change program another important test.

Table 1.

Problem-Solving Dynamics

of News and Editorial Meetings

	1		2		3		4		5		6		7		8		9		10	
Number of meetings observed	1		2		3		4		5		6		7		8		9		10	
Number of units on each level	200		160		150		100		200		178		200		100		160		80	
Behavioral categories	N	%	N	%	N	%	N	%	N	%	N	%	N	%	N	%	N	%	N	%
Owning up to ideas	112	55	118	74	101	67	71	71	137	69	138	77	140	70	75	75	103	64	57	73
Open to new ideas Experimenting with new ideas	57	29	20	12	32	21	6	21	48	24	26	14	30	15	17	17	26	14	7	08
Not helping others to own up to their ideas	31	16	22	14	17	12	11	8	15	07	14	09	30	15	8	08	31	22	16	19
Helping others to own up to their ideas																				
Concern for ideas	78	39	69	43	87	58	65	65	159	79	97	56	113	56	46	46	76	48	32	40
Conformity to ideas Individuality related to ideas	94	47	78	50	61	41	25	25	41	21	80	43	86	43	44	44	81	50	47	59
Antagonism at the idea level	27	14	13	07	2	01	2	10			1	01	1	01			0	02	1	01

The Feedback Session as a Validity Check of the Living System Model

~~~~~~
~~~~~~

Two ways have been identified to use the transcript of the feedback session as a possible validity check for the diagnosis of the living system. The first possibility is to have someone score the meetings and see to what extent the quantitative scores matched those presented in Table 1, Appendix A. This was done, and the scores were not significantly different, statistically, in any category except one (open i). However, the use of these scores as a validity check may be seriously questioned because the feedback session was designed and chaired by the interventionist. The feedback session may have represented a different milieu. The relatively high openness scores were due to the fact that the members asked many questions about the report. The fact that there were a few units where feelings were expressed could be related to the interventionist's expression of his own feelings and a few of the clients' responses.

A more appropriate validity check would be to compare the issues discussed by the executives and to note the degree to which they agreed or disagreed with the issues identified in the diagnosis. This was done as follows. A typed transcript was made from the tape recordings of the feedback session. Any long speeches by the interventionist were cut out. The transcript was then given to a disinterested professional colleague to analyze.* (This colleague was employed by different universities; he was not organizationally dependent upon me in any way; and he knew nothing about the design of the study.) The only thing he was told was that the protocol represented a transcription of a feedback session. He was asked to go through the entire manuscript and note (1) the issues discussed (giving the page and paragraph); and (2) whether there was agreement or disagreement with the interventionist.

Sixty-five different issues were identified. In fifty-nine issues, the clients agreed with the interventionist *and* presented further examples to document the findings. In six episodes there was disagreement expressed with the diagnosis. The first twenty issues discussed during these episodes are presented in Table 2. There is, as one may see, a high degree of agreement between the issues identified by the writer during his diagnosis of the living system and the comments made by the executives where given an opportunity to confront the diagnosis.

* Dan Johnson, Jr.

Table 2.

Agreement and Disagreement with Issues in the Report

Issue	Agree or disagree	No. of people	Was issue in report?
1. Questions become orders	agree	2	yes
2. Brain picking	agree	2	yes
3. Lack of experimentation	agree	2	yes
	disagree	2	yes
4. Competitiveness	agree	5	yes
5. Win-lose dynamics	agree	4	yes
6. Rigged meetings	agree	1	yes
	disagree	1	yes
7. Internal dynamics can affect writer's view of reality	agree	2	yes
8. Creation of deadline and crisis	agree	2	yes
9. Overstaffed	agree	2	yes
10. Lack of value of X-type meeting	agree	3	yes
11. Problem of demotions	agree	5	yes
	disagree	1	yes
12. Secrecy in management	agree	4	yes
	disagree	1	yes
13. Decreasing loyalty to organization	agree	3	yes
14. Commitments to decisions may be illusive	agree	2	yes
15. Problems are overly magnified	agree	4	yes
16. Subterfuge in management	agree	4	yes
	disagree	1	yes
17. Conflict is suppressed	agree	3	yes
18. Value of openness	agree	4	yes
19. Organization can become compliant	agree	3	yes
	disagree	1	yes
20. Administration as a second-class process	agree	6	yes

References

Argyris, C. *Integrating the Individual and the Organization,* New York: Wiley, 1954.

Argyris, C. *Some Causes of Organizational Ineffectiveness Within the Department of State.* Occasional Paper 2. Washington, D.C: Center for International Studies, Department of State, 1967.

Argyris, C. "The Incompleteness of Social Psychological Theory," *American Psychologist,* 1969, 24 (10), 893–908.

Argyris, C. *Intervention Theory and Method: A Behavioral Science View.* Reading, Mass.: Addison-Wesley, 1970.

Argyris, C. *Management and Organizational Development.* New York: McGraw-Hill, 1971.

Argyris, C. *The Applicability of Organizational Sociology.* London: Cambridge University Press, 1972.

Argyris, C., and Schön, D. A. *Theory in Practice: Increasing Professional Effectiveness.* San Francisco: Jossey-Bass, 1974.

Balk, A. *A Free and Responsive Press.* New York: Twentieth Century Fund, 1972.

Blake, R., Shepard H., and Mouton, J. *Managing Intergroup Conflict in Industry.* Ann Arbor, Mich.: Foundation for Research on Human Behavior, 1965.

Brewster, K. Speech to the American Association for the Advancement of Science. In *The Wall Street Journal,* Jan. 19, 1970, p. 12.

Brucker, H. *Communication Is Power.* New York: Oxford University Press, 1972.

Gardner, J. "America in the Twenty-Third Century." *The New York Times,* July 27, 1968.

Hohenberg, J. *The Free Press/Free People.* New York: Columbia University Press, 1971.

Levinson, H. *The Great Jackass Fallacy.* Cambridge, Mass.: Graduate School of Business, Harvard University, 1973.

Moynihan, D. P. "The Presidency and the Press." *Commentary,* Mar. 1971, 41–52.

National Commission on the Causes and Prevention of Violence. *Mass Media and Violence,* Vol. 11. Washington, D.C.: Government Printing Office, 1969.

Penthouse Interview. "Geraldo Rivera." Mar. 1973, 56–60ff.

Pool, I. de S., and Shulman, I. "Newsmen's Fantasies, Audiences, and Newswriting." *Public Opinion Quarterly,* 1959, *23* (2).

Pool, I. de S. "Newsmen and Statesmen: Adversaries or Cronies." In W. L. Riverts and M. J. Nyhan (Eds.), *Aspen Notebook on Government and the Media.* New York: Praeger, 1973.

Raskin, A. H. "What's Wrong with American Newspapers?" *New York Times Magazine,* June 11, 1967, 28ff.

Reston, J. *The Artillery of the Press.* New York: Harper and Row, 1966.

Rosenthal, R. M. "Save the First Amendment." *New York Times Magazine,* Feb. 11, 1973, 16–47ff.

Simon, H.A. *The Science of the Artificial.* Cambridge, Mass.: M.I.T. Press, 1969.

Sulzberger, A. O. "The *Times* Bars Support to Panel for Monitoring News Media." *The New York Times,* Jan. 16, 1973, 39M.

Swanson, G. E. "Agitation Through the Press: A Study of the Personalities of Publicists." *Public Opinion Quarterly,* 1956, *20* (2), 441–456.

Swanson, G. E. "Agitation in Face-to-Face Contacts: A Study of the Personalities of Orators." *Public Opinion Quarterly,* 1957, *21* (2), 288–294.

"Symposium: Journalism and Mischief." *The American Scholar,* 1968, *37* (4), 627–641.

Ways, M. "What's Wrong with News? It Isn't New Enough." *Fortune,* Oct. 1969, 110–111ff.

Wicker, T. "The Reporter and His Story: How Far Should He Go?" *Nieman Reports,* Sept. 1972, 15–19.

Index